Preventing Sexual Violence

The LAW AND PUBLIC POLICY: PSYCHOLOGY AND THE SOCIAL SCIENCES series includes books in three domains:

Legal Studies—writings by legal scholars about issues of relevance to psychology and the other social sciences, or that employ social science information to advance the legal analysis;

Social Science Studies—writings by scientists from psychology and the other social sciences about issues of relevance to law and public policy; and

Forensic Studies—writings by psychologists and other mental health scientists and professionals about issues relevant to forensic mental health science and practice.

The series is guided by its editor, Bruce D. Sales, PhD, JD, ScD(hc), University of Arizona; and coeditors, Bruce J. Winick, JD, University of Miami; Norman J. Finkel, PhD, Georgetown University; and Valerie P. Hans, PhD, University of Delaware.

* * *

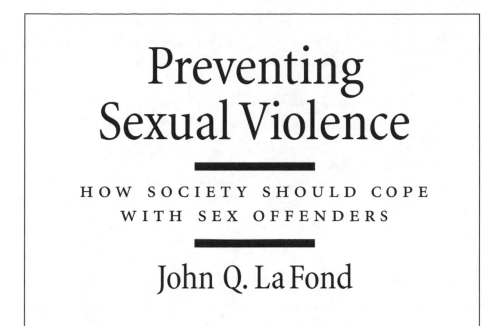

Preventing Sexual Violence

HOW SOCIETY SHOULD COPE WITH SEX OFFENDERS

John Q. La Fond

AMERICAN PSYCHOLOGICAL ASSOCIATION
WASHINGTON, DC

Published by
American Psychological Association
750 First Street, NE
Washington, DC 20002
www.apa.org

To order
APA Order Department
P.O. Box 92984
Washington, DC 20090-2984
Tel: (800) 374-2721
Direct: (202) 336-5510
Fax: (202) 336-5502
TDD/TTY: (202) 336-6123
Online: www.apa.org/books/
E-mail: order@apa.org

In the U.K., Europe, Africa, and the Middle East, copies may be ordered from
American Psychological Association
3 Henrietta Street
Covent Garden, London
WC2E 8LU England

Typeset in Goudy by World Composition Services, Inc., Sterling, VA

Printer: United Book Press, Baltimore, MD
Cover Designer: Berg Design, Albany, NY
Technical/Production Editor: Kristen S. Boye

The opinions and statements published are the responsibility of the authors, and such opinions and statements do not necessarily represent the policies of the American Psychological Association.

Library of Congress Cataloging-in-Publication Data

La Fond, John Q.
  Preventing sexual violence : how society should cope with sex offenders / John Q. La Fond.
      p. cm. — (The law and public policy)
  Includes bibliographical references and index.
  ISBN 1 59147 172 9 (alk. paper)
  1. Sex crimes—United States. 2. Sex offenders—United States. 3. Sex crimes—United States—Prevention. 4. Sex offenders—Rehabilitation—United States. 5. Sex offenders—Legal status, laws, etc.—United States. 6. Recidivism—United States—Prevention. I. Title. II. Series.

HV6592.L3 2005
364.15′3—dc22   2004016370

British Library Cataloguing-in-Publication Data
A CIP record is available from the British Library.

Printed in the United States of America
First Edition

To Evelyn,
For her love and friendship

CONTENTS

PREFACE

Sex offenders are America's most hated public enemy. People believe they are lifelong predators who will seek out new victims as long as they live. Media accounts of vicious new sex crimes committed by sex offenders who have been released from prison—often against vulnerable, young children—fan the flames of public rage. Heartrending stories about Jesse Timmendequas, a convicted sex offender, killing young Megan Kanka in New Jersey, or Early Shriner raping and sexually mutilating a young boy in Tacoma, Washington, have struck a responsive chord in all of us.

The public has demanded action and politicians have responded, passing new laws designed to prevent sex offenders from committing any more sex crimes. This aggressive strategy is based on a jurisprudence of dangerousness and prevention. Sex offenders are seen as so likely to commit many more sex crimes during their lifetimes that everybody believes that special steps must be taken to stop them *before* they do.

However, it is my belief that, although these measures were enacted out of genuine and understandable concern about these horrible crimes, some false assumptions are being made. As a result, the proposed solutions have too often not been grounded in hard facts and careful analysis. Crucial factual assumptions such as the following form the basis of most sex offender laws in the United States:

- There has been an epidemic of sex crimes in America over the past decade or so.
- The criminal justice system has failed miserably in preventing sexual violence.
- Sex offenders are more dangerous than other criminals and will commit many more crimes than other offenders, and certainly more sex crimes.

- Experts can identify which sex offenders are *really* dangerous and which are not.
- Most sex offenders target "strangers" rather than people they know.
- Mental health professionals can effectively treat these criminals, significantly reducing their risk of committing more sex crimes.
- Special programs can be developed to manage sex offenders in the community, denying sex offenders access to victims and ensuring that they will not commit new crimes.
- Ordinary people should be enlisted in this fight; they can take useful steps to defend themselves and their children.
- Drugs that reduce sexual desire will also reduce sexual recidivism; convicted sex offenders should be forced to take them if they want to return to the community.
- These new laws will reduce sex offending, help solve sex crimes, and make our neighborhoods safer.

Beginning in about 1990, states launched new initiatives designed to prevent sex offenders from committing more crimes. Some of these initiatives were designed to confine dangerous sex offenders for a very long time. Others were designed to help the community protect itself, to monitor sex offenders more intensively after they have been released from prison, or to change sex offenders' biology.

Many states have enacted much harsher sentences for sex offenders. They are being given longer sentences and are actually serving more of their sentences in prison. So many sex offenders are being confined that sex offenders are the second largest "growth industry" in the American prison system.

Every state in the country has a law requiring most convicted sex offenders to register with the police and tell them where they live. They must also inform the police whenever they move. In many states they must also furnish pictures, fingerprints, and DNA samples. There is also a federal register for sex criminals. Lawmakers assume that registration will deter offenders from committing new crimes and will help the police solve any that are committed. Every state also has a law that allows or requires the police to notify the community about dangerous sex offenders who live nearby. These laws seek to empower the community to protect itself from hazardous neighbors.

Sixteen states have enacted a novel sex offender commitment law that allows the state to civilly commit especially dangerous sex offenders called *sexually violent predators* (SVPs) who are about to be released from prison. These offenders are confined and treated in a secure facility for an indeterminate period and may be released only if they are no longer likely to commit another sex crime. As of spring 2002, some 2,229 men (and a few women and juveniles) had been committed to these prisonlike hospitals or were awaiting their commitment trial. Very few SVPs have been given conditional release, and even fewer have been given final release.

Several states have passed "chemical castration laws" that require selected sex offenders, as a condition of parole, to take drugs that eliminate their sex drive. If they refuse, they must serve their entire sentence. Other states are considering these laws. Sexual predators often must take these drugs if they ever hope to be conditionally released into the community. This approach assumes that men who have no sexual appetite will not commit sex crimes.

Some states have developed aggressive systems for monitoring sex offenders in the community and denying them access to potential victims. They use treatment providers, experts who give frequent lie-detector tests, and specially trained parole officers who specialize in supervising sex offenders. This team approach to implementing a risk-management strategy allows authorities to increase or decrease control over sex offenders, depending on ongoing risk assessments.

I must confess that for many years I have been skeptical of many of these new initiatives. Too often, politicians have enacted them in response to yesterday's tragic headline. Some strategies, in my opinion, threatened basic constitutional values by allowing the state to punish people for what they *might* do rather than for what they had done. Others seemed to invite people to take the law into their own hands or have required the misuse of powerful drugs to change basic human biology. After listening to my criticism, many people asked me, "Well, what would *you* do?" I came to realize that it is easier to be a constant critic than a constructive problem solver. I determined that I had a moral and intellectual responsibility to propose effective solutions rather than to simply curse the darkness.

This book examines what we know—and what we do not know—about sex offenders, victims, and sex crimes. It attempts to determine whether the current wisdom on which these new laws are based is accurate. Enough time has passed since these laws were first enacted to see whether they work and are cost-effective. In short, I examine the new weapons we are using to fight sex offenders and then discuss what we should—and should not—do to win this war.

I hope every reader will find this book stimulating, thoughtful, and helpful and that it will prove a useful resource for anyone interested in preventing sex crimes. Lawmakers and policymakers will find hard facts and analysis that are indispensable in designing sound public policy and passing effective crime-prevention measures. Mental health experts, who are increasingly called on to diagnose and treat sex offenders, to conduct risk assessments in individual cases, and to contribute in this important public policy arena will find this book of immense value. Judges and lawyers as well as law enforcement personnel, including prosecutors, police, and probation and parole officers, should read this book to understand both the constitutional and the forensic issues generated by these new laws.

Academics, researchers, and students interested in how the law should respond to sexual violence will find this book the most up-to-date and complete summary of what we know about sex offending and how the law has responded. Parents, school officials, and others will find this book invaluable in helping them protect our children from sex offenders. In summary, anyone interested in this difficult and complex subject will learn a great deal from this book.

This book covers a broad range of issues, including state-of-the-art research on sex offenders, sex crimes, and victims; cutting-edge constitutional analysis of new laws; and intensive public policy evaluation. Although these topics are formidable, this book is easy to read. As much as possible, I have avoided jargon and clutter.

Sex crimes and sex offenders are an emotional subject and evoke a wide range of public policy responses. This book attempts to separate fact from fiction, and effective responses from futile gestures. In short, it is a clarion call to fight sexual violence as effectively as possible, using strategies that are based on sound information. This book can help prevent future sexual violence.

ACKNOWLEDGMENTS

I would like to thank the extremely capable research assistants at the University of Missouri–Kansas City School of Law, who have helped me so much over the years. They include Rebecca Abeln, Diane Cotroneo, Christin Keele, Jin Liu, Paige Nicols, and Tina Parsley. Norma Karn, my secretary, has been a constant source of support, and Marcia Pinkman has continually encouraged me to keep writing.

I profited from many constructive comments made by my colleagues in a faculty workshop, especially suggestions made by Nancy Levit and Irma Russell. Pam Benton, Kathleen Hall, and Larry MacLachlan, very talented research librarians at the University of Missouri–Kansas City School of Law, have been an invaluable resource.

I am also grateful to my editor, Ed Meidenbauer, who has made many insightful suggestions to improve this book.

I have learned so much from so many people over the years while thinking about this difficult subject. I thank you all.

Preventing
Sexual Violence

INTRODUCTION

Society is enraged by sex offenders and the crimes they commit. Over the past decade or so, the United States has mobilized its crime-fighting forces, adding innovative weapons to its arsenal to meet this new danger. Sex offenders are the targets of this latest crusade against crime. Drawing on American ingenuity, new strategies have been developed to cope with the increased threat posed by sex offenders. Only by reviewing the historical context in which this latest round of law reform took place can we understand just how powerful and exceptional these novel weapons are.

THE REHABILITATIVE IDEAL

Sex offenders have been on the American radar screen before. In the 1960s, many states enacted sexual psychopath laws based on similar laws passed by several states in the late 1930s.[1] These laws allowed many sex offenders to be diverted from the criminal justice system into treatment programs. This strategy fit comfortably with the primary emphasis the criminal justice system then placed on rehabilitating offenders. Experts believed that crime was largely caused either by external social forces like poverty, or by internal pathology, like mental illness. Sexual offenders were seen

---

[1] SAMUEL JAN BRAKEL ET AL., THE MENTALLY DISABLED AND THE LAW (3rd ed. 1985).

primarily as individuals who suffered from a mental disorder that caused them to commit these horrible crimes. Mental health professionals, especially psychiatrists, were convinced they could accurately diagnose and effectively treat these mental pathologies, curing sex offenders so they could be safely be released into the community.

PUNISHMENT, NOT TREATMENT

Unfortunately, experts did not know why sex offenders were committing these crimes. Moreover, there was little evidence to support this claimed ability to diagnose and treat "sick" sex offenders. By the early 1980s, a solid consensus had developed in the United States that experts could not identify any specific group of sex offenders as sexual psychopaths by acceptable medical standards and that no treatments had proved to reduce sexual recidivism.[2] To make matters worse, many sex offenders committed to treatment programs spent less time in confinement than they would have if they had served their prison sentences, and other "patients" committed more sex crimes after they had "successfully" completed these treatment programs.[3] The public lost confidence in sexual psychopath programs. Treatment instead of punishment for sex offenders was discarded. By the early 1980s, most states had formally abolished or virtually abandoned their sexual psychopath programs.

NEW STRATEGIES TO COMBAT SEX OFFENDERS

In the 1970s and 1980s, additional forces for dramatically changing how society responded to sex offenders gathered momentum. Feminist voices successfully argued for changing how sex crimes, particularly rape and sexual assaults, were defined and prosecuted.[4] The old laws protected overly aggressive male sexual behavior and minimized women's right to sexual autonomy. Rape laws were dramatically revised to make conviction easier.[5] "Rape

---

[2] Id.

[3] See John Q. La Fond, Washington's Sexually Violent Predator Law: A Deliberate Misuse of the Therapeutic State for Social Control, 15 U. Puget Sound L. Rev. 655 (1992).

[4] See, e.g., Susan Estrich, Rape, 95 Yale L. J. 1087 (1986).

[5] See Leigh Bienen, Rape III–National Developments in Rape Reform Legislation, 6 Women's Rts. L. Rep. 170, 170–213 (1980). New statutory definitions focused primarily on the behavior of the aggressor rather than on his state of mind. Often, the new laws did not require women to use physical force to resist; this change sought to reduce the risk of physical injury to victims. Law Enforcement Assistance Administration, Battelle Memorial Institute Law and Justice Study Center, Forcible Rape 7 (Prosecutor's Volume 1977). They also abolished spousal immunity, an old common law doctrine that prevented prosecution of a husband for using force to engage in sexual activity with his wife. Some scholars question whether these reforms will result in

shield" laws were enacted to make it much harder for defense lawyers to explore the sexual history of victims, who were usually women, and thereby attack their credibility.[6] In the 1980s, sex offenders were considered fully responsible for their crimes, just like any other criminal. They fully deserved their prison sentences. Some states provided treatment for sex offenders who wanted it, while they were in prison. But sex offenders would not be released early from prison simply because they had participated in treatment programs.[7]

These important law reform measures for sex crimes were consistent with the abrupt shift from the rehabilitative model of the 1960s and 1970s to a responsibility-and-punishment model that swept America in the 1980s. "Law and order" had become an important social movement. The criminal justice system implemented a "just deserts" ideology of punishment. Criminals should be punished for their past acts with *fixed* sentences that were proportional to the harm they had inflicted on their victims and on society.[8] Many states increased their sentences for crimes, especially sex crimes. Other states, however, set rather low sentences.[9]

EVEN TOUGHER MEASURES

Despite these tough "law and order" measures, during the 1990s citizens throughout the country became even more alarmed over the menace to community safety that sex offenders posed. Although numerous factors contributed to this communal rage, the primary catalyst was a small number of serious crimes committed by convicted sex offenders against children.

Horrible Crimes Against Children

In 1987, convicted sex offender Earl Shriner was released from a Washington State prison even though, while incarcerated, he had drawn pictures of torture chambers and told other inmates of the terrible sex crimes against children he would commit after his release. Authorities had tried to have Shriner civilly committed to a mental health facility at the end of his prison term, but the court refused to commit him because he was not

---

the conviction of innocent people. *See, e.g.,* Stephen Schulhofer, *Rape-Reform circa June 2002: Has the Pendulum Swung Too Far?* 989 ANNALS N.Y. ACAD. SCI. 276 (2003).

[6] Vivian D. Berger, *Man's Trial, Woman's Tribulation: Rape Cases in the Courtroom,* 77 COLUM. L. REV. 1 (1977); J. Alexander Tanford & Anthony Bocchino, *Rape Victim Shield Laws and the Sixth Amendment,* 128 U. PA. L. REV. 544 (1980).

[7] La Fond, *supra* note 3.

[8] JOHN Q. LA FOND & MARY L. DURHAM, BACK TO THE ASYLUM: THE FUTURE OF MENTAL HEALTH LAW AND POLICY IN THE UNITED STATES (1992).

[9] La Fond, *supra* note 3.

mentally ill. Two years later, Shriner carried out the threats he had made in prison. He cut off the penis of a 6-year-old boy in Tacoma, where Shriner was then residing, raped him, and left him to die.[10] The community was aghast. How could public officials let such a dangerous convicted sex offender out of prison? Surely, there must be some way to keep dangerous sex offenders locked up even after they had served their sentences.

In 1993, Richard Allen Davis, a career criminal living in California, abducted Polly Klaas from a slumber party and then killed her.[11] In 1994, Jesse Timmendequas, a convicted sex offender released on parole and living in a halfway house in a residential community in New Jersey, sexually assaulted and killed Megan Kanka. Her parents had not been informed that the men living across the street from them were convicted sex offenders.[12] Citizens in New Jersey were outraged that public officials had not notified Megan's parents and others in the neighborhood that these sex offenders lived nearby and posed a serious threat to their children. Megan's parents said that had they been warned about these men, they would have been much more vigilant in protecting her. In their minds, this terrible crime could have been easily prevented.

These horrendous crimes received extensive media coverage. They also galvanized parents of the victims, and their families and friends, to form political action groups—including foundations named for child victims of terrible sex crimes, such as Jacob Wetterling, Nicole Megan Kanka, and the Klaas Kids—to lobby politicians and the media to demand changes in the law. These efforts were amazingly successful.[13]

Public Outrage

The public outrage over these horrendous sex crimes—some of which had been *predicted* and were, in the eyes of many, *preventable*—proved beyond a reasonable doubt that society needed to do much more to keep convicted sex offenders from committing more sex crimes. To many people, these cautionary tales were simply the tip of the iceberg. They believed there was a national epidemic of sex offenses being committed by dangerous sex offenders released too soon from prison without any control by the police or warning to the public. The public believed that sex offenders were much more dangerous than other criminals and that they committed numerous

---

[10] *See* David Boerner, *Confronting Violence: In the Act and the Word*, 15 U. Puget Sound L. Rev. 525 (1992) and sources cited therein.
[11] Vlae Kershner & Carolyn Lockhead, *Politicians React With Calls for Stiffer Sentences*, The S.F. Chron., Dec. 7, 1993, at A4.
[12] *Man Charged in 7-Year-Old Neighbor's Killing*, N.Y. Times, Aug. 1, 1994, at B5.
[13] Stuart Scheingold et al., *The Politics of Sexual Psychopathy: Washington State's Sexual Predator Legislation*, 15 U. Puget Sound L. Rev. 809 (1992).

sex crimes, often preying on children. Clearly, something drastic had to be done to save our children.

Pressure on Politicians

Politicians were compelled to take action. In June 1989, Booth Gardner, then Governor of Washington, convened a special task force to study how Washington's laws should be changed, under intense political pressure both from victims' rights groups and the media.[14] The case of Earl Shriner became the paradigm case: Dangerous sex offenders must not be allowed to commit another sex crime. One nonnegotiable demand made by law reform advocates was that very dangerous sex offenders would, one way or another, not be released from prison to commit another horrendous sex crime. Another demand was that people had a right to know when a dangerous sex offender was released from prison and living in their community. This task force made a number of recommendations to protect the community from dangerous sex criminals.

In 1990, the Washington legislature responded to this intense pressure to guarantee community safety.[15] It enacted virtually all of the task force's recommendations and passed a comprehensive set of laws called "The Community Protection Act."[16] The more aggressive and controversial of these included much longer prison sentences,[17] a novel civil commitment law for sexually violent predators, mandatory registration for virtually all sex offenders, and community notification laws. These statutes became models that other states used to enact their own versions. Legislatures in other states soon followed, introducing similar reforms.[18]

More recently, some states have adopted more draconian measures, even changing the human biology of dangerous sex offenders to prevent new sex crimes. In 1996, California added a powerful and controversial weapon to its crime-fighting arsenal: a "chemical castration" law that requires sex offenders convicted of certain crimes, as a condition of parole, to take drugs that reduce their male hormone levels and thus reduce their sex drive.[19] If they refuse, these offenders are kept in prison until they have

---

[14] For a thorough discussion of this process and the law reform initiated by it, see *Predators and Politics: A Symposium on Washington's Sexually Violent Predators Statute*, 15 U. PUGET SOUND. L. REV. 506 (1992). For a complete description of the Task Force's work, see TASK FORCE ON COMMUNITY PROTECTION: FINAL REPORT TO BOOTH GARDNER, GOVERNOR, STATE OF WASHINGTON (1989).

[15] Scheingold, *supra* note 13.

[16] The Community Protection Act, WASH. REV. CODE ANN. § 4.24.550 (1990).

[17] For example, in the early 1990s, Washington State on average doubled the maximum sentences for most sex crimes. La Fond, *supra* note 3.

[18] *See also* Jonathan Simon, *Managing the Monstrous, Sex Offenders and the New Penology*, 4 PSYCHOL. PUB. POL'Y & L. 452 (1998).

[19] *See* Chapter 6.

served their full prison sentence. Several other states, including Florida, Montana, and Oregon, have enacted chemical castration laws like California's that require many sex offenders to take drugs designed to significantly reduce their sex drive.[20] Other states are now using these drugs to treat and control sex offenders.

THE JURISPRUDENCE OF DANGEROUSNESS

Some commentators have characterized the laws enacted during this cycle of law reform aimed directly at sex offenders as implementing a "jurisprudence of dangerousness."[21] These criminals were perceived to be extremely dangerous during their entire lifetimes, and special approaches were critical to protect future victims from such ongoing threats. These laws represented an important shift in crime-fighting strategies in two important ways.

Confinement to Prevent Sex Crimes

First, earlier crime control strategies had embraced a "just deserts" ideology of punishment, which held that individuals should "pay their debt to society" by serving a prison term appropriate for the harm they *had committed*. Now, the emphasis shifted to social defense: The law must *prevent* future sex crimes. Extended confinement would be used to prevent sex offenders from committing more sex crimes. So long as a convicted sex offender was extremely dangerous, society was justified in confining him. In addition, aggressive measures to monitor and manage less dangerous sex offenders in the community would be required.

Community Self-Defense

Second, the community, not just the police, prosecutors, and other public players in the criminal justice system, must be empowered to safeguard itself from dangerous sex offenders. No longer would the community rely solely on the government to protect citizens against sex offenders. Vital information about dangerous sex offenders living in towns and cities must be provided to public officials and, in many cases, to neighbors so they could protect their children from these predators. Community protection

---

[20] *Id.*
[21] Michael Petrunik, *The Hare and the Tortoise: Dangerousness and Sex Offender Policy in the United States and Canada*, 2003 Can. J. of Criminology & Crim. Just. 43, Christopher Slobogin, *A Jurisprudence of Dangerousness*, 98 Nw. U. L. Rev. 1 (2003).

must be given priority over individual rights. Self-defense was a fundamental right of all citizens.

EMPIRICAL ASSUMPTIONS

Policymakers have made a number of crucial assumptions in formulating this public policy and enacting specific laws targeting sex offenders since about 1990. Following are some of these assumptions.

Sex offenders are a particularly dangerous group of criminals. They are more likely to commit new crimes than other criminals. They are also specialists who will commit sex crimes more frequently than other criminals. Sex offenders are constantly on the prowl for new victims and spend an entire lifetime committing these offenses. Most sex crimes are committed against strangers and not by people known to the victim.

Sex offenders' peculiar penchant for committing sex crimes explains the epidemic of sex crimes that has been sweeping America. Children are especially vulnerable and extensively victimized. Sex crimes inflict special harm on all victims, leaving lasting scars both physical and psychological.

A small group of sex offenders is *extremely* dangerous and *will* commit more sex crimes if not confined. Experts can identify who they are. Special measures are required if these risky individuals are to be prevented from sexually reoffending. Sex offenders can be treated to change their attitudes and behavior and stop them from committing more sex crimes. These same experts can also tell us when their patients have been successfully treated and can be released safely into society. Drugs can change their sexual behavior, thereby substantially reducing their sexual recidivism.

THE DYNAMICS OF LAW REFORM

Stories as Paradigms

Terrible crimes often generate instant and widespread law reform in the United States. These unusual and compelling cases become representative of all cases.[22] Law reform must promise they will not happen again. The political imperative for politicians to "do something" after criminal calamities is certainly understandable. No elected official will dare tell voters that the government cannot stop crime. Too often, however, policymakers ignore facts and "shoot from the hip." In this case, problems caused by hasty law

---

[22] La Fond, *supra* note 3.

reform without sufficient information and deliberation were compounded. Many states simply copied laws enacted in other states with minimal examination of their probable consequences.

Claims of New Expertise

Many of these new laws assume new expertise. And many experts came forward, claiming to possess new knowledge and skills that justify these new laws. For example, many of these measures suppose that some violent sex offenders have mental disorders and that experts can identify, diagnose, and treat those offenders. Other strategies take for granted that experts can identify which sex offenders are dangerous and likely to reoffend and which sex offenders are safe to be released. Thus, valid and reliable diagnoses, accurate predictions of dangerousness, and effective treatment are lynchpins of many of these new legal strategies.

Pros and Cons

Supporters claim these new laws, though harsh, are absolutely necessary to prevent convicted sex offenders from committing more sex crimes. Opponents reply that they violate the Constitution and are expensive and ineffective. In any event, it is clear that citizens are infuriated by repeat sex offenders and will insist on passing whatever laws they believe are necessary to prevent new sex crimes against new victims.

THE NEED FOR REASONED REFLECTION

The fierce public anger and virtually unanimous political consensus that these new public policy initiatives were essential for community protection left little opportunity for reasoned reflection on whether they are based on sound empirical knowledge and whether they actually work. Indeed, some observers have argued that law reform, including many of these measures, enacted in response to isolated, highly publicized, and emotionally charged crimes, is likely to be misguided and create as many problems as it tries to solve.[23]

Enough time has passed to allow passions to cool and to acquire empirical evidence on the impact of these new crime-fighting strategies. It is time to find out whether these aggressive measures have proved to be a wise and effective public policy that protects the community against dangerous sex offenders.

---

[23] Scheingold, *supra* note 13.

In this book, I review what we know—and what we do not know—about sex offenders. I then examine in depth several of the more controversial new laws designed to prevent sexual recidivism to see whether they achieve their goal. I identify measures that seem to work and to be worth keeping, as well as some measures that should be adjusted or discarded. Finally, I suggest changes in public policy that should be made to make the community safer.

Are Sex Offenders Really Dangerous?

Chapter 2 examines this fundamental question in depth and provides a "state-of-the-art" answer. Why do sex offenders commit these crimes? Do convicted sex offenders commit more crimes than other criminals? Do they commit more sex crimes? Can experts tell us which sex offenders pose the greatest risk of committing another sex crime?

Can Sex Offenders Be Treated?

A pivotal question for policymakers is whether sex offenders can be treated. Despite pronounced skepticism in the 1970s and 1980s about the efficacy of sex offender treatment, professional groups argued during this more recent cycle of law reform that new expertise has been developed that can reduce the rate of sexual recidivism. In reliance on these promises, innovative prison treatment programs are being provided in some state prisons. Newly enacted sexual predator laws require that states treat sex offenders committed under them. Many sex offenders are also being treated in the community. We need to know whether treatment, in fact, is effective in preventing sexual reoffending. Chapter 3 describes the current treatments for sex offenders and then rigorously examines the available evidence to see whether they work.

The Criminal Justice System

States have been aggressively using the criminal justice system to convict and imprison sex offenders, to keep many of them in jail for a long time, and to limit their right to come and go in the community after their release. This book describes and then examines these strategies and the empirical assumptions that shaped them. Is there an epidemic of sex crimes in the United States? Are children more often being sexually victimized by strangers or by people they know? Is the criminal justice system failing to protect the community against dangerous sex offenders? Are even longer sentences, including more lifetime sentences, needed?

Registration and Notification Laws

As mentioned earlier, every state has enacted a sex offender registration law. There is also a national sex offender registry. These laws apply to most sex offenders and are expensive to implement. Thus, we need to know whether there is any evidence that these laws actually do make our communities safer.

Every state also has passed a community notification law, which allows or requires public officials to disclose to the community the names of convicted sex offenders. Many states allow anyone to access their names and addresses by the Internet. Do these laws provide crucial information that allows neighbors to watch out for their children and prevent sex crimes? Or, do they simply create more anxiety and fear? Needless to say, community notification can make it more difficult for convicted sex offenders to earn a living and provide homes for their families. Occasionally, it can provoke vigilante justice. How much do notification laws cost? Are they effective? Chapter 4 describes how these laws work and how much they cost. It also analyzes the constitutional challenges to both registration and notification laws. Finally, it recommends changes that should be made to make our communities safer.

Civil Commitment to Fill Gaps

Sexual predator laws were born out of necessity. Some way to confine dangerous sex offenders due to be released from prison had to be invented. Since 1990, 16 states have enacted sexual predator laws that allow civil commitment of sex offenders after the criminal justice system can no longer confine them.

Chapter 5 describes these laws and explains how they work. It also discusses why supporters believe these laws are essential to protect the public and why critics claim they are terrible public policy and should be abolished. These laws are extremely expensive. Do they work? Are they worth the $100,000 a year it costs to keep each of these selected sex offenders in a prison that is also a hospital? Are alternative strategies available that can provide effective protection against more sex offenders at less cost?

Chemical Castration

Some state legislatures have pushed the constitutional envelope to the breaking point. As noted earlier, several states have enacted "chemical castration" laws, which require convicted sex offenders to take drugs that reduce their sex drive if they want to be released from prison on parole. A Colorado law *requires* judges to order some child molesters to take sex-drive-reducing drugs as a condition of parole, without requiring a clinical examination to determine whether these drugs are medically appropriate for each offender. These drugs are effective in reducing male sex drive; however, they can also have serious side effects and have not been approved by federal regulatory agencies for this purpose.

Do these laws reduce sexual reoffending? Even if they do, these laws and this treatment approach raise serious constitutional, moral, and philosophical questions. Chapter 6 examines how these drugs work and analyzes whether the evidence supports the claim they can reduce sexual recidivism. It also analyzes the constitutional issues raised by chemical castration laws and the policy arguments both for and against their use. It then makes balanced recommendations on this controversial subject.

Risk Management

New strategies based on the concept of risk management, like "community containment" in Colorado and "lifetime probation" in Arizona, are being used to prevent sex offenders from committing more sex crimes. Under the containment approach, many sex offenders living in the community are subject to intensive community supervision by a team that includes a parole officer, a treatment provider, and a polygraph operator. Using surveillance, lie detectors, and other control and assessment methods, officials periodically evaluate them to ascertain their current risk of reoffending. Officials can then increase or decrease the control exercised over these individuals in light of that risk evaluation. Rather than make a one-time prediction of whether a sex offender will commit another crime, this strategy allows officials to gather information about the offender on an ongoing basis and make any necessary adjustments in supervision.

Scholars have also proposed the creation of a new "sex offender reentry court" modeled after specialized problem-solving courts for drug offenders, people with mental illness, and domestic violence abusers. In this court, a judge, together with the teams like those used in community containment, would manage the risk of releasing sex offenders into the community and ensuring they do not reoffend. The judge would use his or her sentencing and release power to manage risk and create incentives for offenders to participate in treatment and change their attitudes and behavior. These courts have been effective with other types of offenders. Chapter 7 takes a good look at these approaches.

Recommendations

Finally, chapter 8 recommends what society *should* do to prevent sexual violence. Many new laws aimed at sex offenders have been enacted since

1990. Some of them seem to work and are cost-effective. They make sense. Other laws do not seem to reduce sexual recidivism or are extremely expensive. Worse, some laws may even make society less safe.

EFFECTIVE SOLUTIONS

Everybody feels passionate about the need to protect our loved ones from becoming victims of sex crimes. Because of this emotional background, how society should cope with sex offenders is a difficult subject. Informed and reasoned public deliberation is critical if we are to respond in ways that effectively prevent future sex crimes, while also honoring our commitment to constitutional values. It makes sense to concentrate our limited resources on those strategies that have the best chance of saving future victims from damaging sex crimes. This book provides a framework for that much-needed national conversation.

1

SEX CRIMES, VICTIMS, AND OFFENDERS

Society is terrified of what it believes is a new epidemic of sex crimes sweeping the country. Far too often, children seem to be the victims of these heinous acts. Has the number of sex crimes increased dramatically in the past 2 decades? Do sex offenders target children in large numbers? Do these criminals prefer to victimize strangers or people they already know? Do sex crimes inflict extraordinary damage on victims that require harsher punishment? These and other important questions must be answered as accurately as possible if we are to formulate effective strategies to prevent new sex crimes.

There is a great deal of research on these crucial issues. It is time to review what we know. First, I look at what we know from official crime statistics. Then, I discuss what victims tell us. Finally, I examine what offenders say about their crimes and their victims.

THE CONTROVERSY OVER MEASURING SEX CRIMES

It is not clear that we actually know how many sex crimes have actually been committed in this country. Attempts to accurately measure the extent of rape and other forcible sex crimes have evoked heated debate. Estimates can fluctuate wildly. For example, estimates of the number of rapes committed in the United States range from 80,000 to 700,000 annually.[1] This tremendous discrepancy can be explained by the different methods used to count these crimes. The number of rapes and other sex crimes reported to law enforcement authorities is far lower than the number of such crimes reported by victims and sex offenders in surveys.

Police Crime Rate Statistics

One way to measure crime is to count how many crimes are reported to the police each year. Measured by these reports to law enforcement agencies, crime rates in the United States increased dramatically beginning in the 1960s and soared until about 1980. The rate of violent crime increased almost 50% between 1971 and 1980.[2] However, sex crimes, including rape, increased over a longer period, from 1976 to 1992, when they reached their peak. The highest rate of forcible rapes reported to the police since 1976 occurred in 1992, when there were 84 rapes per 100,000 women, or about 1 for every 1,200 women.[3]

Around 1990, this escalating trend suddenly reversed, and serious crime in the United States started to decline significantly. The number of reported rapes from 1992 dropped 14% by 1995, when 97,460 forcible rapes were reported to law enforcement agencies. This was the lowest total since 1989.[4] The number of forcible rapes reported to law enforcement in 2001, 90,863, dropped even more; it was the lowest total reported since 1985.[5] When 1993 figures are compared with 1995 figures for forcible rape and sexual assaults, experts estimate that the "number of offenses experienced by victims . . . dropped by a quarter and the per capita rate of rape and sexual assault dropped 30%."[6] However, the number of forcible rapes reported in 2002 increased to 95,136, a 4.7% increase over 2001.[7] In summary, serious sex crimes exploded from about 1976 to 1992. However, they have decreased dramatically since about 1992.

---

[1] BUREAU OF JUSTICE STATISTICS, U.S. DEPT. OF JUSTICE STATISTICS, U.S. DEPT. OF JUSTICE, CRIMINAL VICTIMIZATION IN THE UNITED STATES—STATISTICAL TABLES, at Table 2, *Personal Crimes* (2001).

[2] FEDERAL BUREAU OF INVESTIGATION, U.S. DEPT. OF JUSTICE, CRIME IN THE U.S.: UNIFORM CRIME REPORTS FOR THE UNITED STATES (1971, 1980, 1988).

[3] BUREAU OF JUSTICE STATISTICS, U.S. DEPT. OF JUSTICE, SEX OFFENSES AND OFFENDERS, AN ANALYSIS OF DATA ON RAPE AND SEXUAL ASSAULT (1997).

[4] *Id.* Many of the statistics contained in the references for this chapter were derived from samples, specific time periods, law enforcement agency reports, victim surveys, and similar sources. Even though they do not, therefore, describe precisely sex crimes, offenders, victims, and other salient factors for the entire time period, the data will be presented as generally representative. This will avoid the necessity of qualifying all data described in this text.

[5] Bureau of Justice Statistics, *supra* note 1.

[6] Bureau of Justice Statistics, *supra* note 3, at 2.

[7] Federal Bureau of Investigation, *supra* note 2, at sec. II *Crime Index* (2003).

These statistics indicate that the public had good reason to be alarmed by increasing sexual violence during the 1980s and early 1990s. But they also suggest that sexual violence has abated significantly since then and that the public's continued fear, although understandable, is not as well founded.

Victim Surveys

Researchers also count sex crimes by conducting victim surveys. In somewhat simple terms, they ask people whether they have ever been the victim of a sex crime. This approach assumes, correctly, that not every victim will report the crime to the police. Thus, victim surveys generally indicate that more sex crimes are committed than are actually reported to law enforcement authorities.

Victim surveys invariably show that the incidence of serious forcible sex crimes is far higher than official crime-reporting statistics show. For example, in 1995 the National Victim Center and Crime Victims Research and Treatment Center reported that 13.4% of all adult American women had been victims of rape. It also estimated that 683,000 forcible rapes occurred in 1992. In more terrifying terms, the Center estimated that every minute 1.3 forcible rapes occur; 78 occur every hour; and 1,871 occur every day.[8]

Other studies also support the conclusion that many more sex crimes are committed in this country than are reported to the police. The American Psychological Association's Task Force on Male Violence Against Women estimated that between "14% and 25% of adult women have endured rape according to its legal definition."[9]

National Crime Surveys (NCS) conducted in 1994, 1995, and 1998 indicate that only 32%—one out of three—of sexual assaults committed against individuals age 12 or older were reported to the police.[10] Other researchers concluded that 84% of a large group of women, 4,008 adults, who identified themselves as victims of rape, had not reported the crime to law enforcement authorities.[11]

Some studies report an even higher incidence of rape. For example, a controversial study by Koss and her colleagues found that 27% of college women had been victims of at least one rape (or attempted rape) since the

---

[8]NATIONAL CENTER FOR VICTIMS OF CRIME & CRIME VICTIMS RESEARCH AND TREATMENT CENTER, RAPE IN AMERICA: A REPORT TO THE NATION (1992).
[9]Lisa A. Goodman et al., *Male Violence Against Women: Current Research and Future Directions*, 48 AM. PSYCHOLOGIST 1054, 1054–58 (1993).
[10]CENTER FOR SEX OFFENDER MANAGEMENT, RECIDIVISM OF SEX OFFENDERS, at 2 (2001).
[11]National Center for Victims of Crime & Crime Victims Research and Treatment Center, *supra* note 8.

age of 14.[12] This figure is extremely high when compared with the reports of victimization in NCS victim surveys, which indicated that only 1.4% of women had been victims of rape or attempted rape. Critics of the Koss study attacked its methodology and rejected its findings as mere advocacy.[13] Supporters retort that many women tend to blame themselves for what happened or deny that what occurred was actually rape.[14]

A more recent study by the National Institute of Justice examined violence against women on college campuses, including rape, sexual assault, and stalking. It concluded that 2.8% of the women surveyed reported they had been the victim of either a completed rape (1.7%) or an attempted rape (1.1%). The victimization rate was 27.7 rapes per 1,000 females.[15]

Some critics argue that the manner in which questions are posed in these surveys overstates the rate of sexual victimization.[16] Supporters, on the other hand, claim that, if anything, the number of actual sex crimes remains significantly underreported. Indeed, a comprehensive report from the Bureau of Justice indicates that in 1994 and 1995, only one of three victims of rape or sexual assault reported the crime to a law enforcement agency.[17] Victims who did report sex crimes to the police most often did so to prevent the offenders from committing new crimes against them. Those who did not report most often said that they considered the crime to be a personal matter.[18]

It may seem counterintuitive that victims of rape do not report this heinous crime to law enforcement authorities, but victims describe a number of cogent reasons for not reporting, including fear that they will be victimized again by the offender or harmed by his family or friends, that the offender may be a family member or friend who supports the victim, that others may find out, that no one will believe them, and that the criminal justice system will just make things worse. In addition, many victims are ashamed or feel guilty as a result of the sexual assault.[19]

---

[12] Mary P. Koss et al., *The Scope of Rape: Incidence and Prevalence of Sexual Aggression and Victimization in a National Sample of Higher Education Students*, 55 J. OF CONSULTING & CLINICAL PSYCHOL. 162 (1987).

[13] Neil Gilbert, *The Phantom Epidemic of Sexual Assault*, 103 THE PUB. INT. 54, 58 (1991).

[14] ROBIN WARSHAW, I NEVER CALLED IT RAPE (1988).

[15] Bonnie S. Fisher et al., U.S. DEPT. OF JUSTICE, RESEARCH REPORT: THE SEXUAL VICTIMIZATION OF COLLEGE WOMEN, at 10 (2000), *available at* http://www.ncjrs.org/pdffiles1/nij/182369.pdf.

[16] *See, e.g.*, Gilbert, *supra* note 13; Neil Gilbert, *The Campus Rape Scare*, WALL ST. J., June 27, 1991, at A14. *See also* KATIE ROIPHE, THE MORNING AFTER: SEX, FEAR, AND FEMINISM ON CAMPUS (1993). The victim survey for sex crimes was revised and phased in from January 1992 through 1993 and has been used since then. The instrument expanded the scope of sexual events covered beyond rape and attempted rape to include sexual assaults and other unwanted sexual contacts. The Bureau of Justice concluded that the "new questionnaire would produce estimates of rape and sexual assault that were 4 times higher than previously measured." Bureau of Justice Statistics, *supra* note 3, at 1.

[17] Bureau of Justice Statistics, *supra* note 3, at v.

[18] *Id.* at 2.

[19] Center for Sex Offender Management, *supra* note 10, at 3.

Incest victims are reluctant to report sex crimes to the police because they fear their families will be disrupted. The closer the relationship between the female victim and the offender, the greater the likelihood that the police will not be told about the rape or sexual assault.[20] When the offender was a current or former husband or boyfriend, about 75% of the attacks were not reported to police; this compares with 54% not being reported if the attacker was a complete stranger. It is doubtful that techniques can be developed to increase significantly the rate at which sex crimes are reported to authorities; consequently, recidivism rates for sex crimes are likely to be seriously understated.[21]

Crimes Against Children

It is now commonly accepted that sex crimes committed against minors are underreported.[22] Yet the research does not always support this common assumption. For example, in a 1994 study sponsored by the National Institute of Justice, a telephone survey of 2,000 children from ages 10 to 16 found that 3.2% of girls and less than 1% of boys had experienced sexual abuse.[23]

Although it is unknown how representative these samples may be, existing research does provide informative statistics on sex crimes committed against children. Data compiled by the National Incident-Based Reporting System (NIBRS) reveal information about certain types of sex offenses committed against children from 1991 to 1996.[24] Juveniles (children under age 18) accounted for 67% of all sexual assault victims reported to law enforcement. Thus, there is solid evidence indicating that sex offenders do, in fact, target children more often than adults.

The distribution of child victims by age differed with the type of sex crime. For instance, the risk of being a victim of forcible rape peaked at ages 10 to 14. The risk of being a forcible sodomy victim peaked at age 4, and at ages 3 to 4, the risk of being sexually assaulted with an object peaked. On the basis of the NIBRS data, a boy is most likely to be the victim of sexual assault at the age of 4 (but this risk is half the risk of girls at the age

---

[20] BUREAU OF JUSTICE STATISTICS, U.S. DEPT. OF JUSTICE, RAPE AND SEXUAL ASSAULT: REPORTING TO POLICE AND MEDICAL ATTENTION, 1992–2000, at 3 (2002).
[21] Center for Sex Offender Management, *supra* note 10, at 3.
[22] Robert A. Prentky et al., U.S. DEPT. OF JUSTICE, CHILD SEXUAL MOLESTATION: RESEARCH ISSUES (1997), *available at* http://www.ncjrs.org/pdffiles/163390.pdf. Incidence is also difficult to estimate because sex offenses often involve nonsexual offenses like kidnapping and other varieties of sexual violations, providing an array of charges that may be brought against an offender. When conviction is based on a lesser or nonsexual offense, for example, incidence measures are made inaccurate.
[23] *Id.* (*citing* David Finkelhor & Jennifer Dziuba-Leatherman, *Children as Victims of Violence: A National Survey*, 94 PEDIATRICS 413, 413–20 (1994).
[24] Howard N. Snyder, *NIBRS Statistical Report: Sexual Assault of Young Children as Reported to Law Enforcement: Victim, Incident, and Offender Characteristics* (2000), *available at* http://www.ojp.usdoj.gov/bjs/pub/pdf/saycrle.pdf.

of 4), while a girl is most likely to be a victim of sexual assault at 14. Girls ages 14 to 17 were victims of sexual assault at a rate 10 times greater than boys in the same age range. As these disturbing statistics indicate, very young children are too often victims of sexual attack.

Who Commits Sex Crimes Against Children?

The NIBRS data also provide information about sex offenders who victimize children.[25] Not surprisingly, males commit most sex crimes against children. They committed 96% of the sexual assaults against children reported from 1991 to 1996. Females committed 12% of the sexual assaults against children under the age of 6 and 6% of the sexual assaults against children ages 6 to 12. Only 3% of offenders were female in sexual assaults against juveniles ages 12 to 17.

Minors, including young children, also commit sex crimes against other children. Minors under the age of 12 comprised 16% of juvenile offenders who had committed sex crimes against children. Fortunately, they usually did not commit forcible rapes. However, juvenile offenders under the age of 12 committed 23% of all forcible sodomies reported from 1991 to 1996.

A substantial proportion of those committing sex offenses against children know their victims.[26] Of the offenders who victimized children under the age of 6, 49% were family members;[27] 42% of offenders against children ages 6 to 11 were also family members, as were 24% of offenders against children ages 12 to 17. Forty-eight percent of offenders were acquaintances of children under 6; 53% were acquaintances of children ages 6 to 11, and 66% acquaintances of juveniles ages 12 to 17. In general, relationships between victims and offenders were similar for males and females. Thus, children are much more likely to be sexually victimized by people they know than by strangers. As I discuss later, some of the recent crime prevention strategies target sexual violence by strangers, thereby missing the more likely offenders.

Solving Sex Crimes

In 1995, law enforcement agencies reported that about 50% of all reported forcible rapes were cleared by an arrest.[28] In 1995, law enforcement authorities made an estimated 34,650 arrests for forcible rape and 94,500 for other sex offenses. Arrests for rape and other sex offenses crested in

---

[25] Id.
[26] Id.
[27] Most of the offenders against children under 6 years old were family members.
[28] Bureau of Justice Statistics, supra note 3, at v.

1991, when 148,120 individuals were arrested.[29] Of course, not all arrests result in convictions. And, as we saw earlier, many sex crimes are never even reported to the police and are never investigated. Thus, the police never apprehend many sex offenders, and many of those who are apprehended are never convicted and punished. In light of this information, it is clear that society should emphasize strategies that effectively prevent the commission of sex crimes.

THE GENDER OF OFFENDERS AND VICTIMS

Victims

Overwhelmingly, sex crimes are committed by males against females.[30] The Department of Justice estimates that 94% of victims of rape and sexual assault were female.[31] Males had a much lower rate of victimization. For example, in 1994, victims reported one rape or sexual assault for every 270 females; the rate for males was significantly less, about one rape or sexual assault for every 5,000 males age 12 or older. Because men are much less likely to be the victims of sex crimes, male policymakers may have trouble empathizing with the pervasive fear of sexual violence that dominate women's daily lives.

Offenders

Males commit almost all of the sex crimes committed in this country. Of every 100 persons arrested or convicted for rape, 99 are male. Six in 10 are white, and the average age is in the early 30s. Offenders who were age 30 or older were involved in 4 out of 10 rape/sexual assaults. In about 1 out of 4, offenders were under age 21. Juveniles comprised about 16% of those arrested for forcible rape in 1995 and 17% of those arrested for other sex crimes. Females constituted 8% of offenders arrested for sex crimes other than rape. It is no surprise, then, that almost all sex offenders committed under sexual predator laws are men.[32]

Very little is known about the incidence, prevalence, and nature of sex offenses committed by women. One reason is that, historically, women have seldom been charged with sex crimes other than prostitution;[33] this

---

[29] *Id.* at 8.

[30] For a recent compilation of scholarship on female sex offenders, *see* Catherine F. Lewis & Charlotte R. Stanely, *Women Accused of Sexual Offenses*, 18 Behav. Sci. & L. 73 (2000).

[31] Bureau of Justice Statistics, *supra* note 20, at 1.

[32] *See* chapter 5.

[33] Adele Mayer, Women Sex Offenders: Treatment and Dynamics (1992).

has resulted in scarce data being compiled on women as sex offenders. Yet, we do know that women commit serious sex crimes. According to the Bureau of Justice Statistics, in an average year from 1993 to 1997, about 1 in 50 violent sex offenders (including rape and sexual assault) were women.[34] Approximately 1% of convicted offenders admitted to state prisons in 1996 for rape and sexual assault were women.[35] From 1991 to 1996, in all reported incidents of child sexual abuse, 12% of perpetrators who had committed sexual assault against children under 6 years of age were female.[36]

Women as a group traditionally have not been viewed as potential sex offenders, due in part to the stereotypical presumption that the typical offender is male and the typical victim female. Because there is little reliable empirical research on female sex offenses, courts have been hesitant to sentence convicted female offenders as harshly as their male counterparts.[37] But as social and cultural values regarding women's sex roles have changed, so have conceptions of female offenders. Researchers speculate that the number of reported sex offenses by women will continue to increase as detection of female-committed offenses increases[38] and the legal system adapts to the changing public perception of women as potential sex offenders.

VICTIM–OFFENDER RELATIONSHIP

Most victims of sex crimes know their attackers. Three out of four rape/ sexual assault victimizations involved offenders (both single and multiple-offender incidents) with whom the victim had a prior relationship, such as a family, intimate, or acquaintance relationship.[39] Yet, only about 1 in 4 of offenders who victimized their own child or stepchild was imprisoned.[40]

Strangers were involved in only about 20% of sexual offense victimizations when there was only a single offender. (When multiple offenders were involved, a much less frequent occurrence than a single offender, strangers accounted for 76% of the crimes.)[41] In almost 90% of rapes involving victims

---

[34] Lawrence A. Greenfield & Tracy L. Snell, U.S. Dept. of Justice, Women Offenders, at 2 (1999), *available at* http://www.ojp.usdoj.gov/bjs/pub/pdf/wo.pdf.

[35] *Id.* at 10.

[36] Snyder, *supra* note 24, at 8.

[37] *See, e.g., In re* Care & Treatment of Coffel, 117 S.W.3d 116 (Mo. Ct. App. 2003), where the court reversed a judgment ordering civil commitment of a female offender because there was insufficient empirical evidence on female sex offenders from which any qualified expert witnesses could reliably predict her likelihood of reoffending. The available data on women sex offenders was not substantial enough to support a finding that Coffel was a sexually violent predator. *Id.* at 38.

[38] Mayer, *supra* note 33.

[39] Bureau of Justice Statistics, *supra* note 3, at 4.

[40] *Id.* at 26.

[41] *Id.* at 4.

younger than 12, the victim knew the offender.[42] In 43% of those cases, police reported that a family member had been the offender.

Strangers commit fewer than 10% of all child molestations.[43] The majority of sex crimes against children are committed by fathers (20%), stepfathers (29%), other relatives (11%), and acquaintances (30%).[44] Unfortunately, the majority of child molestations by nonstrangers may not even be reported to the police or on victim surveys.[45]

THE HARM SEX CRIMES CAUSE

By anyone's standards, sexual assault causes great harm to the victim. Damage is psychological and physical, which is traumatic enough, but there are also economic and other longer term effects.

Violence to the Victim

In 1993, victims of rape and sexual assault comprised about 4% of the victims of violence and about 6% of crimes in which medical assistance was provided. Most observers agree that if a woman is raped, she has some sort of physical injury. Consequently, 100% are physically injured; however, most rape victims do not receive treatment for their injuries. Of those who sought medical attention, 5% had suffered a serious injury, including severe lacerations, fractures, internal injuries, or unconsciousness.[46]

Use of Weapons

Contrary to popular belief, sex offenders use weapons much less frequently than other violent offenders, who use a weapon in about 30% of their offenses. Most violent sex offenders do not use a weapon while committing a sexual offense. Rapists reportedly use a firearm in about 5% of those crimes, while sexual assaulters use a knife in 2% of their crimes. They used physical force in 80% of those crimes. Rapists are more likely to use a gun in rapes involving a stranger as victim (i.e., in about 10% of them). This compares with the use of a gun in about 2% of rapes involving rape of a family

---

[42]Id. at 11.

[43]Leonore J. Simon, *The Myth of Sex Offender Specialization*, 23 NEW ENG. J. ON CRIM. & CIV. CONFINEMENT 387 (1997).

[44]Leonore Simon et al., *Characteristics of Child Molesters: Implications for Fixated-Regressed Dichotomy*, 7 J. OF INTERPERSONAL VIOLENCE 211 (1992).

[45]C.S. Widom & R. Shepard, *Accuracy of Adult Recollections of Early Childhood Abuse*, in RECOLLECTIONS OF TRAUMA: SCIENTIFIC EVIDENCE AND CLINICAL PRACTICE (J.D. Read & S. Lindsay eds., 1997).

[46]Bureau of Justice Statistics, *supra* note 3, at 12.

member.[47] In summary, violent sex offenders are much less likely to use a deadly weapon committing sex crimes when compared with other violent offenders.

Economic Loss

About 1 in 11 of victims of rape or sexual assault incurred economic loss as a result of the crime. The average economic loss was $200, and almost 7% of the victims said they lost time from work.[48]

Psychological Damage

More important, victims of sex crimes suffer serious psychological harm. Thirty percent of rape victims have experienced at least one major depressive episode in their lifetime; in contrast, only 10% of women who had never been victims of a violent crime have had a serious depressive episode.[49] Victims of rape are also more likely to have problems with drugs or alcohol.[50]

Rape victims often show long-term symptoms of chronic headaches,[51] fatigue,[52] sleep disturbance,[53] recurrent nausea,[54] decreased appetite,[55] eating disorders,[56] menstrual pain,[57] sexual dysfunction,[58] and suicide attempts.[59] Sexual assault also significantly increases the probability of substance abuse.[60]

Posttraumatic Stress Disorder

Almost one third of rape victims experience posttraumatic stress disorder at some time during their lives. This is 6.2 times more than women

---

[47]*Id.*

[48]*Id.* at 5.

[49]Dean G. Kilpatrick, *National Violence Against Women Prevention Research Center, The Mental Health Impact of Rape, available at* http://www.nvaw.org/research/mentalimpact.shtml.

[50]*Id.*

[51]*See, e.g.,* Mary P. Koss & L. Heslet, *Somatic Consequences of Violence Against Women,* ARCHIVES OF FAMILY MEDICINE, Sept. 1992, at 1:53–59; Kimberly K. Eby et al., *Health Effects of Experiences of Sexual Violence for Women With Abusive Partners,* 16 HEALTH CARE FOR WOMEN INTERNATIONAL 563, 563–76 (1995).

[52]Eby, *supra* note 51, at 563–76.

[53]*Id.*

[54]*Id.*

[55]Dean G. Kilpatrick et al., *Mental Health Correlates of Criminal Victimization: A Random Community Survey,* 53 J. OF CONSULTING & CLINICAL PSYCHOL. 866, 866–73 (1985).

[56]H.S. Resnick et al., *Health Impact of Interpersonal Violence, sec. II: Medical and Mental Health Outcomes,* 23 BEHAV. MED. 65, 65–78 (1997).

[57]Koss & Heslet, *supra* note 51, at 1:53–59.

[58]J.M. Golding, *Sexual Assault History and Women's Reproductive and Sexual Health,* 20 PSYCHOL. OF WOMEN Q. 101, 101–21 (1996).

[59]Kilpatrick, *supra* note 55, at 866–73.

[60]Dean G. Kilpatrick et al., *A 2-Year Longitudinal Study of the Relationships Between Violent Assault and Substance Use in Women,* 65 J. OF CONSULTING & CLINICAL PSYCHOL. 834, 834–47 (1997).

who had never been crime victims developed this disorder.[61] Someone who has personally experienced actual or threatened death or serious injury during a rape or sexual assault can repeatedly and painfully reexperience the traumatic event in "flashbacks" or "nightmares." These individuals may try to avoid situations, people, or activities they associate with it, which can retrigger horrible memories of the crime. Their emotional responses may feel deadened or, conversely, they may be constantly hypervigilant or overly aroused in other ways, such as experiencing difficulty in sleeping or concentrating.[62] In this debilitating way, they may relive the horror of the crime in any number of emotion-wrecking ways.

Other Consequences

Victims also suffer in other ways, including unwanted pregnancy,[63] sexually transmitted diseases,[64] and even death.

Sex crimes cast a shadow of fear over women that intrudes into their daily lives, often influencing choices over where they go, with whom, and at what time. In many ways, the threat of sexual victimization pervasively constrains women's freedom of movement.[65] It is not surprising that fear of being raped by a stranger drives women's fear of crime.[66]

Summary

Sex crimes do real damage to their victims, most of whom are female. Many of these victims suffer physical, economic, and psychological damage of immense, even catastrophic, dimension. This damage can last a lifetime.

---

[61] See, e.g., Kilpatrick, supra note 49; Sue Boney-McCoy & David Finkelhor, Prior Victimization: A Risk Factor for Child Sexual Abuse and for PTSD-Related Symptomatology Among Sexually Abused Youth, 19 CHILD ABUSE & NEGLECT 1401 (1995); Sue Boney-McCoy & David Finkelhor, Psychosexual Sequelae of Violent Victimization in a National Youth Sample, 63 J. OF CONSULTING & CLINICAL PSYCHOL. 726 (1995); B.O. Rothbaum et al., A Prospective Examination of Post-Traumatic Stress Disorder in Rape Victims, 5 J. OF TRAUMATIC STRESS 455 (1992); Dean G. Kilpatrick et al., Victimization, Posttraumatic Stress Disorder, and Substance Use and Abuse Among Women, available at http://www.nida.nih.gov/PDF/DARHW/285-308_Kilpatrick.pdf.
[62] AMERICAN PSYCHIATRIC ASSOCIATION, THE DIAGNOSTIC AND STATISTICAL MANUAL OF MENTAL DISORDERS, IV–TR (4th ed., text revision 2000). (hereinafter, DSM–IV–TR), at 463–68.
[63] Melissa M. Homes et al., Rape-Related Pregnancy: Estimates and Descriptive Characteristics From a National Sample of Women, 175 AM. J. OF OBSTETRICS & GYNECOLOGY 320, 320–24 (1996).
[64] See, e.g., Koss & Heslet, supra note 51, at 1:53–59L; Resnick, supra note 56, at 65–78.
[65] See, e.g., Margaret T. Gordon & Stephanie Riger, The Female Fear: The Social Cost of Rape (1991); Elizabeth A. Stanko, Intimate Intrusions (1985).
[66] Nancy A. Crowell & Ann W. Burgess, Understanding Violence Against Women (1996).

SEXUAL ASSAULTS AGAINST ADOLESCENTS AND CHILDREN

Whereas rape and sexual assault of adult women have received a lot of media attention, and rightly so, most sexual assaults are committed against underage victims. This is an emotional topic, one tangled with the horrifying fact of underreportage and the knowledge that these assaults usually cause long-term damage to children.

Sex Crimes Reported to the Police

Crimes against juveniles are the large majority (67%) of the sexual assaults investigated by law enforcement agencies. The more frequently reported types of sex crimes include forcible fondling (45% of all reported cases) and forcible rape (42%); the less frequently reported sexual assaults include forcible sodomy (8%) and sexual assault with an object (4%).[67] Many of the victims of sexual assault were very young. One of 7 victims was under the age of 6, and more than one third of all victims of all sexual assaults were under 12. A quarter (25.1%) of the victims of all sexual assaults between ages 6 and 11 were male.[68]

Approximately 80% of rape victims were under the age of 30, and about *half* of those were under 18. Indeed, the risk of being the victim of a forcible rape increases dramatically from age 10 to 14, when it is the *highest*.[69] In 15% of reported rapes, the victims were under 12, and another 29% were between 12 and 17.[70] Thus, 44% of the victims of rape were *under* the age of 18.

Self-Reports by Sex Offenders

Imprisoned rape and sexual assault offenders reported that 2 out of 3 of their victims had been under 18 in crimes involving a single victim and 4 out of 10 rapists said that their victim had been a child. About 80% of sexual assaulters disclosed that their victim was under 18.[71] Most imprisoned offenders who had committed a crime against a child were imprisoned for a sex crime. A large majority of incarcerated prisoners whose victims were under 18 had committed sexual assault or molestation. Offenders reported committing forcible rapes against children *unknown* to them in only 11.9%

---

[67] Snyder, *supra* note 24, at 2.
[68] *Id.*
[69] *Id.*
[70] Bureau of Justice Statistics, *supra* note 3, at 11.
[71] *Id.* at 24.

of the cases and in only 11.3% of sexual assaults.[72] Thus, their victim was typically a child whom they knew; they did not randomly target strangers.[73]

Victim Surveys

Surveys also indicate a higher sexual victimization rate for children than official estimates. In a national telephone survey of 2,000 children between ages 10 and 16, 3.2% of the girls and 0.6% of the boys reported sexual abuse involving physical contact. These reports indicated rates of child sexual victimization that "far exceed those reported in official government victimization statistics."[74] For example, the rate of rape was about five times higher than the estimate of 0.1% reported in the National Crime Survey. One study (although highly criticized) found that the typical sex offender molests an average of 117 children, most of whom never report the crime.[75] Although the exact extent of their sexual victimization is impossible to establish, it is clear that children and juveniles are frequently the victims in sex offenses.

Harm to Children

Children, who comprise a significant proportion of sex crime victims, can suffer in even more perilous ways than adult victims. Like adult victims, they can be subjected to physical force or the threat of weapons. They also suffer special kinds of harm. Long-term effects of child abuse can include serious psychological impairment of emotions, including fear, anxiety, depression, anger, hostility, and poor self-esteem.[76] Many also develop a pronounced inability to trust other persons, inhibiting the development of interpersonal relationships. Sexual victimization may also negatively impact the development of a healthy sexuality.[77]

Young girls coerced into sex are three times more likely to develop psychiatric disorders, including posttraumatic stress disorder and eating disorders, or alcohol and drug abuse as adults than are girls who have not been

---

[72]Lawrence A. Greenfield, U.S. Dept. of Justice, at 10 (1996).

[73]Id. at iii.

[74]Finkelhor & Dziuba-Leatherman, supra note 23, at 415.

[75]See Sally Squires, Who Would Sexually Abuse a Child? Study Looks at 67,000 Cases, WASH. POST, June 18, 1986, at T07, available in 1986 WL 2038702 (referencing a study funded by the National Institute of Mental Health and conducted by Dr. Gene Abel, psychiatrist and professor at Emory University). But see chapter 2.

[76]Angela Brown & David Finkelhor, Impact of Child Sexual Abuse: A Review of the Research, 99 PSYCHOL. BULL. 66, 69–70 (1986).

[77]Mavis Tsai & Nathaniel Wagner, Therapy Groups for Women Sexually Molested as Children, 7 ARCHIVES OF SEXUAL BEHAV. 417, 422–24 (1978).

sexually abused.[78] The literature also suggests a correlation between child abuse and teenage prostitution.[79]

Boys who are sexually abused have a suicide rate 1½ to 14 times higher than boys who have not been sexually abused.[80] More ominous, many researchers believe that early sexual abuse can contribute to boys themselves becoming sexual abusers later on in life.[81] In surveys, sexual assault offenders were substantially more likely than any other category of offenders to report having experienced physical or sexual abuse while growing up. (On the other hand, two thirds of sexual assault offenders reported that they had never been physically or sexually abused as a child.)[82]

Sex Crimes and Murder

Sexual motivation is almost never the primary motive for murder. Since the late 1980s, murders involving rape or a sex offense as the primary motive have declined from 2% of murders to less than 1%.[83] Perhaps contrary to high-profile media cases, sex offending seldom leads to the death of the victim.

USING THE CRIMINAL JUSTICE SYSTEM
TO PREVENT SEX CRIMES

There is strong evidence that society is using the criminal justice system aggressively against sex offenders. Over the past 2 decades or so, a number of states have enacted indeterminate sentencing laws with harsh punishment for repeat sex offenders.[84] Other states have increased prison terms for sex offenders.[85] Washington State has increased its sentencing

---

[78] Kenneth S. Kendler et al., *Childhood Sexual Abuse and Adult Psychiatric and Substance Use Disorders in Women: An Epidemiological and Cotwin Control Analysis*, 57 Archives of Gen. Psychiatry 953 (Oct. 2000).

[79] *See, e.g.*, Laurie Schaffner, *Female Juvenile Delinquency: Sexual Solutions, Gender Bias, and Juvenile Justice*, 9 Hasting's Women's L. J. 1, 23 (1998) (studies suggest relationship between early sexual abuse and delinquent behaviors, including prostitution, on the part of teenagers); Charles A. Phipps, *Children, Adults, Sex and the Criminal Law: In Search of Reason*, 22 Seton Hall Legis. J. 1, 83 (1997) (teenage prostitution one of several negative consequences of sexual abuse of a child) and Mimi H. Silbert & Ayala M. Pines, *Entrance Into Prostitution*, 13 Youth & Soc'y 471 (1982) (of 200 street prostitutes interviewed, most under the age of 21, 60 percent reported having been the victims of incest and sexual abuse at the ages of 3 to 16).

[80] William C. Holmes & Gail B. Slap, *Sexual Abuse of Boys: Definition, Prevalence, Correlates, Sequelae and Management*, 280 J. of the Am. Med. Ass'n 1855 (1998).

[81] *Id.*

[82] Bureau of Justice Statistics, *supra* note 3, at 23.

[83] *Id.* at 27.

[84] *See, e.g.*, Colo. Rev. Stat. §16-13-203 (1996).

[85] In 1990, Washington State, for example, on average doubled the sentences for sex offences. *See* Community Protection Act, Wash. Rev. Code Ann. § 4.24.550 (1990).

ranges for sex offenders six times. Some states have increased penalties for crimes, such as burglary, that are "sexually motivated."[86]

"Three Strikes and You're Out"

Many states have enacted mandatory life sentencing laws, often called "one, two, three strikes and you're out" laws. The purpose of these laws is straightforward: Repeat serious offenders should be removed from society for life.[87] Between 1993 and 1995, 24 states and the federal government enacted "three-strike" statutes that enhanced sentencing for repeat offenders.[88] Some of these laws require a mandatory life sentence if the defendant is convicted of a specified number of qualifying felonies. Serious sex crimes, including most sex offense felonies, generally qualify as a "strike" in these laws.[89] Thus, many repeat sex offenders can be sentenced to very long mandatory sentences, including life imprisonment.[90]

Sex Offenders in Prison

Since 1980, the average annual growth in the number of prisoners incarcerated in the United States has been 7.6%. Yet, the number of prisoners sentenced for violent sexual assault other than rape increased by nearly 15%—faster than any other category of crime except drug trafficking. From 1980 to 1994, the prison population increased by 206%; the number of imprisoned sex offenders increased by 330%.[91] In 1980, 20,500 prisoners in state prisons (6.9% of all prisoners) were serving time for rape or sexual assault. By 1994, the number of sex offenders in the system had jumped to 88,000 (9.7% of the state prison population).[92]

Length of Sentences for Sex Offenders

In 1992, over two thirds of convicted rapists received a prison sentence. Of these, the average term imposed was just under 14 years, and about 2% of convicted rapists received a life sentence. Between 1985 and 1993, the

---

[86] Lucy Berliner, *Sex Offenders: Policy and Practice*, 92 Nw. U. L. Rev. 1203, 1215 (1998).

[87] National Institute of Justice, U.S. Dept. of Justice, *Three Strikes and You're Out: A Review of State Legislation Series*, at 3 (1997).

[88] *Id.*

[89] *Id.* at 2; *see also* Berliner, *supra* note 86, at 1215.

[90] Mandatory life sentences with no possibility of parole are imposed on offenders who have "struck out" in Georgia, Indiana, Louisiana, Maryland, New Jersey, North Carolina, South Carolina, Tennessee, Virginia, Washington, and Wisconsin. *See* National Institute of Justice, *supra* note 87, at 8.

[91] Bureau of Justice Statistics, *supra* note 3, at 17.

[92] *Id.* at 18.

average time served by convicted rapists in state prisons increased from about 3 years to 5 years, thus increasing the percentage of sentence served from about 38% to about 50%. For sex offenders released from prison between 1985 and 1993, there has been an increase in the average length of stay in prison and in the percentage of the sentence served in confinement prior to release.[93]

Plea-Bargaining Versus Trial

Sex offense defendants are more likely to receive a prison term if they have a jury trial than are defendants tried by a judge or who enter a guilty plea. The average prison term for defendants tried by a jury is 13 years longer than the average sentence imposed on those who plead guilty to rape.[94] Thus, as it does for other types of offenders, the practice of plea-bargaining may result in sex offenders receiving inducements for waiving their constitutional right to trial. These benefits may include, for example, being charged with less serious crimes or reduced counts, receiving shorter sentences, or avoiding serving any time in jail or prison.

Community Control

Law enforcement is also aggressively monitoring more sex offenders in the community. On any day there are about 234,000 offenders convicted of rape or sexual assault under the care, custody, or control of corrections agencies. Almost 60% of these offenders are being conditionally supervised in the community.[95] Sex offenders comprise about 4% of convicted offenders on probation and about 3% of offenders in local jails. They constitute about 10% of offenders in state prisons and 1% in federal prisons.[96]

CONCLUSION

Although we know less about sex crimes, offenders, and their victims than we need to know, a solid knowledge base is available for policymakers for developing effective strategies for coping with sex offenders.

---

[93] Id. at 19.
[94] Id. at 14.
[95] Id. at 15.
[96] Id. at 16–17.

An Epidemic of Sex Crimes?

Based on official police records, sex crimes did increase dramatically over the past several decades until about 1993, when they started to decline significantly. Yet, victim surveys still suggest that a significant number of forcible sex crimes are committed that are not reported to the police. How to resolve these conflicting indicators is difficult, if not impossible. Perhaps the truth is that, although there are more forcible sex crimes experienced by victims than are officially reported, the overall number of such crimes is declining, as official police reports suggest.

If this is true, what caused this sudden reversal? Did innovative strategies, like special civil commitment for sex offenders, mandatory registration, community notification, and chemical castration, significantly cause this welcomed change in course? Or, did other, more traditional strategies, like aggressive prosecution and longer prison sentences, change the tide? Or, have all of these strategies played a role in the recent reduction in sex crimes and in reducing the danger posed by sex offenders? These are extremely important questions, and we are still waiting for definitive answers.

The Primacy of the Criminal Justice System

In all probability, aggressive use of the criminal justice system played the most significant role in reducing sex-offending. Crime rates for most other violent crimes also declined during approximately the same period. This is not surprising. During the early 1980s, sentences for most serious crimes were increased and more offenders were sentenced to longer prison terms. The number of people confined in jails and prisons in the United States increased significantly.[97] Although establishing a cause-and-effect relationship between longer prison sentences and crime reduction may be impossible, it is likely that they played a key role in reducing sex crimes.

The criminal justice system has also responded aggressively to punish and prevent sex crimes. An increase has been seen in both the average length of confinement for sex offenders and in the proportion of their sentence that sex offenders must serve before they are released.[98] More sex offenders are being monitored in the community; yet many sex offenders are never arrested or convicted for their crimes.

More aggressive use of the criminal justice system should be the primary means of preventing sexual violence. It is an effective strategy for reducing

---

[97]*Id*. at 17–18.
[98]*Id*. at 19.

sex crimes. Having said that, we should be concerned about the high number of sex crimes that are not cleared. Sex offenders who are not arrested, convicted, and sent to prison remain free to commit more sex crimes. Advances in science, like DNA testing, need to be used more aggressively in investigating sex crimes. As DNA samples are collected from convicted sex offenders,[99] solving some sex crimes, especially rape, should become easier.

In chapters 7 and 8, I critique some criminal justice strategies that are overly broad and unnecessarily incarcerate some sex offenders for long periods of time while allowing other sex offenders to serve too little time. I also explore new criminal justice strategies that show great promise for providing effective protection for prospective victims.

Offenders and Victims

Offenders who know their victims commit most sex crimes; strangers do not commit them. Preventive strategies should acknowledge the established risk that victims are more likely to be sexually harmed by people they know. Our current preoccupation with using strategies for preventing sex offenders from committing sex crimes against strangers, like sexual predator and community notification laws, may be woefully misdirected. Instead, strategies to prevent, detect, and punish sex crimes should focus on places and institutions in which victims, especially young victims, are too easily available for sexual exploitation. Schools, churches, day care centers, camps, college campuses, and other similar environments provide extensive opportunities for sex offenders to find, groom, and take advantage of victims.

Females constitute 99% of sex crime victims. Children and adolescents are disproportionately victims of sex crimes. Too many of these horrible crimes remain secrets forever. We must take these crimes more seriously and rethink how we can make it easier for victims, especially children, to tell someone in a position to respond that they have been sexually victimized. Strategies that encourage victims to report and to cooperate with law enforcement agencies in prosecuting sex crimes must be emphasized. Victims of sex crimes also need help in coping with the severe harm done to them by offenders. The harm done to children by sex crimes can continue over the course of their lives. More must be done to help them heal and live productive, healthy lives.

Men commit the vast majority of sex crimes. Although we do not know why men commit sex crimes,[100] initiatives to change how the culture

---

[99] See chapter 4 for a discussion of how some states collect DNA samples as part of sex offender registration laws.
[100] See chapter 3.

views male sexuality and how men acquire their sexual attitudes are important areas for future research.[101]

Sexual violence is an extremely serious problem. Too many women and children are victims of sex crimes. But what about sex offenders? Are they especially dangerous? Do they commit more crimes than other criminals? In the next chapter, I explore what is known about sex offenders.

---

[101] See Julie Shapiro, *Predators and Politics: A Symposium on Washington's Sexually Violent Predators Statute, Sources of Security*, 16 U. PUGET SOUND L. REV. 843 (1992) (includes discussion of "culture of violence" and its possible relationship to acts of sexual violence).

2

ARE SEX OFFENDERS
REALLY DANGEROUS?

A driving force for many of the law reform initiatives launched in the past decade or so is the assumption that sex offenders pose an extreme ongoing threat to commit more sex crimes against more victims, especially children. The public believes that sex offenders commit many more crimes, particularly sex crimes, than other types of criminals. Policymakers have confidence that experts can identify those sex offenders who pose a special threat of committing another sex crime and who should, therefore, be targeted for special protective measures. Many of the recently enacted legal strategies to protect the community also rely on these assumptions.

But do we really know enough about sex offenders to support these common assumptions and to justify these legal strategies? There are many important questions that must be answered accurately if we are to effectively protect the community. Why do sex offenders commit sex crimes? Are sex offenders more dangerous than other criminals? Do they commit more *sex* crimes? Can we accurately identify which sex offenders will commit another sex crime if nothing is done to stop them? Can we tell which sex offenders will *not* commit another crime if left alone? In this chapter, I try to answer these difficult yet essential questions.

WHY DO SEX OFFENDERS COMMIT SEX CRIMES?

The Etiology of Sex Offending

What causes sex offenders to commit sex crimes? The short and honest answer, unfortunately, is that we do not know for certain. Researchers have suggested a number of plausible explanations, and the search for clear answers continues. But the question remains extremely important, and efforts to answer it must continue.

Answering that question could help us in several important ways. First, potential offenders could be identified *before* they actually commit sex crimes, providing timely and effective intervention and protecting prospective victims of sex crimes. Second, more effective treatment could be provided to sex offenders, enabling them to change their criminal attitudes and behavior. Third, we could more efficiently and effectively monitor sex offenders who live in the community by using appropriate risk management techniques to prevent them from reoffending.

Theories

Although there are no scientifically established answers, a number of current theories attempt to explain why sex offenders commit sex crimes.

Psychoanalytic/Psychiatric Theories

Early theories hypothesized that early childhood experiences, including family relationships, later caused offenders, who are mostly men, to commit sex crimes. Becker and Murphy concluded that this theory is probably not correct. They said, "early writers focused on infantile sexuality, castration anxiety, and the oedipal complex."[1] In the psychiatric view, sex offenders were sick individuals whose behavior was caused by individual mental pathology.[2] Basically, there was little to no support for such theories, and "they have generally fallen by the wayside."[3]

Family Dynamics

Researchers have suggested that family dysfunction, like confused mother–daughter roles or family isolation, may have caused incest offen-

---

[1] Judith V. Becker & William D. Murphy, *What We Know and Do Not Know About Assessing and Treating Sex Offenders*, 4 PSYCHOL. PUB. POL'Y & L. 116, 119–20 (1998).
[2] Owen D. Jones, *Sex, Culture, and the Biology of Rape: Toward Explanation and Prevention*, 87 CAL. L. REV. 827, 831 (1999).
[3] Becker & Murphy, *supra* note 1, at 120.

ders to commit sex crimes against the family. Again, there is little empirical support for this view.[4]

Culture, Patriarchy, and Misogyny

Sometimes labeled as the *feminist view*, this approach generally posits that society itself causes sexual aggression and victimization. In this view, men, who commit most sex crimes, learn from a male-dominated culture how to use sexual aggression to exploit and subordinate women and keep them in their place. Women, in turn, accept the role of victim. Causation is external to the individual; it is located primarily in patriarchal cultural attitudes and social traditions, which socialize men to be potential rapists. Consequently, "sex" crimes should really be considered crimes of "violence" against women.[5] In this view, attitudes such as sexual stereotyping and rape myth play a role in sexual offending.[6]

Some research indicates that some sexually aggressive people (primarily college students) do have these attitudes. However, no research has established that this hypothesis applies to more violent rapists. Others disagree with this view. In their judgment, sexual motivation is an important component of rape.[7]

Mating Strategies

Another theory suggests that the mating strategies of men differ significantly from those of women. Women are believed to be more likely than men to seek monogamous and lasting sexual relationships. Men, on the other hand, may be relatively more interested in novelty and less interested in stability. Thus, some men may be less willing to compromise with women's romantic and sexual preferences. Instead, they simply coerce women into sex, uninhibited by the suffering of their partner.[8]

Evolution

Other researchers suggest that rape can be considered an adaptive feature of evolution or as a by-product of other adaptive characteristics.[9] In

---

[4] *Id.* (citing P.M. Crittenden, *Research on Maltreating Families: Implications for Intervention*, THE APSAC HANDBOOK ON CHILD MALTREATMENT (J. Briere et al., eds., 1996).

[5] Jones, *supra* note 2, at 838–840.

[6] Becker & Murphy, *supra* note 1, at 120 (1998) (citing Susan Brownmiller, *Against Our Will: Men, Women, and Rape* (1975)).

[7] C.T. Palmer, *Twelve Reasons Why Rape Is Not Sexually Motivated: A Skeptical View*, 25(4) J. OF SEX RES. (1988), at 512–530.

[8] Grant T. Harris et al., *Appraisal and Management of Risk in Sexual Aggressors: Implications for Criminal Justice Policy*, 4 PSYCHOL. PUB. POL'Y & L. 73, 82 (1998) (citing DAVID M. BUSS, THE EVOLUTION OF DESIRE: STRATEGIES OF HUMAN MATING (1994, 2003)).

[9] J. Archer & A.E. Vaughan, *Evolutionary Theories of Rape*, 3(1) PSYCHOL. EVOLUTION & GENDER (2001), at 95–101. Feminists disagree with this view. *See* J.A.Vega & Wheeler, *Naturalism and Feminism: Conflicting Explanations of Rape in a Wider Context*, 3(1) PSYCHOL. EVOLUTION & GENDER (2001), at 47–85.

this view, reproductive success was, at least in earlier times, enhanced by certain individual characteristics. Rape[10] is such a trait because, by circumventing the woman's mating preferences, it allows the man to increase the number of women with whom he mates and therefore increases his reproductive success.[11] In this view, sexual motivation is necessary (although not sufficient) for the act of rape to occur.[12] This view is descriptive, not normative. It does not argue that men are determined to rape or that rape is inevitable, nor does it justify or excuse rape.[13]

Biology

Some researchers have suggested that biological factors, especially research focusing on regions of the brain or neurotransmitters, may cause people to engage in sexually deviant behavior.[14] The research, so far, does not establish a causal connection between biology and sexually deviant conduct.[15]

Victims of Sexual Abuse

One current and controversial theory states that past victims of sexual abuse themselves become future sexual abusers. Research indicates that about 30% of adult sexual offenders were sexually abused as children.[16] This information is somewhat confounding for several reasons.

First, it is higher than the rate of sexual victimization in the general population. This would suggest that past sexual abuse *might*, indeed, be causally related to future sex offending. On the other hand, the vast majority of children who were sexually abused do *not* themselves become sex offend-

---

[10] In this context, rape would have the more narrow meaning of forced vaginal copulation with a female. It would not include other types of rape. *See* Jones, *supra* note 2.

[11] Randy Thornhill & Craig T. Palmer, *A Natural History of Rape: Biological Bases of Sexual Coercion* (2000); *see also* Randy Thornhill, *The Biology of Rape*, 39 Jurimetrics J. 137 (1999).

[12] Craig T. Palmer et al., *Is It Sex Yet? Theoretical and Practical Implications of the Debate Over Rapists' Motives*, 39 Jurimetrics J. 271 (1999).

[13] Jones, *supra* note 2.

[14] Becker & Murphy, *supra* note 2, at 120 (citing D. Blumer, *Changes of Sexual Behavior Related to Temporal Lobe Disorders in Man*, 6 J. of Sex Res. (1970) 173–180; R. Langevin, *Sexual Anomalies and the Brain* (1990), in Handbook of Sexual Assault: Issues, Theories, and Treatment of the Offender 103–113 (W. L. Marshall et al., eds., 1991). Martin P. Kafka, *Successful Antidepressant Treatment of Nonparaphiliac Sexual Addictions and Paraphilics in Men*. 52 J. of Clinical Psychiatry 60–65 (Feb. 1991).

[15] Becker & Murphy, *supra* note 1, at 120.

[16] Various studies, primarily using self-reporting, have examined the relationship between childhood physical abuse and childhood sexual abuse and subsequent sexual offending. These studies tend to demonstrate a direct correlation between past physical or sexual abuse and sexual offending. *See, e.g.*, L. Merril & C. Thomson, *Childhood Abuse and Premilitary Sexual Assault in Male Navy Recruits*, 69 J. of Consulting & Clinical Psychol. (April 2001), at 252–261; S. Dhawan & W. Marshall, *Sexual Abuse Histories of Sexual Offenders*, 8 J. of Research & Treatment (Jan. 1996); C. Kruttschnitt, *A Sociological Offender-Based Study of Rape*, 30 Sociological Quarterly (Summer 1989), at 305–329.

ers.[17] Moreover, girls are abused four or five times more often than boys, yet women make up only a small proportion of the adults who abuse children.[18] This finding strongly suggests that past sexual abuse does not cause someone to become a sex offender. Second, 70% of adult sex offenders were *not* victims of past sexual abuse. This percentage would suggest that past victimization is not necessarily causally related to future sex offending, at least in most cases.

In any event, this information should be viewed in a careful and balanced way. Being the victim of past sexual abuse appears to put an individual at greater risk of sexual offending, but it is not necessary for someone to become a sex offender.

Mental Disorder

Mental health professionals have concluded that some people with certain types of recurring, deviant sexual drives suffer from a mental disorder, generally called a *paraphilia*. The fourth edition of the *Diagnostic and Statistical Manual of Mental Disorders* (*DSM–IV–TR*) defines paraphilias in this way: recurrent, intense, sexually arousing fantasies, sexual urges, or behaviors generally involving nonhuman objects or involving the suffering or humiliation of one's partner, children, or other nonconsenting persons that occur over a period of 6 months or more. The fantasies, urges, or behaviors cause significant distress or impairment in social, occupational, or other areas of functioning.[19]

There is a dispute among professionals as to whether rapists suffer from a paraphilia. The *DSM–IV–TR* does not include rapists within this disease category. However, many professionals believe that a subset of rapists do suffer from this mental disorder.[20]

In any event, some offenders have strong abnormal sexual drives (e.g., they find children sexually attractive and sexually arousing, or they may take pleasure in the suffering of others). Of course, a diagnosis of a mental disorder does not explain why the individual has this abnormal desire for a sexual partner or object. It simply describes this desire; it does not provide any help in identifying the cause of this desire.

---

[17] Becker & Murphy, *supra* note 1, at 120–21 (*citing* R.K. Hanson & S. Slater, *Sexual Victimization in the History of Sexual Abusers: A Review*, 1 ANNALS OF SEX RESEARCH 485–99 (1988).

[18] Arnon Bentovim, *Why Do Adults Abuse Children?* 307 BRITISH MED. J. 144–145 (1993). The difference between boys and girls may be due to how each gender responds to abusive behavior. Girls tend to internalize it and blame themselves. Boys tend to externalize it and may seek to make others feel the powerlessness they felt.

[19] AMERICAN PSYCHIATRIC ASSOCIATION, THE DIAGNOSTIC AND STATISTICAL MANUAL OF MENTAL DISORDERS, IV–TR (4th ed., text revision, 2000) (hereinafter *DSM–IV–TR*), at 566–67.

[20] Becker & Murphy, *supra* note 1, at 118.

Having a deviant sex drive puts individuals in a very difficult situation. Like most humans, they are sexual beings who have a sex drive and seek sexual intimacy and gratification. But, depending on their particular desire, having sex with their preferred sexual partner may be against the law. Thus, for example, they must refrain from fulfilling their sexual urges with children or run the risk of being punished by the criminal law if they act on them.[21] Although deviant sexual urges can be very powerful, scholars believe that most individuals who suffer from a paraphilia do, in fact, refrain from engaging in criminal activity to satisfy them.[22]

Psychopathy

Psychopathy is a personality disorder characterized by a collection of interpersonal, affective, and behavioral features.[23] Specifically, psychopaths tend to be individuals who are extremely self-centered, try to manipulate others for their own gain, and like to dominate other people. Often psychopaths exhibit short-lived, shallow emotion and a marked lack of empathy for the rights or feelings of others or guilt for the bad things they do. Psychopaths typically engage in impulsive and irresponsible conduct that is sensation seeking. Researchers have suggested that some sexually aggressive and coercive male psychopaths have a "life strategy" characterized by "aggression, risk taking (chronic, low arousal and need for stimulation), lack of empathy (callousness), deception, and high mating effort."[24]

Studies have produced some evidence that psychopathy in sex offenders increases the risk they will commit another violent sex offense.[25] Consequently, psychopathy is often assessed as a predictive factor of recidivism.[26]

Faulty Moral Reasoning and Inept Social Skills

Some researchers believe that rapists and other sex offenders do not morally comprehend[27] or simply ignore[28] the fact that they are harming their

---

[21] A recent controversial issue involving paraphilic behavior and the criminal law is sado-masochism. Some individuals take sexual pleasure in inflicting physical pain on their partners. Conversely, some individuals take sexual pleasure in having physical pain inflicted on them. Should the criminal law prohibit mutually consenting adults from engaging in sexual sado-masochism? See Monica Pa, *Beyond the Pleasure Principle: The Criminalization of Consensual Sadomasochistic Sex*, 11 TEX. J. WOMEN & L. 51 (2001).

[22] Park Elliot Dietz, *Sex Offenses: Behavioral Aspects*, 4 ENCYCLOPEDIA OF CRIME & JUST. 1485, 1490 (1983).

[23] The more current diagnostic term for this disorder is *antisocial personality disorder*.

[24] Harris et al., *supra* note 8, at 83.

[25] *Id.*

[26] R.C. Serin et al., (2001) *Psychopathy, Deviant Sexual Arousal, and Recidivism Among Sexual Offenders*, 16(3) J. OF INTERPERSONAL VIOLENCE (2001), at 234–246.

[27] J.H. Greer et al., *Empathy, Social Skills, and Other Relevant Cognitive Processes in Rapists and Child Molesters*. 5 AGGRESSION AND VIOLENT BEHAVIOR (Jan–Feb 2002), at 99–126.

[28] P.M. Valliant, T. Gauthier, D. Pother, R. Kosmyna, *Moral Reasoning, Interpersonal Skills, and Cognition Of Rapists, Child Molesters, and Incest Offenders*, 86 PSYCHOLOGICAL REPORTS (Feb. 2000), at 67–75.

victims. Others suggest that sex offenders lack social skills; consequently, they are unable to negotiate social situations, respond appropriately to behavioral cues, and seek consensual sexual partners.[29]

Other Possible Causes

Researchers also suggest other causal theories. Some suggest that rape is frequently used for revenge or for punishment, or that it is also an unexpected criminal opportunity that materializes while the offender is engaged in another crime, such as a burglary or robbery.[30] Others view rape as a property crime and sex as a commodity that men steal.[31]

There is also a direct relationship between alcohol use and rape. It is quite possible that drinking loosens inhibitions against engaging in wrongful conduct.[32] Developmental events in their lives may teach some men that manipulation, coercion, and violence are valid ways to conduct social relationships.[33]

Summary

There is no generally accepted scientific explanation of why sex offenders commit sex crimes. Indeed, it is very possible that there are a number of different and independent causes.[34] If so, this suggests that a variety of identification, prevention, treatment, and monitoring methods may be needed to reduce sexual victimization. For the moment, policymakers must await further research before we know with confidence the answer (or answers) to that question. This, of course, does not mean that there are no effective strategies to prevent sexual reoffending.

DO SEX OFFENDERS SPECIALIZE IN SEX CRIMES?

Recently, researchers have questioned the validity of the assumption that sex offenders specialize in the type of sex crime they commit or the

---

[29] R.E. Hopkins, *An Evaluation of Social Skills for Sex Offenders*, 19 Issues in Criminological and Legal Psychol. (1993), at 52–59; P.M. Valliant & D.H. Antonowicx, *Rapists, Incest Offenders, and Child Molesters in Treatment: Cognitive and Social Skills Training*, 36 Int'l J. of Offender Therapy & Comp. Criminology (Fall 1992), at 221–230.

[30] D. Scully & J. Marolla, *Riding the Bull at Gilley's: Convicted Rapists Describe the Reward of Rape*, in James M. Henslin, Down to Earth Sociology: Introductory Readings 45–60 (11th ed., 2001); Diana Scully, Understanding Sexual Violence: A Study of Convicted Rapists (1990), at 141–42.

[31] See Katherine K. Baker, *Once a Rapist? Motivational Evidence and Relevancy in Rape Law*, 110 Harv. L. Rev. 563, 603 n.223 and sources cited therein (1997).

[32] See *id*. at 604.

[33] N.M. Malamuth & M.F. Heilmann, *Evolutionary Psychology and Sexual Aggression*, in Handbook of Evolutionary Psychology (C. Crawford & D.L. Krebs eds., 1998), at 515–542.

[34] Harris et al., *supra* note 8, at 81.

type of victims they choose. Simply put, some scholars do not believe that sex offenders commit only sex crimes. Historically, sex offenders have been assumed to be distinguishable from other criminals because they have underlying mental disorders or psychopathy that cause them to commit specific types of sex crimes and that specific treatment for these conditions will decrease their dangerousness.[35] This assumption is in discord with some criminological studies that show most sex offenders commit a *variety* of violent offenses (including nonsex crimes), and even a variety of sex crimes as opposed to specializing in one type.[36] Criminological evidence shows that sex offenders are not limited to committing just sex crimes, but commit nonsex crimes as well. Even more intriguing, some research shows that sex offenders, like rapists, do not specialize in the type of sex crime they commit, but commit a variety of sexual offenses.[37] Thus, sex offenders may be a lot like other offenders.

These findings suggest that the legal system's reliance on psychological theory to assess and predict dangerousness of sex offenders may be tenuous at best, and that, in any event, policies concerning the appropriate treatment for sex offenders must take this into consideration.[38] If the underlying pathology of sex offenders is indistinguishable from that of other nonsexual offenders, then a psychological basis for categorization and treatment of sex offenders is unreliable. Moreover, the potential for false positives (incorrect predictions that particular offenders will commit another particular offense) suggests that the criminal justice system actually discriminates against sex offenders, who may be no different than other violent offenders.

ARE SEX OFFENDERS DANGEROUS?

Do sex offenders commit more crimes than other types of criminals? Do they commit more sex crimes? Because current legal strategies assume that sex offenders are particularly likely to commit more crimes than other criminals, it is important to know whether this is true.

Recidivism

Probably the most useful (or at least the most manageable) approach in answering this question is to consider how many new crimes sex offenders

---

[35] L.M.J. Simon, *An Examination of the Assumptions of Specialization, Mental Disorder, and Dangerousness in Sex Offenders*, 18 BEHAV. SCI. & L. 275 (2000), at 275–308.

[36] *Id.* at 277. The general criminological theory of sex offending is that violent offenders exhibit a lifelong, versatile pattern of violent crime featuring impulsive conduct that receives immediate gratification.

[37] *Id.* at 282.

[38] *Id.*

commit. To do this, researchers establish "recidivism rates" for sex offenders (i.e., the rate at which they commit new crimes). In addition, researchers must decide whether they will measure only new *sex* crimes committed by convicted sex offenders or whether they will measure *all* new crimes they commit, including nonsex offenses.

Researchers must also decide whether they will include both minor and serious crimes or only serious crimes.[39] They must also determine how long they will follow the career of selected offenders to learn whether they will commit another crime. Generally speaking, the longer the follow-up period, the more opportunities for reoffending and the higher the recidivism rate is likely to be.[40]

Measuring new offenses in this manner allows comparison of the rates at which sex offenders commit new *sex* crimes or other crimes and the rates at which other types of criminals reoffend. If sex offenders do have an especially high rate of reoffending, then they should be considered more dangerous than other types of criminals who have a lower recidivism rate. Using special efforts to prevent sex offenders from committing more sex crimes that society does not use for other types of criminals would be justified.

If, on the other hand, their recidivism rate is similar to, or even lower than, that of other types of criminals, then *as a group* sex offenders should not be considered more dangerous than other criminals. And, society may want to rethink the wisdom of using special crime prevention strategies for all sex offenders.[41]

As I soon discuss in this chapter, there are insurmountable obstacles to achieving complete accuracy in measuring accurate recidivism of criminal offenders, especially sex offenders. Nonetheless, this approximate information allows policymakers to evaluate the dangerousness of various types of criminals and the efficacy of the criminal justice system and other strategies for preventing criminals from committing new crimes.

Defining *Sex Offenders*

Sex offenders are not all alike. In fact, there are different types of sex offenders. Some commit violent sexual rapes and assaults on strangers. Others commit sex crimes against members of their own families. Often their victims are young children, and the sexual abuse may continue for a

---

[39] Ctr. for Sex Offender Mgmt., *Recidivism of Sex Offenders*, at 3 (2001).
[40] *Id.* at 4.
[41] V.L. Quinsey, *Sexual Aggression: Studies of Offenders Against Women, in* 2 LAW AND MENTAL HEALTH: INTERNATIONAL PERSPECTIVES (D.N. Weisstub ed., 1984), at 140–172.

long time. And, there are other offenders who engage in unusual sexual activity, such as exposing themselves or voyeurism.[42]

To consider all of these different types of offenders and their offenses under a single descriptive category of "sex offenders" is misguided. If all sex offenders are lumped into a single category, researchers will not be able to distinguish the recidivism rates for each group accurately. Thus, we will not know how many new sex crimes each type of offender is likely to commit. Instead, researchers will "average" the recidivism rates for different groups into a single rate.

This practice will also prevent researchers from identifying different risk factors for each type of offender. Consequently, it will be more difficult to determine how much risk of reoffending each specific type of sex offender poses.[43] It may also prevent policymakers from targeting the most dangerous type of sex offender by using carefully tailored strategies to prevent them from committing more sex crimes.

Measuring Recidivism

Experts have attempted to measure how many new crimes convicted criminals commit. They do this in several ways.

Official Records

Most methods use official police or court records, such as records for arrest, conviction, or incarceration. Researchers study these data to determine how often a convicted offender has been rearrested, convicted, or sentenced to jail or prison for specific crimes or as a result of parole violation.[44] They then compute how likely criminals in general or specific types of criminals, such as sex offenders or burglars, will commit another crime and what crime they will commit.

Relying on official records does not establish accurate recidivism rates for criminals, for a number of reasons. This method detects only those crimes that have been reported to the police and that then lead to the individual's arrest, conviction, or incarceration. Using arrest records will generate the highest rate of recidivism (compared with using conviction or incarceration)

---

[42]See DSM–IV–TR supra note 19: 302.4, Exhibitionism, which involves the exhibition of one's genitals to a stranger, and 302.82, Voyeurism, which involves observing unsuspecting individuals, usually strangers, who are naked, in the process of disrobing, or engaging in sexual activity.
[43]Ctr. for Sex Offender Mgmt., supra note 39.
[44]Using parole or probation violation is a blunt measure because researchers must know what specific behavior the criminal engaged in to warrant his being returned to prison. Unless the individual actually committed a new sex crime, rather than violated another condition of his parole or probation (like using drugs or alcohol), then this event will not necessarily indicate that he committed another sex crime. See id. at 2.

because police need to have only "probable cause" or a reasonable factual basis for believing the suspect has committed a crime. Using conviction rates will generate a lower recidivism rate than using arrest records, because the prosecutor must have sufficient evidence to establish the offender's guilt beyond a reasonable doubt in a criminal trial. Moreover, using subsequent incarceration is the most restrictive measure, because many people convicted of a crime are not sentenced to jail or prison. Thus, this method will generate a lower recidivism rate than using either arrest or conviction records.

As I noted in chapter 1, many sex crimes, perhaps a majority, are not even reported to the police.[45] Even when reported, the police do not necessarily arrest someone, for any number of reasons. For example, the police may not have sufficient evidence to establish probable cause and, consequently, cannot secure an arrest warrant. Even if the police do arrest someone, the case does not always go to trial. Prosecutors may dismiss the charges for many reasons, including their professional determination that they do not have sufficient evidence to convict. Often, individuals charged with a sex crime may plea bargain with prosecutors. In many cases, a criminal defendant may plead guilty to a charge that does not include a sex crime or he may plead guilty to a less serious sex crime. Thus, even conviction records do not necessarily reflect accurately what type of crime the offender actually committed. Of course, these problems are pervasive in researching recidivism rates for all types of criminals and all types of crimes. Nonetheless, relying on official records can generate useful information.

Victim Surveys

As I mentioned in chapter 1, researchers can ask people how often they have been a victim of a crime. These victim surveys indicate that many sex crimes are not even reported to law enforcement authorities.

Because of these difficulties it is impossible to accurately establish actual recidivism rates for any type of offender. But it is possible to estimate with some accuracy recidivism rates for different types of criminals and to have some sense of comparative rates of reoffending among different types of offenders.

Self-Reports by Sex Offenders

Researchers also use other methods to determine recidivism, like self-reporting. Criminals are asked to disclose (usually on a confidential basis) how many crimes they have committed.[46] Often this method indicates that

---

[45] See chapter 1.
[46] See chapter 1 for a description of selected sex offender surveys.

offenders, especially sex offenders, commit more crimes than the police know about.

DO SEX OFFENDERS COMMIT MORE CRIMES?

Surprisingly, official law enforcement records indicate that sex offenders, as a group, are *not* especially dangerous. In fact they commit *fewer* new crimes than many other types of criminals.

A major study published in 1989 of all state prisoners released in 11 states in 1983 showed that, when measured by rearrest for the same crime, rapists had a relatively low rate of rearrest for rape; only 7.7% of released rapists were rearrested for rape. In clear contrast, 33.5% of larcenists were rearrested for larceny; 31.9% of released burglars were rearrested for burglary; and 24.8% of drug offenders were rearrested for drug offenses. Only murderers had a lower recidivism rate for the same crime than rapists.[47]

This trend was affirmed in a study published in 2002. In this study of recidivism rates for sex offenders released from 15 state prisons, 9,691 men serving sentences longer than 1 year were tracked for 3 years after their release in 1994.[48] This population represented about two thirds of all male sex offenders released from state prisons in the United States that year. Recidivism was measured by the rate of rearrest, reconviction, and reimprisonment in the 3 years following release.

Approximately 29% of the offenders studied had been arrested previously for a sex crime. More than half of them had at least one prior conviction. Of these, 13.9% had been convicted of a violent sex offense and 4.6% had been convicted of child molestation. Overall, sex offenders had shorter criminal histories than nonsex offenders released in 1994. The prior arrest record for the released sex offenders was about half the rate of nonsex offenders released that same year.[49] Generally, the rearrest rate for *any* crime (sexual or nonsexual) for sex offenders, 43%, was significantly *lower* than for nonsex offenders, 68%.[50] Most recidivism by sex offenders

---

[47] Bureau of Justice Statistics, Special Report, Recidivism of Prisoners Released in 1983, at 5 (1989). *See also* Lita Furby et al., *Sex Offender Recidivism: A Review*, 105 Psychol. Bull. 3 (1989).
[48] Patrick A. Langan et al., *Recidivism of Sex Offenders Released From Prison in 1994* (2003), *at* http://www.ojp.usdoj.gov/bjs/pub/pdf/rsorp94.pdf. [hereinafter, *Langan et al.*] The data were collected from prisons in Arizona, California, Delaware, Florida, Illinois, Maryland, Michigan, Minnesota, New Jersey, New York, North Carolina, Ohio, Oregon, Texas, and Virginia.
[49] *Id.* at 11. Sex offenders had been arrested at an average rate of 4.5 times prior to their sentences at the time of release, whereas nonsex offenders averaged about 8.9 prior arrests. The data produced mixed results as to an association between the length of time served for a sentence for a sex crime and the level of recidivism. *Id.* at 19.
[50] *Id.* at 14.

in the 3 years following release occurred in the first year after release. Within 6 months following release, 16% of them were rearrested for a new crime.[51]

DO SEX OFFENDERS COMMIT MORE *SEX* CRIMES?

The short answer is yes. This same study reconfirms that sex offenders, as a group, have relatively low rates of committing another sex crime. Approximately 5% of the released sex offenders were rearrested for a new *sex offense* (forcible rape or sexual assault) within 3 years.[52] Only 3.5% of all released sex offenders were *convicted* for a new *sex* crime within 3 years of release. Although sex offenders are less likely to commit any crime than nonsex offenders, they are more likely to commit another *sex offense* than are nonsex offenders. Only 1.3% of nonsex offenders were rearrested for committing a sex crime within 3 years of release during the study period. Thus, sex offenders were four times more likely (5.3% vs. 1.3%) to be arrested for a sex crime within 3 years of their release.

Even though sex offenders are more likely to commit sex crimes than nonsex offenders, surprisingly, nonsex offenders (a much larger group in the study) accounted for 87% of the estimated sex crimes committed by all the prisoners who were released in 1994. Released sex offenders committed only 13% of these estimated sex crimes.[53] Thus, society will not prevent sex crimes by focusing only on convicted sex offenders.

This study also confirms that a history of past sex offending indicates a greater risk of future sex offending. Sex offenders who had been arrested for two or more sex crimes were twice as likely to be arrested for a new sex crime after their release when compared with sex offenders who had a history of only one prior sex crime arrest.[54] The findings also suggest that an offender's specific history of sex offending indicates a greater risk that he will commit the same type of sex crime. Child molesters in the study were more likely to be arrested for child molestation than sex offenders who had no prior arrest for this crime (6.4% vs. 1.7%). Furthermore, offenders who had been arrested for sexual assault had a 6.9% rate of rearrest for sexual assault compared with 1.9% for sex offenders who had not been arrested for this crime.

---

[51] *Id.* at 16. The younger the sex offender was upon release, the higher the rate of recidivism. *Id.* at 18.
[52] *Id.* at 24.
[53] *Id.*
[54] *Id.* at 28.

Two Canadian researchers, Hanson and Bussiere, conducted a review of 61 studies that followed sex offenders to determine whether these individuals reoffended and, if they did, what type of crime they committed. By combining all of these studies, these researchers in effect looked at recidivism rates for 23,393 sex offenders. The overall sexual offense rate was 13.4% for a follow-up period of 4 to 5 years. Thus, only 13.4% of these 23,393 sex offenders committed another sex offense in the 4- to 5-year period after they committed a sex offense.[55] In this same study, 18.9% of the rapists committed another sex crime during the follow-up period, whereas 12.7% of the child molesters committed another sex crime during that period.

Other researchers have reached somewhat similar results. Quinsey, Lalumiere, and their colleagues reviewed the research literature and established weighted averages for various subgroups of sex offenders. For example, they estimated that rapists had a 22.8% likelihood of reoffending and that child molesters' rate was 20.5%.[56] Some scholars have concluded that incest offenders have quite a low risk of reoffending.[57]

Follow-Up Periods

The rates of sexual reoffending tend to increase the longer the period of follow-up. This is probably to be expected. Simply put, the longer the time that sex offenders are studied, the more likely more of them will be arrested for another sex crime. Child molesters, in particular, seem to be very likely to commit another child molestation crime.[58] In one study, almost 80% of sex offenders with both adult and child victims reoffended sometime over a 20-year follow-up period.[59] However, even with a long follow-up period and meticulous review of records, the "average sexual offense recidivism rate rarely exceeds 40%."[60] Thus, the available evidence does not support the assumption that most sexual offenders are more dangerous than many other types of criminals. It does, however, show that sex offenders are more likely to commit another *sex offense* than are nonsex offenders[61]

---

[55] R.K. Hanson & M.T. Bussiere (1998), *Predicting Relapse: A Meta-Analysis of Sexual Offender Recidivism Studies*, 66 J. OF CONSULTING & CLINICAL PSYCHOL. 348–362.

[56] V.L. QUINSEY ET AL., ASSESSING DANGEROUSNESS: VIOLENCE BY OFFENDERS, BATTERERS, AND CHILD ABUSERS (1995).

[57] V.L. Quinsey et al., *Actuarial Predictions of Sexual Recidivism*, 10 J. OF INTERPERSONAL VIOLENCE 85 (1995).

[58] M.E. Rice & G.T. Harris, *Cross Validation and Extension of the Violence Risk Appraisal Guide for Child Molesters and Rapists*, 21 L. & HUMAN BEHAV. 231 (1997).

[59] Harris et al., *supra* note 8, at 84.

[60] R. Karl Hanson, *What Do We Know About Sex Offender Risk Assessment?*, 4 PSYCHOL. PUB. POL'Y & L. 50, at 67 (1998).

[61] *Id.*

Likelihood of Committing Another Sex Crime

Certain types of sex offenders are more likely to commit another *sex* crime rather than some other type of crime when compared with other offenders. Child molesters, for example, generally do not commit violent offenses. However, child molesters who victimize only children are very likely to commit another sex crime *if* they reoffend. In contrast, rapists tend to commit more nonsexual, violent crimes than child molesters, at least when recidivism rates are based on official records.[62]

On the other hand, a rapist is 10.5 times more likely to be arrested for rape than a nonrapist.[63] Rapists and sexual assaulters are also more likely to repeat the offense for which they were convicted (i.e., a sex crime) than any other type of felon.[64] Thus, violent sex offenders are more likely to commit another violent *sex* crime than other violent offenders, such as offenders who commit assaults or robberies. But remember that sex offenders, as a group, have a relatively low recidivism rate. That is, most of them do not commit *any* more crimes. If they do reoffend, however, they are more likely than other offenders to commit a sex crime. Policymakers must determine whether special strategies should be used to prevent the commission of new crimes in general or whether they should try to prevent new sex crimes.

A Group of Very Dangerous Sex Offenders

Although sex offenders generally have a relatively low recidivism rate, there is a small group of sex offenders who have a very high recidivism rate and are very likely to commit another sex offense. This group is exceptionally dangerous. Hanson concluded that "The rate at which this highest risk subgroup actually reoffends with another sexual offense could be conservatively estimated at 50% and could reasonably be estimated at 70% to 80%."[65] Thus, there is a small number of sex offenders who are extremely dangerous because, without preventive measures, they are very likely to commit another serious sex crime. It is this group of very dangerous sex offenders that poses the most serious threat to community safety and that should be subject to aggressive strategies to prevent new victimization.

---

[62] Harris et al., *supra* note 8, at 85.
[63] Bureau of Justice Statistics, *supra* note 47, at 2.
[64] *Id.* at 6; *see also* BUREAU OF JUSTICE STATISTICS, SEX OFFENSES AND OFFENDERS: AN ANALYSIS OF DATA ON RAPE AND SEXUAL ASSAULT (1997), at 27.
[65] Hanson, *supra* note 60, at 67–68.

WHAT SEX OFFENDERS TELL US

Sex offenders tell us that many of them are more dangerous than police records indicate. One self-report of victimization from nonincarcerated sex offenders is extremely disturbing.

Abel and his colleagues conducted a confidential survey of nonincarcerated sex offenders. These individuals were promised complete confidentiality in exchange for candid disclosures of their criminal history. This approach provides information on sex crimes that are not reported to the police or that did not lead to an arrest or conviction. These 561 offenders reported that they had actually committed 291,737 "paraphilia acts" committed against 195,407 victims.[66] This finding indicates that each offender, on average, committed 520 sexually motivated acts against 348 victims. These numbers are astounding. If these self-reports are to be believed, sex offenders may commit an extraordinarily large number of sex crimes.

These findings, however, must be viewed with a great deal of caution and, perhaps, even skepticism. It is not clear whether those sex offenders surveyed were truthful and whether they were typical of most sex offenders. Furthermore, it should be noted that researchers have failed to replicate these findings using even more sophisticated methods to ensure confidentiality.

This extremely disconcerting information must also be tempered by careful consideration of exactly what constituted a "paraphiliac act." This study used the *DSM–II* and *DSM–III* criteria for "paraphilia." Many of the reported acts involved sexual behavior that is not even a crime, like "transvestism" and "fetishism." Other acts, although criminal, are generally not considered serious sex offenses, such as exhibitionism or voyeurism. Even acts of pedophilia that we might assume to be criminal, such as child molestation (undefined in the study), are not necessarily so. A huge difference exists between fondling a child's genitals and simply touching one on the arm to be sexually aroused. Yet both types of conduct could be considered a "paraphiliac" act. This research does indicate, however, that the average number of rapes committed by the 126 rapists was 7.2. Although small in comparison with the number of deviant acts committed by other paraphiliacs, this number is still very troubling because of the seriousness of this crime.

Official recidivism studies show that sex offenders as a group are less dangerous than most other types of criminals. They commit fewer new crimes than many other types of offenders. If they do commit new crimes, however, they are more likely to commit sex crimes than other offenders.

---

[66] G.G. Abel et al., *Self-Reported Sex Crimes of Nonincarcerated Paraphiliacs*, 2 J. OF INTERPERSONAL VIOLENCE 3–25 (1987).

Thus, a generalized fear that sex offenders are especially dangerous does not seem to be supported by the evidence. Victim surveys and offender self-reports indicate that sex offenders, as a group, are more dangerous than recidivism research indicates.

In any event, there is a small group of sex offenders who do pose a very high risk of committing more serious sex crimes. These individuals are prime candidates for aggressive measures designed to prevent further victimization.

CAN WE TELL WHO IS DANGEROUS?

Can we identify which offenders are very likely to commit another sex crime? And if so, how? In this section, I present the currently used methods of predicting which sex offenders are likely to reoffend. Then I discuss the courts' response to these methods.

Predictive Approaches

There are three general approaches to predicting whether an individual sex offender will commit another sex crime.

Clinical

One approach is the clinical method. A professional, usually a psychiatrist or clinical psychologist, thoroughly examines the individual and reviews the person's history, including criminal record, psychosexual history, and other biographical information. These tasks usually require a personal interview with the offender and, in many cases, interviews with others.[67]

In addition, the evaluator should identify factors possessed by the individual that are known to be correlated with sexual offending. For example, a person may have an extensive history of sexual offending; this characteristic has been identified as correlated with sexual offending. Finally, the expert weighs all that he knows about the individual and then makes a clinical judgment about the likelihood that the offender would commit another sexual offense if he were to live in the community without supervision.

Studies indicate that most clinical judgments about future sex offending are quite poor (i.e., experts are not very good at accurately identifying those

---

[67] For a thorough description of how a mental health professional should evaluate an individual for sexual dangerousness, *see* Roy Lacoursiere, *Evaluating Offenders Under a Sexually Violent Predator Law: The Practical Practice, in* Protecting Society From Dangerous Sex Offenders: Law, Justice, and Therapy (Bruce J. Winick & John Q. La Fond eds., 2002).

individuals who, in fact, will commit another sex crime). A number of experts have conducted studies that review the predictive accuracy of clinical judgments about sexual reoffending and found that the average correlation was 0.10 (i.e., in very general terms, the experts were correct in only about 10% of the cases in which they predicted the individual would commit another sexual reoffense).[68] Thus, it appears that expert predictions of sexual dangerousness based solely on an examination of the individual and his history are quite inaccurate.

Actuarial Approach

This approach is based on a method used by insurance companies to establish risk for their policies and to set rates. Experts identify a group of sex offenders known to have a very high rate of sexual offending. Then the experts see what characteristics this group has in common. It is very similar to looking at a group of men who have had heart attacks at a relatively early age and isolating what characteristics these men share. For example, they may have had high blood pressure, been overweight, and done very little exercise. On the basis of the history of the *group*, experts could then predict with a fair degree of accuracy that all men who have high blood pressure, are overweight, and do little exercise have a 40% greater likelihood of having an early heart attack than a group of men who do not share these characteristics.[69]

Using this approach, researchers have developed several actuarial instruments to assess the risk that groups of sex offenders pose, by identifying characteristics that other *groups* of sex offenders known to have committed a high number of sex crimes had in common.[70] Hanson and Bussiere, for example, developed an actuarial instrument in 1998 that established correlations between certain characteristics and the likelihood of sexual reoffending. They determined that sexual recidivism was "most closely associated with

---

[68] Hanson, *supra* note 60, at 54 (citing R.K. Hanson & M.T. Bussiere (1996), *Predictors of Sexual Reoffender Recidivism; A Meta-Analysis (User Report No. 96-04).* Ottawa, Ontario, Canada: Department of the Solicitor General of Canada; R.K Hanson & M.T. Bussiere, *Predicting Relapse: A Meta-Analysis of Sexual Offender Recidivism Studies,* 66 J. OF CONSULTING & CLINICAL PSYCHOL. 349–362.

[69] This number is purely hypothetical and is designed to illustrate the process. It does not purport to be an accurate statement of risk.

[70] Currently, there are a number of such instruments used to predict the risk of sexual reoffending. They include Static-99, the RRASOR, the MnStOSOT-R, the CARAT, and the PRAS. *See generally* R. Karl Hanson & David Thornton, *Improving Risk Assessments for Sex Offenders: A Comparison of Three Actuarial Scales,* 24 L. & HUM. BEHAV. 119 (2000). Hanson and Thornton found that the Static-99 is more accurate than either the RRASOR or the SAKJ-Min. and that all three tests exhibit similar predictive accuracy for both rapists and child molesters. The correlation coefficient for the Static 99 was 0.33, which represents "moderate" predictive accuracy. *See also* Howard E. Barbaree et al., *Evaluating the Predictive Accuracy of Six Risk Assessment Instruments for Adult Sex Offenders,* 28 CRIM. JUST. & BEHAV. 490 (2001).

sexual deviancy."[71] They also concluded that other factors that correlate fairly well with sexual reoffending include prior sexual offense, failure to complete treatment, antisocial personality, any prior offenses, young age, never married, any unrelated victims, and any male victim.[72] Thus, sex offenders who have many or all of these characteristics also have a higher probability of committing another sexual offense.

Supporters of this approach argue that these predictive instruments are derived from proven statistical methods of calculating risk and that a sufficiently large number of repeat sex offenders have been studied to give them robust predictive accuracy. They maintain that the instruments are objective, thereby avoiding any possibility of error or bias by the person who conducts the evaluation. Supporters also note that when well-trained individuals use these instruments to evaluate the same person, they achieve the same scores for the same individual. This indicates that the instruments have a high degree of consistency. Most important, supporters argue that these instruments can "identify a small subgroup of offenders with an enduring propensity to sexually reoffend."[73]

At the very least, actuarial instruments provide greater assurance that sex offenders will be treated equally (i.e., offenders with similar offense histories generally will be considered equally likely to reoffend). Actuarial instruments reduce much of the variability in predictions that can generate very different results when individual clinicians bring their different training, experience, and normative preferences to the task of assessing sex offenders for risk.

Critics claim that these actuarial tools do not measure any psychological aspect of the individual; they only provide useful information about groups. Thus, these instruments do not provide any information about the individual that is unique, like a measurement of intelligence. Fred Berlin, a noted expert on sex offending, claims that, when applied to other sex offenders to determine who was and was not sexually dangerous, one type of actuarial instrument, the Rapid Risk Assessment for Sexual Offense Recidivism (RRASOR), was abysmal in predicting who would reoffend and who would not.[74]

No serious dispute exists about the fact that these instruments only allow experts to conclude that a particular individual belongs to a *group* with certain risk factors.[75] However, they cannot be used to state authoritatively

---

[71] Hanson, *supra* note 60, at 57–58 (*citing* Hanson & Bussiere, *supra* note 55).
[72] Hanson, *supra* note 60, at 57–58 (*citing* Hanson & Bussiere, *supra* note 55).
[73] Hanson, *supra* note 60, at 67.
[74] *See* testimony of Fred Berlin in *In re* Commitment of R.S., 773 A.2d 72 (N.J. 2001).
[75] *See generally* Terrence W. Campbell, *Sexual Predator Evaluation and Phrenology: Considering Issues of Evidentiary Reliability*, 18 BEHAV. SCI. & L. 111 (2000).

that an *individual* has a certain probability of reoffending.[76] Some argue that individuals should not be judged based on their membership in a group because this is contrary to the American system of individualized justice.

Opponents also assert that actuarial instruments are bound to generate mistakes. For example, even in a group of men at risk for an early heart attack, not every individual will have one. In fact, many may not. This is also true for sex offenders. Many offenders with characteristics indicating that they belong in a high-risk group will not reoffend. Thus, these instruments will produce a number of false positives (i.e., individuals determined likely to sexually reoffend who in fact would not).[77]

Even if experts can identify a range of risk for a group, they do not know where within that range each individual with those characteristics falls. To mathematically compile the range of risk for the group, we need to aggregate individuals into a group calculation. This necessarily distorts any judgment about individual risk.

To illustrate this dilemma, look again at the group of individuals at risk for early heart attack discussed earlier and assume that the group has a 40% risk of having an early heart attack. One individual who is overweight and does not exercise may in fact have a 30% probability of having an early heart attack; another person with the same characteristics may have a 50% probability. (Note how these two risks when combined would yield a 40% risk of early heart attack.) This is also true for sex offenders. Thus, taking into account the characteristics specific to a particular offender, who might otherwise fit within the group of high-risk offenders described by Hanson, that person may have only a 35% individual probability of committing another sex crime, rather than the 50% to 80% probability range of the group; another individual may have a 90% probability. Unfortunately, actuarial risk instruments do not identify the actual risk for any individual. Consequently, there are serious chances of making mistakes when we use groups to predict risk for an individual.[78]

Applying this logic to the group of sex offenders described earlier by Hanson[79] illustrates the problems. Hanson argued that a small group of sex offenders exists for whom the risk of sexual reoffending can be "conservatively estimated at 50% and could reasonably be estimated at 70% to 80%."[80] Even assuming this is true and that we can identify that group accurately, it is also true that between 20% and 50% of them will *not* commit another

---

[76] Becker & Murphy, *supra* note 1.

[77] *Id.*

[78] For an interesting judicial opinion canvassing opinions of experts who support the use of such instruments and experts who oppose such use, *see In re* Commitment of R.S., 773 A.2d 72 (N.J. 2001).

[79] *See* Hanson, *supra* note 60.

[80] *See id.*

sex crime. Moreover, there is no clear basis for determining which individuals will reoffend and which will not. Thus, it is almost certain that we will make many mistakes when experts and others make these predictions. If we considered the entire group to be dangerous and likely to reoffend, we would overpredict dangerousness. Of course, the natural tendency is to "play safe" and to predict that *all* members of the group will reoffend, even though we know that is not true.

Note also that the characteristics used in these actuarial instruments to predict sexual dangerousness are all historical facts, such as age of first offense, number of victims, or gender of victim, which do not change with the passage of time. Thus, they are called *static factors*. So once an offender's history qualifies him for membership in the group of high risk-offenders, he usually stays in that group, because that particular history, except for his age, generally will not change.

Guided Clinical Approaches

Approaches also exist that include various combinations of these two basic ones. For example, some experts use a guided clinical approach. Here, the expert initially uses an actuarial instrument and then adjusts his or her risk calculation after considering other individual factors. This approach allows evaluators to consider changing or dynamic factors about the individual. For example, a clinician could take into account that the individual has participated in treatment for sex offenders to lower his estimate of risk. Some experts maintain that this approach is the most accurate,[81] whereas others maintain that the purely objective approach of an actuarial instrument is superior.[82]

In any event, the two extreme approaches to risk assessment include pure subjective expert judgment on the one hand, as illustrated by clinical assessment, and a purely objective approach, illustrated by use of only an actuarial instrument. The guided clinical approach uses a blend of these objective and subjective methods.

What the Courts Have Said

Defense lawyers have objected to experts using actuarial tools to make predictions of sexual dangerousness in a variety of legal settings, including civil commitment and community notification. They have argued that these devices are unreliable, untested, and arbitrary, and that their use violates fundamental fairness and due process.[83]

---

[81] *Id.*
[82] Harris et al., *supra* note 8.
[83] *See, e.g., In re* Commitment of R.S., 773 A.2d 72 (N.J. 2001).

Many courts have agreed with some of their objections, including claims that actuarial tools are not scientific instruments and have not been proven to be valid by scientific studies. (To be valid, these tests would have to accurately identify dangerous sex offenders prospectively in actual tests. However, no court is going to allow sex offenders identified as dangerous by these tools to be released simply to determine whether the tools in fact did accurately pick out which offenders committed another sex crime.)

Nonetheless, virtually all courts have concluded that expert testimony concerning sexual dangerousness based on actuarial instruments is admissible in sexual predator cases[84] and in classifying the relative dangerousness of sex offenders subject to community notification laws.[85] They have concluded that these actuarial tools are at least as good as, and probably superior to, clinical judgment. Moreover, they are "simply one piece of the adjudicatory puzzle—a reliable tool that aids the court in reaching the ultimate determination of dangerousness."[86]

Despite serious concerns about both the methodology and accuracy of making individual predictions of dangerousness, it is really not surprising that courts have acquiesced and allowed the government to use actuarial instruments. After all, we have passed numerous laws that let the state control individuals considered sexually dangerous in order to protect the community. Without *someone* telling judges, juries, and state officials who *is* "dangerous," these laws could not, as a practical matter, be used. Actuarial devices, although imperfect, are the best tools available at this time. It should come as no surprise, then, that actuarial tools appear to be used in 13 of the 16 states that have passed sexual predator laws.[87] Necessity, once again, may be the mother of invention.

---

[84] *See, e.g., id., aff'd,* 801 A.2d 219 (2002); *In re* Detention of Strauss, 20 P.3d 1022 (Wash. Ct. App. 2001) (upheld use of RRASOR, MnSOST, VRAG, MnSOST-R, and Static-99), *rev. granted sub nom.,* 45 P.3d 534 (Wash. 2002), *aff'd,* 72 P.3d 708 (Wash. 2003); *In re* Detention of Thorel, 45 P.3d 534 (Wash. 2002); *In re* Detention of Holtz, 653 N.W.2d 613 (Iowa Ct. App. 2002) (upheld use of RRASOR, Static-99, MnSOST and MnSOST-R). *See also* Richard Hamill, *Recidivism of Sex Offenders: What You Need to Know,* 15 Crim. Just. 24, 30–32 (2001). *But see* Donna Cropp Bechman, *Sex Offender Civil Commitments: Scientists or Psychics?,* 16 Crim. Just. 24 (2001) (critique of actuarial instruments). For an excellent analysis of these legal issues *see generally* Eric S. Janus & Robert A. Prentky, *Forensic Use of Actuarial Risk Assessment With Sex Offenders: Accuracy, Admissibility, and Accountability,* 40 Am. Crim. L. Rev. 1443 (2003).

[85] *See, e.g., In re* Registrant G.B., 685 A.2d 1252 (N.J. 1996); *In re* Detention of Campbell, 986 P.2d 771 (Wash. 1999), *cert. denied,* 531 U.S.1125 (2001); *Pedroza v. Florida,* 77 So. 2d 639 (Fla. Dist. Ct. App. 2000); *In re* Detention of Walker, 731 N.E.2d 994 (Ill. App. Ct. 2002); *In re* Commitment of Kienitz, 597 N.W. 2d 712 (Wisc. 1999).

[86] *In re* Commitment of R.S., 773A.2d 72 87 (N.J. 2001).

[87] *Id.* (testimony of Denis Doren).

The Context of Prediction

Note that predictions in systems of social control that a sex offender is likely to commit another sex crime are made at a single moment in time, based on information available at that time. Although not usually stated explicitly, these predictions generally are not limited to the immediate future. Instead, they usually involve a fairly long time period, in many cases, the balance of the offender's life. As I discussed earlier, the longer a sex offender lives in the community, the more likely he is to commit another sex crime. Thus, decision makers like judges or juries are likely to conclude that many sex offenders are likely to reoffend *at some time* in their lives. Put differently, the community may fear that sex offenders set free in the community will inevitably commit another sex crime.

Moreover, predictions that a sex offender has an individual or group probability of committing another sex crime assumes that nothing will be done to control the individual while living in the community to prevent him or her from sexually reoffending. As we see later on, there are a number of strategies that can be used to manage the risk posed by any individual offender to reduce the probability that he or she will commit another sex offense.[88]

RECOMMENDATIONS

Be Realistic About Risk

Although the research is limited and in some cases conflicting, it appears that most sex offenders are not dangerous and will not reoffend. Society's overwhelming fear that all sex offenders pose an ongoing threat of committing more serious sex crimes their entire lives is incorrect and, more important, self-defeating.

Many of our current prevention strategies, such as sex offender registration and community notification in some states, target virtually all sex offenders, most of whom are not dangerous and should not be subject to special crime prevention methods. We are wasting limited resources on people who pose no special threat to the community. Moreover, in painting with such a broad brush, we may be creating a public hysteria that is unnecessary and even counterproductive.[89]

---

[88] *See* chapter 7.
[89] *See* chapter 4.

Concentrate on Dangerous Sex Offenders

There is, however, a small group of sex offenders who are very dangerous and do have a lasting proclivity to sexually reoffend. Important strides have been made in accurately identifying who they are. The use of actuarial instruments to evaluate sexual dangerousness, though not without limitations, uses a valid, objective statistical method to identify these offenders. These instruments can be used extensively to identify those sex offenders who should be subjected to special control measures. For example, they can be used in prosecuting and sentencing sex offenders, identifying which sex offenders should have to register with the police or be subject to extended and intensive surveillance in the community.[90] Actuarial instruments should be used to enhance our ability to apply current crime-control strategies to those sex offenders who are at greatest risk of reoffending. Limited resources can then be concentrated on the most dangerous sex offenders, thereby maximizing our chances of preventing sexual violence.

---

[90] *See* chapters 4, 7, and 8.

3

CAN SEX OFFENDERS BE TREATED?

Does treatment reduce the number of sex crimes committed by sex offenders? This is a crucial question in formulating a realistic strategy for protecting society from repeat sex offenders. If experts can, in fact, change sex offenders so that they do not want to commit sex crimes, or even if they still have that desire, so that they avoid reoffending, then investing significant resources in treatment, at least for sex offenders who want to change, makes a lot of sense. If, however, treatment does not work, or even worse, makes these individuals more likely to reoffend, then we should not expect a therapeutic solution to this ongoing threat.

Sex offenders pose a special challenge for treatment. Knowing the cause of deviant behavior provides a sound starting point for developing effective approaches for changing that behavior. Unfortunately, as noted in chapter 2, there is currently no definitive knowledge on exactly why sex offenders commit sex crimes. In all probability, there are many different causal explanations for sexual offending. This ignorance has made the task of developing effective treatment for sex offenders more difficult. It should come as no surprise that in the past there have been promises of effective treatment that were not fulfilled.

In this chapter, I review what is known, and unknown, about treatment for sex offenders and whether it works. Significant attempts have been made in the past to treat sex offenders, and they failed miserably. Today, new strategies are being tried. We are truly in the midst of a "new age" when mental health professionals are extremely optimistic about their ability to change sex offender behavior and reduce sexual reoffending. New promises are being made. Will they be kept?

TREATMENT SETTINGS FOR CONVICTED SEX OFFENDERS

Several approaches typically are used to treat sex offenders. I discuss them in more detail later in this chapter.[1] But, generally speaking, psychological treatment strategies try to change how offenders think about their sexual behavior and its consequences on themselves and their victims. They also help offenders avoid the internal thoughts and fantasies or external situations that are typically associated with their individual pattern of offending. Medical approaches target an offender's sexual drive by prescribing drugs that reduce a man's libido.

Treatment for convicted sex offenders can be provided in a variety of contexts: community-based sentencing alternatives, prison treatment programs, parole and probation treatment programs, and sexual predator programs. I discuss each of these in this section.

Community-Based Sentencing Alternatives

Many convicted sex offenders, especially first-time offenders who commit crimes against children, are given suspended sentences on the condition that they receive treatment in the community under court supervision.[2] While living in their own residences (or sometimes in state-run residential facilities), they periodically see clinicians who provide treatment in a variety of programs. Community treatment allows these individuals to hold a job and maintain their social networks, including family connections in appropriate cases, while also requiring them to participate in therapy designed to change their attitudes and behavior. Usually, probation officers supervise them to ensure that they comply with the conditions of their release, including participating in scheduled treatment. In a study of 10 jurisdictions, researchers concluded that 64% of convicted child molesters received probation and that counseling was required in 61% of those cases.[3]

---

[1] See notes 30–73 infra and accompanying text.
[2] Lucy Berliner, Sex Offenders: Policy and Practice, 92 Nw. U. L. Rev. 1203 (1998) (citing B.E. Smith et al., ABA Center on Children and the Law, the Prosecution of Child and Sexual Abuse Cases (1993)); L. Berliner et al., A Sentencing Alternative for Sex Offenders: A Study of Decision Making and Recidivism, 10 J. Interpersonal Violence 487 (1995).
[3] B.E. Smith et al., ABA Center on Children and the Law, the Prosecution of Child and Sexual Abuse Cases (1993).

Washington State uses this approach. In 1984, it enacted the Special Sex Offender Sentencing Alternative (SSOSA).[4] This law allows charged sex offenders who do not have a prior sex offense conviction to seek community treatment in lieu of incarceration. A judge must consider the interests of the offender, the community, and the victim. Many argue that this type of treatment alternative is essential to encourage victims to report sex crimes and to cooperate in their prosecution. Some evidence exists (although no systematic research) that many child victims do not want to see their abusers punished and sent to prison.[5] This sentencing option also encourages guilty pleas, sparing victims the ordeal of testifying in a criminal prosecution.[6] In 1997, of the 636 sex offenders eligible for sentencing under SSOSA in Washington State, 240 were sentenced to community treatment under the statute.[7]

More recently, these community-treatment diversion programs have come under attack by critics who claim that they treat sex offenders too leniently, allowing them to avoid punishment they deserve. In response, some states have tightened eligibility criteria or imposed mandatory jail time.[8] Not surprisingly, there is anecdotal evidence that, as a result of these changes, fewer successful prosecutions for sex offenses have been brought and fewer sex offenders are in treatment.[9] Strong arguments can be made that both of these results are undesirable.

Treatment for Prisoners

The latest information from the Department of Justice indicates that there were approximately 95,000 sex offenders in state prisons in 1998,[10] with prisoners convicted of rape and sexual assault accounting for about 5% of the total incarcerated population in the United States.[11] Of the 906,000 prisoners serving sentences in state prisons in 1994, 9.7% were

---

[4] WASH. REV. CODE § 9.94A.120(7)(a) (2004).
[5] Berliner, *supra* note 2, at 1213.
[6] *Id.* at 1214.
[7] *Id.* at 1213.
[8] *Id.*
[9] *Id.*
[10] *See* Joan Comparet-Cassani, *A Primer on the Civil Trial of a Sexually Violent Predator*, 37 SAN DIEGO L. REV. 1057, 1068 (*citing* U.S. DEP'T OF JUSTICE, INTRODUCTION TO NATIONAL CONFERENCE ON SEX OFFENDER REGISTRIES, at vii (1998)).
[11] *See* Lawrence A. Greenfield, U.S. DEP'T OF JUSTICE, SEX OFFENSES AND OFFENDERS: AN ANALYSIS OF DATA ON RAPE AND SEXUAL ASSAULT (NCJ-163392) (1997), *available at* http://www.vaw.umn.edu/documents/sexoff/sexoff.html.

violent sex offenders,[12] but other estimates indicate the percentage of sex offenders to be more than 10%.[13]

In 1997, the Bureau of Justice Statistics reported that about 14% of sex offenders in prison were ordered to receive sex offender treatment as a condition of their sentences.[14] One estimate indicates that approximately 1,500 programs and professionals are providing treatment for sex offenders nationwide.[15] More than half of the states (approximately 39) provide prison-based treatment programs for sex offenders,[16] but the majority of incarcerated sex offenders do not receive treatment. For example, in 1993, only about 13% of the 85,000 incarcerated sex offenders were enrolled in treatment programs.[17] More recently, some states have eliminated their treatment program altogether.[18] Washington State has the largest program; in 1998 it had 945 offenders on a waiting list for the 200 spots available.[19]

Modern treatment options for sex offenders vary widely from state to state. Frequently, sex offenders receive suspended sentences on the condition that they participate in court-supervised community-based treatment.[20] Less frequently, though, incarcerated sex offenders may participate in prison-based treatment, which differs markedly from traditional psychological therapy in the community. For example, although traditional psychotherapy is voluntary, and clients are usually motivated to seek help, prison-based therapy is sometimes mandated. In a survey conducted in 2000, about 12 states reported that treatment for incarcerated sex offenders was required.[21] However, in Alaska, treatment is mandatory only if court ordered. In a number of other state programs where treatment is not mandatory, consideration for parole and a determination of "good time" earned toward early release is contingent on treatment. Prisoners in treatment are presumed to

---

[12] Id. The average number prisoners sentenced for violent sexual assaults other than rape annually is nearly 15% since 1980, more than any other category of violent crime.

[13] See Bruce J. Winick, Sex Offender Law in the 1990s: A Therapeutic Jurisprudence Analysis, 4 PSYCHOL. PUB. POL'Y & L. 505, at 546 (1998).

[14] See Berliner, supra note 2, at 1204.

[15] See id. (citing F H KNOPP ET AL., NATIONWIDE SURVEY OF TREATMENT PROGRAMS AND MODELS (1994)); see also H. Musk et al., Pedophilia in the Correctional System, 59(5) CORRECTIONS TODAY (1997) at 24. Musk et al. cite the same figure of 1,500 programs and professionals nationwide serving both pedophiles and nonpedophiles.

[16] See MARY WEST ET AL., COLORADO DEPT. OF CORRECTIONS, STATE SEX OFFENDER TREATMENT PROGRAMS: 50-STATE SURVEY, app. at 10 (2000), available at http://www.doc.state.co.us/admin_reg/PDFs/SO-report-send2.pdf. See also NAT'L INST. FOR CORR., U.S. DEPT. OF JUSTICE, SEX OFFENDER TREATMENT SKILLS FOR CORRECTIONS PROFESSIONALS, app. at 10 (2001), available at http://www.nicic.org/downloads/pdf/2001/sexoff-files/participmanual.pdf.

[17] See Erica Goode, Battling Deviant Behavior, Little Is Known About Causes, But Some Kinds of Treatment Show Promise, U.S. NEWS & WORLD REPORT (SEPT. 19, 1994), at 74–76.

[18] Berliner, supra note 2, at 1214.

[19] Id.

[20] Id. at 1212. See supra notes 2–9 and accompanying discussion.

[21] See West, supra note 16. Twenty-one states reported formal sex offender treatment programs designed just for the prison population.

be in denial of any need for change and do not enjoy confidentiality, as do private clients in therapy.[22] Group therapy is typically used in the prison setting, whereas private clients usually seek individual therapy sessions.

Obviously, treatment programs add to the cost of incarcerating sex offenders. Furthermore, as we saw in chapter 1, sex offenders are serving more prison time and are the second fastest growing group of offenders in our prison system. If treatment is effective in reducing sex crimes, then the money spent on it for prisoners is a good investment. If it is not, then we are wasting precious resources.

Parole and Probation Treatment Programs

Many states require convicted sex offenders to participate in community-based treatment programs as a condition of probation or parole. Offenders may have to see a mental health professional on a regularly scheduled basis, either in a group or in an individual session. Failure to adhere to this condition can result in revocation of probation or parole and their return to jail or prison. In many cases, sex offenders must pay for their treatment unless they are indigent.

Sexually Violent Predator Programs

Since 1990, a number of states have enacted sexually violent predator (SVP) laws, which allow sex offenders who have served their prison sentences to be civilly committed to high-security mental health facilities for control and treatment. Special treatment programs must be established for these individuals. SVP laws are clear that these offenders cannot be released until they are no longer a threat to the community.

As of spring 2002, more than 2,229 men (and a few women) had been committed as SVPs or were awaiting trial. (I examine these laws more extensively in chapter 5.) If treatment is not effective, then it is very unlikely that many of these individuals will be released, and the number of SVPs in custody will continue to grow. Because these laws require the government to provide intensive treatment in a secure environment, they are extremely expensive. Across the country, the average annual cost to treat civilly committed sex offenders ranges from $90,000 to $120,000 per offender.[23]

---

[22] See COUNCIL ON SEX OFFENDER TREATMENT, TEXAS DEP'T OF HEALTH, THE MANAGEMENT OF SEX OFFENDERS, *available at* http://www.tdh.state.tx.us/hcqs/plc/csot_mgmt.pdf (last visited Feb. 6, 2004) (*citing* NAT'L INST. OF CORR., U.S. DEP'T OF JUSTICE, SEX OFFENDER TREATMENT SKILLS FOR PROFESSIONALS 93-S3302 (1993)).

[23] See chapter 5 for a thorough analysis of the cost of SVP laws. *See also* Anita Schlank & Rick Harry, *Examining Our Approaches to Sex Offender & the Law: The Treatment of the Civilly Committed Sex Offender in Minnesota: A Review of the Past 10 Years*, 29 WM. MITCHELL L. REV. 1221, 1221–39 (2003). The difference in cost between incarceration and civil commitment is related to the number

Typically, the cost of treating sexual predators far exceeds the cost of incarceration. Thus, we simply must know if treatment for sex offenders works.

THE PROMISE OF PSYCHIATRY

In the past, both mental health professionals, especially psychiatrists, and policymakers have been very enthusiastic about treating sex offenders rather than punishing them. As I discuss in chapter 5, a majority of states enacted sexual psychopath laws, beginning with Illinois in 1938, to provide treatment for sex offenders in mental health facilities rather than send them to prison.[24] (Of course, even then mental health professionals also treated a number of sex offenders in the community.) Psychiatrists were at the forefront of this therapeutic movement.

Until the 1980s, most treatment programs for sex offenders in state institutions, whether for sexual psychopaths in mental health facilities or for sex offenders in prison, emphasized psychotherapy, sometimes called *talking therapy*.[25] Psychiatrists believed that the cause of sexually deviant behavior often could be traced to early childhood experiences, including relationships between offenders and their parents and siblings.

Sex offenders would meet with a psychiatrist, often in small groups with other sex offenders, and talk about their life experiences and relationships. Often sex offenders would become small-group leaders and lead the discussion. Group therapy allowed other sex offenders to "confront" each other and prevent participants from "conning" the group. It also made treatment more efficient. One-on-one therapy was simply too costly.

Unfortunately, the treatment was poorly described in various studies and appears to have been unstructured. Few controlled studies were conducted. Those that were studied failed to establish that psychotherapy was effective in reducing sexual recidivism.[26] In fact, some studies actually indi-

---

and type of staff required for supervision. Although incarceration is limited to custodial supervision, inpatient treatment facilities require specially trained counselors and other staff to provide intense supervision.

[24] *See generally* SAMUEL JAN BRAKEL & JOHN PARRY, THE MENTALLY DISABLED AND THE LAW (3rd ed. 1985). For a more thorough discussion of these laws, *see* chapter 5.

[25] V.L Quinsey (1977), *The Assessment and Treatment of Child Molesters: A Review*, 18 CANADIAN PSYCHOLOGICAL REVIEW (1977) 204–220; V.L. Quinsey, *Sexual Aggression: Studies of Offenders Against Women*, in LAW AND MENTAL HEALTH: INTERNATIONAL PERSPECTIVES Vol. 1, 84–121 (D. Weisstub ed.) (1984).

[26] Marnie E. Rice & Grant T. Harris, *What We Know and Don't Know About Treating Adult Sex Offenders*, in PROTECTING SOCIETY FROM DANGEROUS SEX OFFENDERS: LAW, JUSTICE, AND THERAPY (Bruce J. Winick & John Q. La Fond eds., 2003). *See also* L. Furby et al. (1998), *Sex Offender Recidivism: A Review*, 105 PSYCHOL. BULL. (1998) 3–30. This study examined "treatments delivered in the 1960s and 1970s that would not meet current standards of practice." R. Karl Hanson et al., *First Report of the Collaborative Outcome Data on the Effectiveness of Psychological Treatment of Sex Offenders*, 14 SEXUAL ABUSE: A JOURNAL OF RESEARCH AND TREATMENT (2002) 169, at 173.

cated that graduates of these programs had *higher* sex offending recidivism rates than sex offenders who were simply sent to prison to serve their time.[27] Gradually, this initial optimism for treating sex offenders faded.[28]

A NEW EXPERTISE EMERGES

As psychiatry retreated from this domain, psychologists and others began to develop different treatment approaches for sex offenders. Many of these approaches are "agnostic" about what causes people to commit sex crimes. Instead, they simply try to change an offender's thought processes, attitudes, desires, and behavior.

There are two broad treatment approaches: psychological and medical. Psychological approaches help offenders to change how they think and how they act. They are more concerned with teaching offenders how to avoid committing sex crimes. Medical approaches, primarily surgical and chemical castration, attempt to diminish sex offenders' sexual motivation or libido.[29] Reducing an offender's sex drive, it is assumed, will reduce his sexual offending.

Psychological Approaches

Most treatment programs for sex offenders use a comprehensive cognitive–behavioral therapeutic model that emphasizes relapse prevention. After the general failure of psychoanalysis to effectively treat sex offenders, behavior modification became the treatment of choice beginning in the late 1970s, and therapists gradually used cognitive methods during the 1980s.[30] Thus, a cognitive–behavioral model emerged together with the application of relapse prevention to sex offenders in a group setting.

---

[27] J.J. Romero & L.M. Williams, *Group Psychotherapy and Intensive Probation Supervision With Sex Offenders*, FEDERAL PROBATION (1983), 47, 36–42. L.V. FRISBIE, ANOTHER LOOK AT SEX OFFENDERS IN CALIFORNIA, RESEARCH MONOGRAPH No. 12 (California Department of Mental Hygiene, 1969); L.V. FRISBIE & E.H. DONDIS, RECIDIVISM AMONG TREATED SEX OFFENDERS, RESEARCH MONOGRAPH No. 5 (California Department of Mental Hygiene, 1965). A 1985 study of the Washington State sexual psychopath program by the state legislature found that, despite the highly selective population participating in these programs, the recidivism rates for offenders who actually completed the program was about the same as that of sex offenders incarcerated without treatment. SEX OFFENDER PROGRAMS AT WESTERN AND EASTERN STATE HOSPITALS, DEPARTMENT OF SOCIAL AND HEALTH SERVICES, REPORT No. 85-16 (December 13, 1985) (reporting to the Washington State Legislature).
[28] For a more detailed analysis of the failure of rehabilitation for sex offenders, *see* John Q. La Fond, *Washington's Sexually Violent Predator Law: A Deliberate Misuse of the Therapeutic State for Social Control*, 15 U. OF PUGET SOUND L. REV. 663–70, at 655 (1992).
[29] J. Michael Bailey & Aaron S. Greenberg, *The Science and Ethics of Castration: Lessons from the Morse Case*, 92 NW. U. L. REV. 1225, 1227 (1998).
[30] M.S. Carich et al., *Sexual Offenders and Contemporary Treatments*, 57(1) J. OF INDIVIDUAL PSYCHOL. 3–17 (2001).

As a result of this intersection between psychiatric and behavioral strategies, contemporary cognitive–behavioral treatment for sex offenders generally involves identifying and defining problematic thought processes associated with inappropriate sexual behavior and changing emotional or behavioral responses to environmental factors, with the goal of preventing future offenses.[31] Offenders in therapy are typically required to keep track of sexual behaviors, fantasies, thoughts, and feelings and to avoid environmental stimuli that reinforce deviant arousal. Although contemporary practice emphasizes cognitive and emotional processes, many specific behavior-modification techniques are used to control sexual arousal.

The most useful sex offender treatment programs are comprehensive and holistic, incorporating various treatment methods that target deviant thinking and behavior patterns specific to offenses committed.[32] A variety of therapeutic methods may be used in sex offender treatment programs, typically involving both behavioral and cognitive techniques. Although treatment options vary from state to state, the following sections describe generally some techniques common among treatment programs aiming to prevent relapse.

Redirecting Sexual Preference

Some sex offenders simply have a deviant sexual preference, and the criminal law punishes sexual conduct involving some of those preferences. For example, some adults are sexually aroused by and attracted to children. Others may take a sadistic delight in humiliating and inflicting physical damage on a woman during a rape. Many of these sexual preferences are clinically diagnosed as paraphilias under the current system of mental disorders.[33] Still other offenders may be diagnosed with a particular psychopathy, a personality disorder characterized by distinct behavioral, emotional, and personal features that support deviant sexual behavior.[34]

As mentioned earlier in chapter 2, we do not know with certainty why some people commit sex crimes. Nonetheless, the human sex drive can be very powerful in animating sexual behavior. A variety of conditioning

---

[31] PHIL RICH, UNDERSTANDING, ASSESSING, AND REHABILITATING JUVENILE SEXUAL OFFENDERS (2003).

[32] See Carich et al., *supra* note 30.

[33] According to the American Psychiatric Association, the essential features of paraphilia are "recurrent, intense sexually arousing fantasies, sexual urges, or behaviors generally involving 1) nonhuman objects, 2) the suffering or humiliation of oneself or one's partner, or 3) children or other nonconsenting persons that occur over a period of at least 6 months. . . ." AMERICAN PSYCHIATRIC ASSOCIATION, THE DIAGNOSTIC AND STATISTICAL MANUAL OF MENTAL DISORDERS (4th ed., text revision 2000) (hereinafter DSM–IV–TR), at 566.

[34] R. Serin et al., *Psychopathy, Deviant Sexual Arousal, and Recidivism Among Sexual Offenders*, J. OF INTERPERSONAL VIOLENCE, 16(3), 234–246 (2001).

strategies try to reduce deviant sexual arousal and reinforce appropriate arousal.[35]

The behavior-modification technique of *covert sensitization* is sometimes used to reduce the effect of deviant stimuli on an individual's sexual arousal and conduct.[36] Through therapist-guided imagery, the offender is directed to imagine his specific deviant behaviors. Instead of leading to the usual pleasurable outcome of sexual satisfaction, however, the therapist directs the offender to imagine the deviant behavior leading to unbearable consequences, such as arrest and incarceration. The offender learns how to imagine these terrible real-world consequences to block the thinking and conduct that in the past has led to his criminal act.[37] Conversely, guided imagery may be used to condition positive responses to appropriate sexual stimuli in the same manner.

Olfactory conditioning is another technique, in which the image of deviant sexual behavior is paired with an unpleasant odor.[38] Sex offenders attracted to young boys, for example, may be shown pictures of young boys and at the same time exposed to the foul smell of ammonia (often just smelling salts) to create a negative association with the deviant stimulus. The off-putting response to offensive odors disrupts the chain of events that, in the past, has led to a pleasurable outcome for the deviant sexual behavior.

Masturbatory satiation is another conditioning technique that involves two components combining cognition and behavior.[39] First, the offender is directed to masturbate to an appropriate fantasy, like sex with a consenting peer, until ejaculation. Then, during the refractory period following orgasm, when another orgasm cannot occur, the offender is directed to masturbate to his deviant sexual fantasies, such as having sex with a child, in an effort to pair his unsatisfying sexual activity with the deviant behavior. Masturbating to sexually appropriate thoughts and visual stimuli is thought to encourage offenders to seek acceptable alternatives to deviant sexual behavior. The erotic quality of the offender's deviant fantasy is diminished, as the pleasure of orgasm is no longer associated with that fantasy.

A phallometric measuring device, known as a plethysmograph, measures the physiological response of a penis to various stimuli and can be used to detect whether sex offenders still have a deviant sexual preference.[40]

---

[35] M. O'CONNELL ET AL., WORKING WITH SEX OFFENDERS (1990), at 99.

[36] AMERICAN PSYCHIATRIC ASSOCIATION, DANGEROUS SEX OFFENDERS: A TASK FORCE REPORT OF THE AMERICAN PSYCHIATRIC ASSOCIATION (Howard Zonana et al., eds., 1999) (hereinafter "APA Task Force Report").

[37] *Id.* at 45 (1999).

[38] *See* O'Connell, *supra* note 35, at 97–98.

[39] R.M. Wood et al., *Psychological Assessment, Treatment, and Outcome With Sex Offenders*, 18 BEHAV. SCI. & THE L. 23, 23–41 (2000).

[40] *See* O'Connell et al., *supra* note 35 at 97–98; *see also* Carich, *supra* note 32.

The plethysmograph measures sexual arousal by monitoring penile circumference through a small gauge fitted to the shaft of the penis. The offender, wearing the gauge, is presented with various stimuli, and his penile response is recorded by the plethysmograph. For example, if visual or auditory material involving young children causes the offender to have an erection, then this response is typically interpreted to mean he still has a sexual appetite for young children. Some experts believe these erection measures are useful in classifying individuals as to the type of paraphilia they have, especially persons with pedophilia, and to target deviant arousal. The tests can also be used to determine which treatment should be used and to measure its effect by taking pre- and posttest measures of arousal.[41]

This device may not be foolproof, however.[42] It is not entirely clear whether some men have learned how to avoid having a sexual reaction by not looking at or listening to the depictions of sexual acts or by distracting themselves while they are being studied, and some studies suggest many sexual offenders are able to inhibit sexual arousal. To counter these deliberate attempts to avoid detection, clinicians use a variety of techniques to spot or prevent such attempts by offenders to conceal their deviant sexual interest while this instrument is being used. Measures to verify that the individual is actually looking at or listening to the stimuli include asking the offender to identify signals that are superimposed on the stimuli and watching their gaze. Clinicians also ask the offender to talk about the stimuli to make sure he is not thinking about something else.[43]

Cognitive Restructuring

Many sex offenders have a distorted view of their behavior and its impact on their victims. Often, these idiosyncratic attitudes (sometimes called *private logic*[44]) allow offenders to excuse their criminal behavior.[45] Distorted views commonly involve cognitive defense mechanisms, such as denial, minimization, rationalization, and justification.[46] For example, some rapists believe that their victims "asked" to be raped, perhaps by dressing or behaving in a certain way, or that most women actually "enjoy" the experience. Some child molesters believe that sexual activity with a child is simply one way of expressing their love for the child and that sex may

---

[41] J.V. Becker & J.D. Murphy (1998). *What We Know and Do Not Know About Assessing and Treating Sex Offenders*. 4 (1/2) PSYCHOL. PUB POL'Y & L. 116–137 (1998).

[42] *Id. See also* G. Hall, *Theory-Based Assessment, Treatment, and Prevention of Sexual Aggression* (1996).

[43] APA Task Force Report, *supra* note 36, at 54.

[44] *See* Carich et al., *supra* note 30.

[45] *See* APA Task Force Report, *supra* note 36, at 70.

[46] *See* O'Connell et al., *supra* note 35.

be a good experience for a young person. Or they may minimize the serious-ness of their actions because they only fondled the child or did not use force. Another typical belief of the sex offender is that he is a helpless victim, which helps rationalize his actions. Cognitive restructuring tries to change the way offenders think about what they have done and to have a realistic understanding that they have committed a terrible act and have inflicted great harm on their victims.

Victim Empathy

Because many offenders leave the scene of their offense right away, they do not see and appreciate the terrible emotional consequences of their behavior on the victim.[47] Consequently, many programs also try to teach sex offenders to have empathy for their victims through understanding how the victims experienced the crime.[48] An offender may write essays or letters to his victim (although correspondence usually is not actually given to the victim) whereby he imagines various factors, such as how the victim felt at the time of the offense, the impact the offense had on the victim's life, or how the offender might feel in the victim's place. Victims may personally describe the horror of their experiences in face-to-face sessions, or indirectly on videotapes, in which they recount the horror of the event for the offender to view. Some programs actually have sex offenders play the role of the victim. The assumption underlying this technique is that recognizing the impact of the sexual offense on the victim will change how the offender thinks about the consequences of his crimes on other people and motivate him to avoid committing future sex offenses.

Social Competency

Some sex offenders exhibit social deficiencies and simply do not know how to interact socially and to seek willing sex partners.[49] Social-skill devel-opment and coping strategies may help to broaden the range of appropriate social functioning for sex offenders and compensate for these deficiencies.[50] This approach helps the offender learn how to establish a social relationship with other adults and how to seek willing sexual partners, but only in the later stages of therapy, after the offender has taken responsibility for his offenses and made progress in treatment. Often, role-playing in a group

---

[47] See APA Task Force Report, *supra* note 36, at 71.
[48] See Becker & Murphy, *supra* note 41.
[49] T. Ward, *Competency and Deficit Models in the Understanding and Treatment of Sexual Offenders*, 36(3) J. OF SEX RESEARCH 298–305 (1999).
[50] See O'Connell et al., *supra* note 35.

therapy setting is used to teach offenders appropriate social skills. Basic sex education and related information may also be provided as part of this therapeutic measure, and offenders may also learn sexual communication skills and learn about sexual intimacy with a peer.[51]

Stress and Anger Management

Other offense-related interpersonal problems common to many sex offenders are often targeted in therapy, including stress and anger management and substance abuse.[52] Many sex offenders cope with stress by committing unlawful sex acts. Others, when angered, may respond with violent sexual behavior. Anger management training teaches offenders to identify the triggers to anger, recognize their typical inappropriate responses to the anger, learn appropriate ways to express this emotion, and reduce the likelihood of future experiences of excessive anger.[53]

Relapse Prevention

Relapse prevention is an application of the cognitive–behavioral model developed for the treatment of addiction and modified for the specific treatment of sex offenders.[54] The aim of relapse prevention is to teach the offender how to use, on a daily basis, coping skills to manage high-risk situations that have led him in the past to commit sexual offenses.[55] Theoretically, specific internal events (such as deviant thoughts, feelings, or fantasies) or external events (such as certain situations or behaviors) reliably precede his commission of a sex crime. These events can be controlled through cognitive–behavioral techniques.[56]

This approach requires the offender to identify his cycle of preceding internal thinking or external high risk factors that usually sets off the chain of events leading to his commission of a sex offense. For example, a sex offender's typical pattern of offending may start with a fantasy about fondling a child. Relapse prevention provides strategies that help him get rid of this fantasy. Or an offender may frequently commit a sex crime after he has consumed alcohol and is alone with a child. The offender learns coping

---

[51]See APA Task Force Report, *supra* note 36.

[52]R.M. Wood et al., *supra* note 39.

[53]See APA Task Force Report, *supra* note 36, at 69; L. Berliner et al., *The Special Sex Offender Sentencing Alternative: A Study of Decision Making and Recidivism*, 10(4) J. OF INTERPERSONAL VIOLENCE 487–502 (1995).

[54]R.M. Wood et al., *supra* note 39.

[55]SEXUAL DEVIANCE: ISSUES AND CONTROVERSIES (T. Ward et al., eds., 2003).

[56]See Wood et al., *supra* note 39.

skills in order to avoid those situations conducive to committing the sex offense and, just as important, how to get out of them before they lead him to commit a sex crime. So a sex offender may try not to consume alcohol while around children, or if he has consumed alcohol and a child is nearby, he may learn that he must leave immediately or make sure that another adult is present.

Medical Approaches

Because sexual offenses are commonly understood to derive at least in part from the physiological responses of the sex drive, it makes sense that society has sought medical approaches to reducing recidivism among sex offenders. In this section I discuss the two most common medical approaches.

Surgical Castration

Castration, the surgical removal of the male gonads (also called an *orchiectomy*), has not been used very much in the United States, but until recently has been used extensively in Europe to reduce the male sex drive and aggression in general.[57] Most studies have not been controlled and included homosexuals who, today, would not be considered sex offenders. Nonetheless, some studies concluded that castration reduced sexual recidivism even among high-risk offenders.[58]

It appears that castration may well reduce sex drive and could thereby reduce sex offense recidivism. Whether incarcerated individuals could give legally effective informed consent is not clear. The inducement of release may simply be too coercive to consider an inmate's "choice" to be truly voluntary.[59] Nor is it clear that the Constitution would permit the government to physically and irreversibly maim a human being for life to prevent future crimes, even if the person did consent.[60] It is very unlikely, however, that the Courts will allow surgical castration to be imposed as *punishment*

---

[57] See Rice & Harris, *supra* note 26.

[58] R. Wille & K.M. Beier, *Castration in Germany*, 2 Annals of Sex Research 103–133 (1989); K. Freund, *Therapeutic Sex Drive Reduction*, 62 Acta Psychiatrica Scandinavica 5–38 (1980); G.K. Stürup, *Treatment of Sexual Offenders in Herstedvester Denmark*, 44 Acta Psychiatrica Scandavia 5–63 (1968).

[59] For a thoughtful discussion of these issues, see Bailey & Greenberg, *supra* note 30; William Winslade et al., *Castrating Pedophiles Convicted of Sex Offenses Against Children: New Treatment or Old Punishment?* 51 SMU L. Rev. 349 (1998). The Wille & Beier study has been extremely influential. According to some experts, it is responsible for the finding in a meta-analysis by Hall in 1995 that medical/hormonal treatment for sex offenders is effective. See R. Karl Hanson et al., *First Report of the Collaborative Outcome Data on the Effectiveness of Psychological Treatment of Sex Offenders*, 14 Sexual Abuse: A Journal of Research and Treatment 169 (2002), at 171.

[60] State v. Brown, 326 S.E.2d 410 (S.C. 1985).

on a convicted sex offender.[61] (I discuss these issues in greater detail in chapter 6.)

Chemical Castration

Drugs can also diminish the male sex drive, thereby reducing sexually deviant behavior. Some drugs prevent or reduce the body from producing the male hormone testosterone. The most common of these are called *antiandrogens*. They accomplish the same sex-drive-reducing effects as surgical castration, but unlike surgery, these effects are reversible by simply discontinuing the medication. Antiandrogens, however, do have unpleasant side effects, including weight gain, fatigue, headaches, less body hair, depression, and gastrointestinal problems.[62] Most men do not like to take them.[63] Other drugs do not block the production of testosterone but instead prevent the body from effectively using this hormone. *Cyproterone acetate* (CPA) is the most common of these drugs; it blocks the intracellular uptake of testosterone and the intracellular metabolism of androgen.[64]

Only one of the antiandrogen drugs, *medroxyprogesterone acetate* (MPA), has been studied in controlled outcome evaluations; even then, the conclusions appear somewhat contradictory.[65] Some research has shown less reoffending by child molesters who took MPA than among those who did not take it.[66] Other research does not support the effectiveness of MPA in reducing sexual reoffending.[67] Some research has also shown no difference in sexual reoffending between offenders who took MPA and those who did

---

[61] Weems v. United States, 217 U.S. 349 (1910); *Brown*, 326 S.E.2d 410 (holding that surgical castration, even if sought by the offender, "is a form of mutilation" and was therefore prohibited by the State Constitution's constitutional prohibition on cruel and unusual punishment); Davis v. Berry, 216 F. 413 (S.D. Iowa 1914) (analogizing Iowa's practice of performing vasectomies on prisoners convicted of two or more felonies to surgical castration since it had the same purpose and effect); Kenimer v. State, 59 S.E.2d 296 (Ga. Ct. App. 1950) (suggesting that castration violated the Eighth Amendment's prohibition on "cruel and unusual punishment"). *See also* Kaimowitz v. Mich. Dep't of Mental Health, (unreported, Cir. Ct. Mich. 1973).

[62] *See* Rice & Harris, *supra* note 26.

[63] R. Langevin et al., *What Treatment Do Sex Offenders Want?* 1 ANNALS OF SEX RESEARCH 353–385 (1988).

[64] *See* APA Task Force Report, *supra* note 43, at 106.

[65] *See* Rice & Harris, *supra* note 26.

[66] J.P. Fedoroff et al. (1992), *Medroxyprogestrerone Acetate in the Treatment of Paraphilic Sexual Disorders.* 18 J. OF OFFENDER REHABILITATION 109–123 (1992) (child molesters treated as outpatients who took MPA and remained in psychotherapy were less likely to reoffend than those who did not take it; however, the authors noted that participants were not randomly assigned, therapists knew which patients were taking MPA, and men taking the drugs may have been more motivated to change).

[67] L.E. Emory et al., *The Texas Experience With Depeprovera: 1980–1990.* 18 J. OF OFFENDER REHABILITATION 125–139 (1992) (recidivism rates between two groups of sex offenders, one taking MPA, the other not, were not significantly different; they were also surprisingly high for those taking MPA because they were low-risk offenders and were highly motivated). *See* Rice & Harris, *supra* note 26.

not.[68] There is also some research suggesting that sex offenders who take these drugs may have a *higher* recidivism rate than those who do not, though it should be noted that offenders in the study on medication might have had a higher risk of reoffending and thus have been stronger candidates for medication.[69]

Other drugs that modify the serotonin transmitter system in the central nervous system have been used to treat sex offenders. They include antidepressants like clomipramine, fluoxetine, and others. These pharmacological agents can reduce depression, anxiety, aggression, and obsessive–compulsive behavior, while causing relatively mild side effects. Although they may reduce the frequency and intensity of sexually deviant fantasies when combined with psychosocial treatments, their effectiveness in reducing sexual recidivism has not yet been established.[70]

Researchers have reached contrary conclusions about the efficacy and wisdom of using pharmacological strategies to reduce sexual recidivism. A Task Force Report prepared by the American Psychiatric Association concluded, "The pharmacological treatment of the paraphilias (including sex offenders) with antiandrogens and hormonal agents is successful in reducing recidivism rates through the reduction of sexual fantasies, sexual drive, sexual arousal, and sexual behavior."[71]

However, Rice and Harris, two noted Canadian researchers, after reviewing the available evidence, concluded that few sex offenders will take testosterone-reducing drugs voluntarily, and even fewer will take them for an extended period. Although agreeing that the research does indicate that those few offenders who take the drugs as part of their treatment have lower reoffense rates, they nonetheless decided, "There is, as yet, no convincing reason to believe that the drugs cause reductions in reoffending. The small proportion of sex offenders who remain in treatment might just be especially highly motivated."[72]

As I point out in chapter 6, some states now require many sex offenders to take these drugs as a condition of their release and parole from prison. Those who refuse must serve their full prison terms. Those strategies not only raise serious Constitutional and ethical questions, they may also rest on a false assumption that these drugs will reduce sexual recidivism.

---

[68] See Rice & Harris, *supra* note 26; *The Use of Medtroxyprogesterone Acetate to Assist in the Treatment of Sexual Offenders*. 4 ANNALS OF SEX RESEARCH 117–129; N. McConaghy et al., *Treatment of Sex Offenders With Imaginal Desensitization and/or Medroxyprogesterone*, 77 ACTA PSYCHIATRICA SCANDAVICA 199–206 (1988).

[69] R.K. Hanson et al., *Where Should We Intervene? Dynamic Predictors of Sex Offense Recidivism*, 27 CRIM JUSTICE & BEH 6–35 (2000).

[70] SEXUAL DEVIANCE: ISSUES AND CONTROVERSIES, at 265–66 (T. Ward et al., eds., 2003); *see* APA Task Force Report, *supra* note 43, at 116–118.

[71] See APA Task Force Report, *supra* note 43, at 118.

[72] See Rice & Harris, *supra* note 26, at 107.

EVALUATING TREATMENT EFFECTIVENESS

Outcome Measures

To study whether treatment for sex offenders is effective, researchers must first determine what result or "outcome" is expected from treatment.[73] In most cases, mental health professionals expect that treatment will reduce sexual reoffending by their patients. (Of course, they may have other expectations, such as a reduction in all violent reoffending, not just sex offenses, or a reduction in specific types of sex crimes, such as child molesting.) Most treatment efficacy studies examine whether treated sex offenders commit fewer sex crimes than untreated offenders do. (All of these studies are of male sex offenders because women make up a very small percentage of sex offenders.[74])

Measuring Outcomes

As I noted in chapter 1, it is difficult to accurately determine whether a convicted sex offender commits another sex crime. Researchers use official records for arrest, charging, or conviction of sex crimes committed by offenders who have received treatment to measure sex offender recidivism. Although objective, these records will invariably undercount the actual number of sex crimes committed by these men.[75] Nonetheless, these data are probably the best information available and generally are used to determine whether treatment reduces sexual recidivism or, put differently, whether treatment for sex offenders is "effective." Self-reporting by sex offenders on whether they commit sex crimes after they receive treatment is generally not used in treatment efficacy studies, because too many sex offenders deny, distort, or minimize their criminal behavior.[76]

Control Groups

The ideal scientific method for studying treatment efficacy would require researchers to randomly select from a single group of sex offenders individuals who receive treatment (the experimental group) and those who

---

[73] See generally Rice & Harris, supra note 26; Grant T. Harris et al., Appraisal and Management of Risk in Sexual Aggressors: Implications for Criminal Justice Policy, 4 PSYCHOL. PUB. POL'Y & L. 73 (1998); see Becker & Murphy, supra note 41.

[74] G.G. Abel et al., Sexually Aggressive Behavior, FORENSIC PSYCHOLOGY AND PSYCHIATRY: PERSPECTIVES AND STANDARDS FOR INTERDISCIPLINARY PRACTICE (J. Curran et al., eds., 1986).

[75] See chapter 1 for a discussion of this problem.

[76] See Rice & Harris, supra note 26.

do not (the control group).[77] Then, both groups would be studied after their release to compare their respective recidivism rates for sex crimes and other crimes. This approach isolates the impact of treatment on sexual recidivism from other variables that might affect sexual recidivism, such as choice, age, or race.

Studies that use random assignment and a control group are called *controlled studies*. They provide the best evidence on this important question. Studies that do not use random assignment and a control group can shed some light on whether treatment for sex offenders is effective in reducing sexual recidivism, but their results are problematic because they do not isolate the causal variable that is being studied: treatment.

Unfortunately, most studies of treatment efficacy for sex offenders have not involved this rigorous research design. Instead, most researchers have used a group of sex offenders that are similar to the group that received treatment and compared the recidivism rate for the treated sex offenders with a similar group who were not treated. In most cases, these two groups were not randomly assigned. Although limited by their design, these studies can provide useful information.

Simply determining whether men commit fewer sex crimes *after* they receive treatment than they did before is not enough to gauge whether treatment is effective. Researchers must also compare sexual recidivism rates for the treated group with those of a similar group of sex offenders who did *not* receive treatment or received a *different* type of treatment (i.e., the *control group*). This practice allows researchers to compare sex offenders who are very similar to one another except for the fact that some of them were not treated or were given a different treatment. Researchers can then determine whether a particular type of treatment, rather than other factors like age or the passage of time, made a difference in reducing sexual reoffending.

Refusers and Dropouts

Some research suggests that excluding treatment refusers and dropouts from analyses may grossly overestimate treatment effectiveness.[78] For example, many men refuse treatment. If they are *excluded* from the "treatment" group, while men who would have refused treatment if offered it are included in the comparison group, then treatment efficacy will be significantly overestimated. Some experts also argue that including only those who complete

---

[77] Marnie E. Rice & Grant T. Harris, *The Size and Sign of Treatment Effects in Sex Offender Therapy*, 989 ANNALS N.Y. ACAD. SCI. 428 (2003).

[78] *See* Rice & Harris, *supra* note 26 (*citing* E.B. FOA & P.M.G. EMMELKAMP, FAILURES IN GROUP BEHAVIOR (1983)).

the program as "treated," and excluding the recidivism rates of those who dropout or are expelled from the program, will significantly overstate the effectiveness of treatment.[79] However, it can also be argued that it only makes sense to include persons who actually complete treatment as "treated," because they are the only ones who have received the full benefit of the therapeutic program.

Voluntary Versus Involuntary Treatment

Most of the recent studies on treatment efficacy involve sex offenders who voluntarily consented to be treated.[80] These studies did not purport to measure whether *involuntary* treatment was effective. This fact is important to remember because, as I note in chapter 5, sexually violent predator laws essentially impose treatment on sex offenders who did not, at least initially, consent to the treatment. We still do not know—and to be truthful, have not even studied—whether treatment is effective in reducing sexual reoffending when it is imposed on people rather than sought by them. It is hoped that states that have enacted sexual predator programs will study this question.

DOES TREATMENT REDUCE SEXUAL RECIDIVISM?

Numerous studies have been trying to find out whether treatment reduces sexual recidivism. Studies on psychotherapy were virtually unanimous: There was no basis for concluding that talk therapy resulted in fewer sex offenses committed by sex offenders who received that treatment than by similar offenders who did not receive it. As noted earlier, new treatments for sex offenders have been tried since approximately the 1980s. Although these treatments are relatively new, sufficient time has elapsed to permit research on this question to be conducted.

Community-Based Treatment in Washington State

Researchers compared recidivism rates for offenders sentenced to community treatment under SSOSA with rates of other sex offenders who were eligible for that program but were not allowed to participate. Both groups had comparable recidivism rates for committing another sex crime during

---

[79] See Rice & Harris, *supra* note 26.
[80] The term *voluntary* does not always accurately describe reality. For example, many sex offenders sought commitment to a sexual psychopath program to avoid serving a criminal sentence in prison. Thus, in a formal sense, these men were treated on a "voluntary" basis. In reality, the threat of imprisonment undoubtedly influenced their decision to seek commitment and treatment as a sexual psychopath.

an average release time of 3.5 years: 5%. SSOSA did not reduce sexual recidivism. It did, however, seem to reduce recidivism for nonsexual offenses. SSOSA participants had a 7.3% felony reconviction rate for nonsex crimes, compared with nonparticipants, who had a 16.3% felony reconviction rate for the same period.[81] Because of design flaws, however, this study does not authoritatively establish whether community treatment is effective in reducing sexual recidivism.

Prison Treatment Programs

Some researchers have compared recidivism rates for sex offenders who have participated in prison treatment programs with a comparable group of sex offenders who have not. In Kentucky, sex offenders who had participated in a prison treatment program had a sexual recidivism rate of 3.4%, compared with a sexual recidivism rate of 8.7% for sex offenders who had not been treated, or almost three times the rate of treated offenders.[82] A Canadian study, which compared matched treated and untreated groups of sex offenders, had a readmission rate of 33.9% for the untreated group and 14.2% for the treated group.[83] Again, because of methodological limitations, these studies suggest, but cannot prove, that prison treatment programs reduce sexual recidivism.

California's SOTEP Program

Probably the most ambitious and scientifically sound study to date on whether treatment reduces sexual recidivism was conducted by Janice Marques and her colleagues in California.[84] The California Sex Offender Treatment and Evaluation Program (SOTEP) used a cognitive–behavioral approach, which combined training in relapse prevention, relaxation, social skills, and stress and anger management, with substance abuse counseling, behavioral treatment for deviant preferences, and aftercare. It targeted child molesters and rapists who were incarcerated. The program began in 1985 and was scheduled to end in 1995.

The project was extremely well designed. The individuals who had volunteered for treatment were randomly assigned into one group that

---

[81] Berliner, *supra* note 2, at 1213.

[82] J.M. BARNES & K.D. PETERSON, THE KENTUCKY SEX OFFENDER TREATMENT PROGRAM (1997).

[83] Berliner, *supra* note 2, at 1214 (*citing* T. NICHOLAICHUCK & A. GORDON, TREATMENT REDUCES SEXUAL RECIDIVISM: CLEARWATER OUTCOME DATA SUMMARY (1996) (Paper presented at the annual ATSA meeting, Chicago, IL)).

[84] J.K. Marques et al. (1993). *Findings and Recommendations From California's Experimental Treatment Program*, SEXUAL AGGRESSION: ISSUES IN ETIOLOGY, ASSESSMENT, AND TREATMENT 143–66 (G.C. Hall et al., eds., 1993) J.K. Marques et al., *Effects of Cognitive–Behavioral Treatment on Sex Offender Recidivism*, 21 CRIM. JUST. & BEHAV. 28–54 (1994).

received treatment and a second group that did not. Sex offense recidivism rates for these two groups were compiled and were compared with the recidivism rates for another control group consisting of matched sex offenders (i.e., incarcerated offenders with a very similar offense history, offense subtype, and personal characteristics) who received no treatment. Follow-up lasted between 5 and 14 years. The researchers also followed offenders who dropped out of treatment, and compiled their recidivism rates. There was high attrition, 35%, in the treatment group, and dropouts were especially likely to have a subsequent arrest for a sex crime or for a violent crime.

The study found that volunteers who had sought treatment and received it had very similar recidivism rates (in 1994, 25% of the treatment group had committed a new sex crime or other violent crime) to those who also had volunteered for treatment but did not receive it (in 1994, 24% to 27% of the untreated control group had committed a new sex crime or other violent crime).[85] Thus, no positive effect for treatment was found. Offenders who had completed treatment, especially child molesters, did have a lower recidivism rate for *nonsexual* violent offenses than untreated volunteers. More recent effects of this program reported by Marques and Day are weaker than those reported in 1994.[86]

Meta-Analysis

We have described specific research projects that have been conducted on a particular treatment approach to see whether it reduces sexual reoffending. This type of research is useful and does shed some limited light on this question. However, researchers have found that they can use a statistical method called *meta-analysis* to integrate many separate studies on this question into a single study. This practice allows them to draw general conclusions on this question by aggregating virtually all sound prior research on the same question. Meta-analysis is more powerful because the number of participants studied is increased significantly and the number of variables that can be studied is also increased.[87] As a result, researchers find out more useful information, and with more confidence, than would be discovered in any single study.

---

[85] J.K. Marques et al., *Effects of Cognitive–Behavioral Treatment on Sex Offenders' Recidivism. Preliminary Results of a Longitudinal Study.* 21 CRIM. JUST. & BEHAV. 28–54 (1994).

[86] J.K. MARQUES ET AL., SEX OFFENDER TREATMENT EVALUATION PROJECT: PROGRESS REPORT (California Department of Mental Health, 1998).

[87] For a good description of a meta-analysis and its advantages, see R. Karl Hanson et al., *First Report of the Collaborative Outcome Data on the Effectiveness of Psychological Treatment of Sex Offenders,* 14 SEXUAL ABUSE: A JOURNAL OF RESEARCH AND TREATMENT 169 (2002). *See also* THE HANDBOOK OF RESEARCH SYNTHESIS (H. Cooper et al., eds., 1994).

The Results: We Do Not Know for Sure Whether Treatment Works

Although an earlier meta-analysis of sex offender treatment studies by Hall found a small, statistically significant, positive effect from treatment,[88] this study has been subsequently reviewed by other researchers who have criticized it and questioned its conclusions.[89] In their view, the most methodologically sound studies included in Hall's study show no treatment effect.

It is important to understand the significance of these studies. They simply conclude that, as of now, no sound evidence exists that positively proves that treatment for sex offenders reduces their sexual reoffending. The research does *not* establish that treatment does *not* work. Simply put, we do not know whether treatment works: It may or it may not.

The Agnostic View

After a more recent review of the available literature, two eminent Canadian researchers concluded that there is simply not enough high-quality research to answer this question.[90] They concluded, "Simply put, the effectiveness of adult sex offender treatment has yet to be demonstrated."[91] In their view, we must remain agnostic about whether treatment reduces sexual reoffending.

The Cautiously Optimistic View

However, some researchers now believe there is some empirical basis for modest optimism that treatment does reduce sexual recidivism. An international committee of experts reviewed the available research on the effectiveness of psychological treatment in reducing sexual reoffending.[92] It conducted a meta-analysis of 43 studies with a combined sample of 9,454 sex offenders. Most of the studies examined rapists and child molesters and had an average follow-up period of 4 to 5 years. It concluded that "the balance of available evidence suggests that current treatments reduce recidivism, but that firm conclusions await more and better research."[93] The group found

---

[88]G.C.N. Hall, *Sexual Offender Recidivism Revisited: A Meta-Analysis of Recent Treatment Studies*, 63 J CONSULT. & CLIN. PSYCHOL. 802–809 (1995).

[89]M.E. Rice et al., *Treating the Adult Sex Offender*, TREATING ADULT AND JUVENILE OFFENDERS WITH SPECIAL NEEDS 291–312 (J.B. Ashford et al., eds., 2001); N. McConaghy, *Methodological Issues Concerning Evaluation of Treatment for Sexual Offenders: Randomization, Treatment, Dropouts, Untreated Controls, and Treatment Studies*, 11 SEXUAL ABUSE: A JOURNAL OF RESEARCH AND TREATMENT 183–193 (1999).

[90]*See* Rice & Harris, *supra* note 26.

[91]*Id.* at 109.

[92]R. Karl Hanson et al., *First Report of the Collaborative Outcome Data on the Effectiveness of Psychological Treatment of Sex Offenders*, 14 SEXUAL ABUSE: A JOURNAL OF RESEARCH AND TREATMENT 169, 169–194 (2002).

[93]*Id.* at 187.

that, on average, adult sex offenders who received cognitive–behavioral treatment, and adolescent sex offenders who received systemic treatments that address family needs and other social systems that influence young offenders, were less likely to reoffend than sex offenders who did not receive treatment. Specifically, they found that contemporary treatments were associated with a "significant reduction in both sexual recidivism (17% to 10%) and general recidivism (51% to 32%)." The committee also found that community treatment appeared to be as effective as institutional treatment. In addition, sex offenders who left treatment were at higher risk of reoffending than sex offenders who completed treatment. Somewhat surprising, however, was that the committee also found that sex "offenders who refused treatment were not at higher risk for sexual recidivism than offenders who started treatment."[94]

Despite this guarded optimism, the committee stressed that its findings should be interpreted cautiously because there were few high-quality research studies, the treatment effects in reducing sexual recidivism were not large in absolute terms (7%), and their findings provide little direction on how to improve treatment for sex offenders. It also noted that not all treatment programs are effective; consequently, public officials should not assume that any treatment is better than no treatment. In addition, no treatment program can assure a complete cessation of offending.

Another Approach for Measuring Treatment Efficacy

Other prominent Canadian researchers have tried a different approach to evaluating whether treatment reduces sexual recidivism.[95] Howard Barbaree and his colleagues agree with Rice and Harris,[96] who have argued that a random control trial is the most rigorous and accurate method of answering that question, because it ensures that all extraneous factors that could affect recidivism are randomly distributed across the treatment and control groups. Thus, there should be no variables other than treatment that could explain any difference in recidivism rates for the two groups. However, they make a persuasive case that it is virtually impossible to use

---

[94] *Id.* at 187.
[95] HOWARD BARBAREE ET AL., THE EVALUATION OF SEX OFFENDER TREATMENT EFFICACY USING SAMPLES STRATIFIED BY LEVELS OF ACTUARIAL RISK (paper presented at the Association for the Treatment of Sexual Abusers, October 9, 2003, St. Louis, MO.). *See also* chapter 2 of C.M. Langton, Contrasting Approaches to Risk Assessment With Adult Male Sexual Offenders: An Evaluation of Recidivism Prediction Schemes and the Utility of Supplementary Clinical Information for Enhancing Predictive Accuracy (2003) (Unpublished doctoral dissertation, University of Toronto).
[96] Rice & Harris, *supra* note 77.

random control trials in the field of sex offender treatment given the current social and political climate.

Thus, they used an alternative approach. To simplify matters, these researchers studied 468 sex offenders, all of whom were treated at the Warkworth Sexual Behavior Clinic in Ontario while serving custodial sentences. The treatment program offered there is representative of current state-of-the-art treatment programs for sex offenders. Stratifying their group by level of risk, using the Rapid Risk Assessment for Sex Offense Recidivism (RRASOR) and the Static–99, these researchers examined the sexual recidivism rates for the group over an average 5-year follow-up period and compared these rates with what two well-established actuarial instruments, the RRASOR and the Static–99, predicted the recidivism of this group to be.[97] They believe that these instruments might control for extraneous variables that might otherwise explain any difference in recidivism. If the treated group had a significantly *lower* recidivism rate than the actuarial instruments predicted, they believe it is due to treatment rather than other factors. Put another way, the actuarial instruments should accurately predict what the recidivism rate for this group should be if they had *not* received treatment.

Both instruments predicted that the sample would have approximately 70 recidivists over the 5-year period; in fact, there were only 53. Likewise, significant differences existed between the study's observed percentages of recidivists at the various actuarially determined levels of risk and the percentages expected according to the instruments. This research is certainly consistent with the conclusion that treatment can reduce sexual reoffending.

In summary, it seems fair to say that there *is* some basis for concluding that treatment can reduce sexual reoffending, but that a more definitive answer to that question awaits further research.

Treatment Refusal

Ironically, experts now agree that quitting treatment or being expelled from a treatment program is a risk factor for future sexual recidivism.[98] Less agreement can be found on whether refusing to participate in treatment is also a risk factor. After reviewing the available research, Rice and Harris have concluded, "Thus, it is highly probable that, irrespective of the effects of treatment, those who refuse [treatment] represent greater risk than those who volunteer for and complete it."[99]

---

[97] For a more thorough description of these instruments, see chapter 2.

[98] R. Karl Hanson et al., *First Report of the Collaborative Outcome Data on the Effectiveness of Psychological Treatment of Sex Offenders*, 14 SEXUAL ABUSE: A JOURNAL OF RESEARCH AND TREATMENT 169 (2002).

[99] Rice & Harris, *supra* note 77.

SHOULD WE CONTINUE TO TREAT SEX OFFENDERS?

This is a provocative question. As discussed in chapter 2, we are much better at predicting when a sex offender is at high risk of committing another sex crime than we are at reducing that risk by treatment and having confidence in actually reducing that risk. Nonetheless, there are very persuasive reasons why we should continue to provide treatment for sex offenders.

Although more research is clearly needed, many experts now believe that there is sound evidence that treatment can reduce sexual recidivism. Reducing sexual reoffending will make our communities safer. We would be foolish not to use any effective measure available, including treatment, to accomplish this important goal.

Many mental health professionals have been engaged for several decades in devising innovative programs that provide treatment to sex offenders. Their efforts provide a solid base for developing more effective treatment programs. Continued funding of these programs will allow professionals to initiate and improve treatment approaches that may be more effective in reducing sexual violence. It will also allow society to study various approaches in a systematic manner to determine whether specific treatments are effective for specific types of sex offenders.

Many sex offenders want to change: They truly do not want to commit more sex crimes. Without some means of changing their attitudes and modifying their behavior, these men will simply not have any tools they can use to avoid committing new sex crimes. Treatment provides a variety of strategies that sex offenders can use to reduce their risk of sexual reoffense. Without them, many sex offenders may well feel helpless in controlling their sexual behavior. Treatment may increase their confidence, strengthen their resolve, and provide specific steps they can take to avoid reoffending.

Of course, treatment may have a negative impact on sex offenders. A purely therapeutic approach that ignores offender responsibility and changing offender attitudes and rationalizations may encourage sex offenders to think of themselves as "sick" and, therefore, not responsible for their actions.[100] Victims may be angered because it could convey the message that someone who "couldn't help himself" violated them.

Clearly, society must make sure that treatment does not, in any way, minimize individual responsibility for committing a sex crime. Offenders must be told in no uncertain terms that what they did was morally wrong and harmful to the victim. It is simply unacceptable that treatment should either trivialize the harm done to victims or minimize the offender's personal

---

[100] Bruce J. Winick, *Sex Offender Law in the 1990s: A Therapeutic Jurisprudence Analysis*, 4 PSYCHOL. PUB. POL'Y & L. 505 (1998).

responsibility for the choices he made. Most current treatment programs do not have these negative consequences. Cognitive restructuring, for example, seeks to change sex offenders' attitudes and beliefs so that they will realize the harm they have done and accept responsibility for it.[101] Treatment can and does reinforce the same moral teaching that the criminal law seeks to engender. Treatment should also emphasize providing tools that sex offenders can and must use to avoid harming another human being. Relapse prevention does that.

Sexual violence does immense harm. Incarcerating massive numbers of sex offenders for many years to prevent that harm is costly and unnecessary, and that strategy should be reserved for the most dangerous sex offenders. Changing the attitudes and behaviors of offenders who truly want to change appears to be within our reach. Providing treatment for them as soon as possible is a wise investment that should reduce sexual violence. If we do not invest in the development of new therapeutic expertise that protects society and changes offenders, we unnecessarily and unwisely limit our public-safety arsenal.

---

[101] *See supra* notes 44–46 and accompanying text.

4

THE EFFECTIVENESS OF REGISTRATION AND COMMUNITY NOTIFICATION LAWS

Beginning in the 1990s, parents demanded to be allowed to enlist in the crusade to protect their children against dangerous sex offenders. People no longer believed that the criminal justice system could protect them from the pervasive threat posed by these insatiable criminals. But to protect their children, parents needed to know who the enemy was and where he lived. Effective self-defense would require the government to provide this crucial information so that the community could be vigilant and proactive.

In 1994, then-governor of New Jersey Christine Todd Whitman signed "Megan's Law."[1] Modeled after Washington State's 1990 law,[2] this law

---

[1] N.J. Stat. Ann. 2C:7-1 through 2C:7-11. For one account of the history underlying the New Jersey legislation, *see* Kenneth Crimaldi, *"Megan's Law": Election-Year Politics and Constitutional Rights*, 27 RUTGERS L.J. 169 (autumn, 1995). Mr. Timmendequas was subsequently convicted of capital murder and sentenced to death. Timmendequas has since appealed his conviction and sentence without success. *See* State v. Timmendequas, 737 A.2d 55 (1999) (N.J. affirming conviction and death sentence) and State v. Timmendequas, 773 A.2d 18 (2001) (ruling that death sentence was not disproportionate). An article in the Philadelphia Inquirer reports that Timmendequas is still sitting on death row. Ralph Siegal, *After U.S. Ruling, Confining of Sex Offenders Challenged*, PHILA. INQUIRY, Jan. 29, 2002, at B03.

[2] In 1990, Washington became the first state to enact a broad sex offender registration law. WASH. REV. CODE ANN. § 4.24.550 (West 2004), first enacted by Laws 1990, ch. 3, § 117, eff. Feb. 28, 1990. California had enacted the first sex offender registration law in 1944. Lucy Berliner, *Sex Offenders: Policy and Practice*, 92 Nw. U. L. REV. 1203, 1214 (1998).

required most sex offenders to register with the police. It also compelled the state to notify people when dangerous sex offenders moved into their communities.[3] The New Jersey law was inspired by the death of young Megan Kanka, who was molested and murdered by a neighbor, Jesse Timmendequas, who, unknown to her parents, was a convicted sex offender living across the street from her.[4]

Today, every state in the nation has a sex offender registration law and a community notification law, primarily because of a federal law, the *Jacob Wetterling Crimes Against Children and Sexually Violent Offender Registration Program* (hereinafter, "The Jacob Wetterling Act"), passed by Congress in 1994.[5] This law required states to establish comprehensive sex offender registration and community notification programs or lose 10% of some federal law enforcement funds.[6] There is also a national sex offender database maintained by the FBI that provides law enforcement agencies access to state registration information.[7]

Registration and notification laws have generated extensive litigation in federal and state courts, claiming that they violate the constitutional rights of sex offenders. Sex offenders have argued that these laws punish them a second time, violating *ex post facto* and double jeopardy provisions of the Constitution while also violating their rights to privacy and denying them due process.

In this chapter, I examine registration and notification laws. I analyze the various constitutional challenges to these laws, their costs and their effectiveness as law enforcement tools, and their impact on both released offenders and the communities in which those offenders reside. Finally, I answer crucial questions that must be asked. Do they work? Are they doing more harm than good? Should they be changed, or even eliminated?

---

[3] WASH. REV. CODE ANN. § 4.24.550 (West 2004).

[4] See *supra* note 1.

[5] See Jacob Wetterling Crimes Against Children and Sexually Violent Offender Registration Act, 42 U.S.C. §§ 14071 et seq. (1997 & Supp. 2002).

[6] The federal statute directs that states "shall" establish programs for, at a minimum, registering names, identifying factors, residence information, and offense and treatment histories of certain released sex offenders, and that states further "shall release relevant information that is necessary to protect the public concerning a specific person required to register under this section." *Id.* This statute had obligated states to create registration programs since 1994, and authorized public notification of registration information; in May of 1996, President Clinton signed an amendment to this statute providing that public notification is now *required* rather than merely authorized. See more on the distinction between registration and notification laws later in this chapter.

[7] See The Pam Lychner Sexual Offender Tracking and Identification Act of 1996, 42 U.S.C. § 14072 (1997 & Supp. 2002).

REGISTRATION VERSUS NOTIFICATION

Statutes setting forth registration requirements and those setting forth notification requirements are complementary, but *distinct*.

Registration Laws

Sex offender registration laws are not new. In 1947, California passed the first registration law that applied only to sex offenders. However, few states enacted a similar law until the 1990s.[8]

A new generation of laws was enacted in the 1990s. These registration laws require convicted sex offenders to provide the police with current information about themselves and to keep that information up-to-date. Most states also require juvenile offenders to register.[9] These laws assume—incorrectly, as we saw in chapter 2—that all sex offenders are likely to commit another sex crime.

State Registration Information

Generally, registrants must provide current address, telephone number, Social Security number, and employment information. They may also have to furnish fingerprints, a photograph, and a DNA sample.[10] At least 22 states require collection of a DNA sample as part of a registration system.[11]

Number of Registered Sex Offenders

In February 2001, 386,000 sex offenders had registered in 49 states and Washington, DC. This was an increase of 39% from the 277,000 sex offenders registered in April 1998. Registrants by state in 2001 ranged from a low of 473 in Maine to a high of 88,853 in California.[12] Several factors contained in the state registration law affect how many sex offenders must register in any one state, including the number of offenses and conviction date that trigger the legal duty, as well as the duration of the requirement to register.[13]

---

[8] Elizabeth A. Pearson, *Status and Latest Developments in Sex Offender Registration and Notification Laws, in* NATIONAL CONFERENCE ON SEX OFFENDER REGISTRIES, at 45 (U.S. Bureau of Justice Statistics, ed., 1998).

[9] Alan D. Scholle, *Sex Offender Registration,* FBI L. ENFORCEMENT BULL., July 1, 2000 *available at* http://www.fbi.gov/publications/leb/2000/jul00leb.pdf.

[10] HAW. REV. STAT. ANN. § 846E-2(2) (Michie 2004); KAN. STAT. ANN. § 22-4907(b) (2004); OKLA. STAT. ANN. tit. 54, §§ 584(a)(2), 588 (West 2004).

[11] Devon B. Adams, U.S. Dep't of Justice, *Summary of State Sex Offender Registries, 2001,* at 3 (2002), *available at* http://www.ojp.usdoj.gov/bjs/pub/pdf/sssor01.pdf. Massachusetts has a registration and notification law (MASS. GEN. LAWS ch. 6, §§ 178C-178P (Supp. 2002)). However, information from this state was not included in this study.

[12] Adams, *supra* note 11, at 2.

[13] *Id.*

Federal Registration Information

Under the Jacob Wetterling Act, states must collect and track "the name of the person, identifying factors, anticipated future residence, offense history, and documentation of any treatment received for the mental abnormality or personality disorder of the person," as well as fingerprints and a photograph of the person.[14] State authorities must then forward this information to the National Sex Offender Registry.[15] This data bank allows law enforcement authorities to track sex offenders wherever they go.

Purposes of Registration Laws

Registration laws have two primary purposes. First, they are designed to deter sex offenders from committing new sex crimes. Policymakers assumed that sex offenders would be less likely to commit another sex crime if they knew that the police know who they are and where they live and could more readily connect them to any new crime they might commit. Second, these laws are designed to help police solve sex crimes by investigating known sex offenders who live in the area where a sex crime was committed.

Criticisms

Critics contend that these laws are not really intended to prevent or solve sex crimes. Instead, their true purpose is to inflict additional punishment and revenge on sex offenders by further stigmatizing and shaming them. They also claim that these laws will make it difficult, if not impossible, for sex offenders to live in a community because they will not be able to obtain housing or hold a job.

Use of Registration Information

Registration laws require sex offenders to provide this information to law enforcement agencies, which can use it to investigate sex crimes.

Duration of Registration Duty

The mandatory minimum period of registration is 10 years from the date of release, or for life for certain second-time offenders, aggravated offenders, and sexually violent predators.[16]

---

[14]42 U.S.C. § 14071(b)(1)(A)-(B) (2004).
[15]42 U.S.C. §§ 14071(2)(B), 14072 (2004).
[16]42 U.S.C. § 14071(b)(6) (2004). The Attorney General has promulgated guidelines further delineating the obligations of a state that opts to comply with the Act. A.G. Order No. 2095-97 (eff. July 21, 1997).

Compliance

As also required by the Jacob Wetterling Act, all states have passed statutes making an offender's failure to fulfill his or her duty to register at least a misdemeanor crime.[17]

It is not clear, however, what percentage of sex offenders required to register actually does. One study reported a compliance rate of 84%.[18] This may be an optimistic estimate. It is far easier to track compliance for sex offenders being released from prison than to track sex offenders released prior to the effective date of registration laws or sex offenders who move to another residence or state after their release from prison.

Federal and State Standards

The Jacob Wetterling Act provides only a *minimum* set of registration requirements that states must adopt if they do not want to lose significant federal crime-fighting funds.[19] Each state is free to impose more stringent registration requirements on offenders, such as requiring nonsex offenders to register, registration for longer periods of time, or more detailed information.[20] Kansas, for instance, has expanded the class of offenders who must register to include persons convicted of murder and manslaughter and attempts, conspiracies, or solicitations to commit murder, even if these crimes did not involve a sex offense.[21] Washington has extended the time period during which offenders who have committed serious sex crimes must keep their registration current, ranging from 10 to 15 years to life.[22]

Retroactive Application

Usually, state laws also require sex offenders who were convicted *before* the registration law became effective to register, even though many of them may now have families and jobs and have been living safely in the community for years. This retroactive application of the duty to register can impose significant hardship on these citizens.

Notification Laws

Notification laws, in contrast, either authorize or *require* law enforcement to disseminate or make available registration information to various

---

[17] 42 U.S.C. § 14071(d) (2004).
[18] Washington State Institute for Public Policy, *Sex Offenses in Washington State: 1998 Update*, 40 (1998), *available at* http://www.wsipp.wa.gov/rptfiles/chrtbook_98.pdf.
[19] 42 U.S.C. § 14071(g)(2) (Supp. 2002).
[20] 42 U.S.C. § 14071(a)(2)(C) (Supp. 2002).
[21] Kan. Stat. Ann. § 22-4902(d) (2004).
[22] Wash. Rev. Code. Ann. § 9A44.140 (West 2004).

members of the community. They were enacted because many policymakers believed that registration laws alone would not adequately protect the public from sex offenders.[23] All 50 states have also passed notification laws since 1990.[24]

Purposes of Notification Laws

These laws are designed to warn the community that a dangerous sex offender lives nearby, providing essential information that allows people to take proactive self-help measures to protect themselves and their children. Armed with this new knowledge, parents could ensure that sex offenders would not have access to their children. People could also report to the police risky behavior, like talking to young children in playgrounds, which could escalate into sexual offending.[25]

Supporters claim that community notification helps *prevent* new sex crimes by promoting community awareness and encouraging increased vigilance. This, in turn, helps law enforcement, reduces recidivism, and creates a useful sense of community safety. Others claim that the primary purpose of notification laws is to satisfy the state's moral obligation to inform the community that a dangerous sex offender lives in the neighborhood.[26]

Criticisms

Critics claim notification laws are unconstitutional, ineffective, costly, and may do more harm than good. They also argue that prediction of sexual dangerousness (at least as implemented in some laws) is too inaccurate and that notification invites vigilantism, may lull the community into a false sense of security,[27] and may *increase* sex offense recidivism by causing the offender to lose his job, housing, and community support group.[28]

Notification Models

The National Institute of Justice has classified notification laws as generally falling into one of the following four models.[29]

---

[23] *See* Peter Finn, *Sex Offender Community Notification*, NAT'L INST. OF JUST. RES. IN ACTION, Feb. 1997, at 1, *available at* http://www.ncjrs.org/pdffiles/162364.pdf.
[24] Richard G. Zevitz & Mary Ann Farkas, *Sex Offender Community Notification: Assessing the Impact in Wisconsin*, NAT'L INST. OF JUST. RES. IN ACTION, Dec., 2000, at 1, *available at* http://www.ncjrs.org/pdffiles1/nij/179992.pdf; Wayne A. Logan, *Sex Offender Registration and Community Notification: Emerging Legal and Research Issues*, 989 ANNALS OF THE N.Y. ACAD. OF SCI. 337 (2003).
[25] *See* Finn, *supra* note 23.
[26] Lucy Berliner, *Letter to the Editor*, 20 CHILD ABUSE & NEGLECT 1133 (1996); *see also* Berliner, *supra* note 2.
[27] Berliner, *supra* note 2, at 1218 (1998).
[28] Safer Society Program, Public Notification of Sex Offender Release (1998).
[29] *See* Finn, *supra* note 23, at 2.

1. Active Agency-Conducted Notification Based on Individualized Risk Determination. The statute confers discretionary power on a designated agency or individual to decide which offenders will be subject to notification and how extensive the notification will be. Generally, the agency must first evaluate each offender to determine his risk of reoffending and then assign that person a risk classification. Whether notification is made and to whom it is made usually depends on that classification. New Jersey and Washington use this model.[30] However, some states, like Tennessee, allow the police to release relevant information when an offender is considered a "significant danger to the community" and notification is "necessary to protect the public."[31]

EVALUATING RISK. Many states use a guided clinical approach to assessing risk.[32] Officials use some type of objective scoring instrument to initially evaluate risk for each offender.[33] Generally, these instruments assign points for various common factors, such as number of sex offenses, age, and other characteristics that correlate with sexual reoffense. Some of these instruments consider offenders who commit sex crimes against family members to be low risks for reoffending.

Often, officials will also review the details of the sex offense for which the offender was convicted and review his prison history, considering whether he successfully completed a treatment program or was a disciplinary problem. These factors may result in an increase or decrease in his individual risk assessment.

Other states use a less structured approach to risk assessment. In New Jersey, for example, county prosecutors, sometimes collaborating with law enforcement officials, assess the risk that any released offender may reoffend.[34] They consider a nonexclusive list of statutory factors, including the person's criminal history, age, prior choice of victims (children or adults), use of violence during a prior offense or offenses, response to treatment, recent behavior, and so forth.[35]

TIERED CLASSIFICATION SYSTEM. Many states use a three-tier classification system and provide notification based on classification of the offender. In Washington State, local law enforcement agencies classify offenders in

---

[30] N.J. REV. STAT. § 2C7-8 (2004); WASH. REV. CODE ANN. § 4.24.550 (West 2004).

[31] TENN. CODE ANN. §§ 40-39-101 et seq. (1997 and Supp. 2001). This statute permits the state, in order to protect the public "concerning any particular individual," to notify the public by "any means," including written notice and electronic transmission of, or online access to, registration data. *Id.* at § 40-39-106.

[32] *See* chapter 2 for a discussion of actuarial instruments and guided clinical approaches in predicting sexual recidivism.

[33] Scholle, *supra* note 9.

[34] N.J. REV. STAT. § 2C7-8(d) (2004).

[35] § 2C7-8(b).

one of three risk categories: high, moderate, or low.[36] They review available risk level classifications made previously by the department of corrections, the department of social and health services, and the indeterminate-sentence review board.[37] For level III (high risk) offenders, disclosure to the public at large is authorized; for level II (moderate risk) offenders, disclosure to schools, day care providers, and community groups is authorized; for level I (low risk) offenders, only disclosure to other law enforcement agencies is authorized.[38] The means of public notification vary widely.

Because broad discretion may be conferred on local police to assess risk for each offender and to decide how community notification will be conducted, this approach can result in very different treatment of offenders with similar histories within a state.

2. Active Agency-Conducted Notification According to Specified Statutory Categories. The designated agency conducts the public notification, but the statute itself defines which offenders will be subject to notification. Nineteen states use a compulsory approach, which requires offenders convicted of specified sex crimes to register.[39] For example, the Kansas law provides that all offenders subject to registration are also subject to community notification.[40]

ADVANTAGES. Because the law, rather than individuals, determines which offenders are subject to notification, there can be no claims of individualized discrimination. The legislature has already determined which types of offenders pose the greatest risk to the community. It also eliminates the oddity of requiring law enforcement officials to make expert psychological decisions about the future risk a particular individual poses.

DISADVANTAGES. This "self-executing" approach has serious drawbacks. Mitigating circumstances cannot be considered in making these determinations. Thus, this model offers fewer incentives to confined offenders to participate in treatment programs because it will have no effect on public notification.[41]

This model is also likely to be extremely inaccurate. First, individuals usually are not afforded an opportunity to challenge their classification.

---

[36] WASH. REV. CODE ANN. § 4.24.550(3)-(4) (2004).

[37] § 4.24.550(3)-(4).

[38] § 4.24.550(3)-(4).

[39] These states are Alabama, Alaska, California, Connecticut, Delaware, Illinois, Indiana, Kansas, Michigan, Mississippi, Missouri, New Hampshire, Oklahoma, South Carolina, South Dakota, Tennessee, Utah, and Virginia. *See* Wayne A. Logan, *Liberty Interests in the Preventive State: Procedural Due Process and Sex Offender Community Notification Laws*, 89 J. CRIM. L. & CRIMINOLOGY 1167, 1175 n.41 and sources cited therein (1999).

[40] KAN. STAT. ANN. § 22-4909 (2004) (directing that information required by offender registration act "shall be open to inspection in the sheriff's office by the public").

[41] On the other hand, states may create alternative incentives with more immediate appeal, such as the allocation of good time credits or parole eligibility based on an inmate's participation in available treatment programs.

Thus, they cannot correct any erroneous information that may be used, nor can they present evidence that they are not dangerous. Second, it literally precludes state officials from using "state-of-the-art" risk assessment methods to determine which offenders are dangerous and which are not.[42] Consequently, this approach is very likely to result in too many mistaken determinations both of dangerousness and nondangerousness being made, thereby undermining the whole purpose of community notification.

3. *Agency-Supervised, Offender-Conducted Notification.* The offender is required to notify the community himself. Louisiana obligates all released sex offenders to personally notify by mail designated members of the public, including neighbors, local schools, and landlords, and in some cases, to publish notification in the local newspaper[43] or use bumper stickers, yard signs, or handbills.[44] Judges in other states have also required offenders to provide notice in a newspaper.[45]

In Corpus Christi, Texas, a judge ordered 21 sex offenders to post warning signs on their homes and bumper stickers on their cars, telling the public about their crimes.[46] The signs said, "DANGER—Registered Sex Offender Lives Here." The signs also included telephone numbers for reporting "suspicious behavior." Bumper stickers had similar warnings and information. Justifying his actions, the judge concluded that Texas law, which requires that sex offenders' pictures and addresses be posted on the Internet and printed in local newspapers, did not go far enough in protecting people. "A lot of people can't afford to go to the Internet, particularly in poor neighborhoods, and some people just don't read newspapers."[47] Concerning sex offenders who objected to these measures, the judge said, "They have only themselves to blame." Oregon has also used similar warning signs.

Although requiring offenders to notify the public themselves may teach responsibility and humility to offenders and ease the workload of law enforcement, critics claim it frightens the community. Because the offender is the source of the information, it may seem more believable and intimidating. Moreover, because the method does not include community education, people may be more frightened than they should be.[48] It is also likely to

---

[42] *See* chapter 2.

[43] La. Rev. Stat. Ann. § 15:542(1)-(2) (West Supp. 2002).

[44] The Louisiana notification statute further obligates the offenders to "give any other notice deemed appropriate . . . including but not limited to signs, handbills, bumper stickers, or clothing labeled to that effect." La. Rev. Stat. Ann. § 15:542(3) (West Supp. 2002).

[45] A Texas judge ordered an offender to place an ad in a newspaper. *See* Michael Grunwald, *Shame Makes Comeback in Court: Texas Judge Likes to Impose Public Punishment for Crime*, Ariz. Republic, Jan. 11, 1998, at A14, *available in* 1998 WL 7742935.

[46] Ross E. Milloy, *Texas Judge Orders Notices Warning of Sex Offenders*, N.Y. Times, May 29, 2001, at A10.

[47] *Id.*

[48] Finn, *supra* note 23, at 6.

result in extreme variation in how the public is told and what information it receives.

4. Passive Notification Initiated by Public Requests for Information. Information about released offenders is only made available to members of the public who actively seek it.

Community Notification in Practice

Depending on how notification is actually made, community notification systems can also be described as passive, active, or communitywide.[49]

1. Passive Notification. Someone must first be interested in obtaining information from the sex offender registration and then must seek it before notification is made public. In theory, this is the least aggressive system because information about sex offenders is not disclosed until someone asks for it. Critics maintain that registration laws cannot protect the public if the public is not actively provided with this information.[50]

States vary in how people can obtain this data. In Alaska, the Department of Public Safety collects and maintains the information in a central registry and provides it only on formal request by individual members of the public.[51] California hands out CD-ROM disks at public locations, allowing anyone to review the sex offender database.[52] Other states, including New York, allow anyone to call a toll-free or nominal-fee "hotline."[53]

Many states post sex offender registration information on the Internet, where anyone may retrieve it.[54] As of February 2001, 29 states and the District of Columbia had publicly accessible Web sites that contained searchable information on individual offenders. Other states are planning similar Web sites.[55] This is an economical and time-saving method of notification. Because anyone can access Internet sites from anywhere, this unbounded access allows virtual public notification to the world.[56]

---

[49] Scholle, *supra* note 9.

[50] *Id.*

[51] ALASKA STAT. § 18.65.087 (Michie 2004). A fee of $10 may also be charged.

[52] *See* Devon B. Adams, U.S. Dep't of Justice, *Summary of State Sex Offender Registry Dissemination Procedures* 1 (1999), *available at* http://www.ojp.usdoj.gov/bjs/pub/pdf/sssordp.pdf.

[53] *See, e.g.,* Scholle, *supra* note 9; Andrea L. Fischer, Note, *Florida's Community Notification of Sex Offenders on the Internet: The Disregard of Constitutional Protections for Sex Offenders,* 45 CLEV. ST. L. REV. 505 (1997); Jane A. Small, Note, *Who Are the People in Your Neighborhood? Due Process, Public Protection, and Sex Offender Notification Laws,* 74 N.Y.U. L. REV. 1451 (1999).

[54] *See* http://www.dps.state.ak.us/Sorcr/search.asp.

[55] Adams, *supra* note 11, at 3.

[56] For example, Kentucky offender registry information is available online at the KSP Offender Registry Web site (http://kspsor.state.ky.us/), which averages over 15,000 hits a month. In Florida, as well, the general public can access offender registry information via the Internet (http://www.fdle.state.fl.us/), a cite that averages about 5 million hits per month. *Id.* at 8. *See* Wayne A. Logan, *A Study in Actuarial Justice: Sex Offender Classification Practice and Procedure,* 3 BUFF. CRIM. L. REV. 593, 596-97 n.12 (noting that the Internet's "unrestricted geographic sweep . . . arguably possesses the greatest potential for widespread dissemination—even beyond state or local boundaries."); *see also* Small, *supra* note 53.

2. Active Notification. Some state laws specify the geographic area that must be notified.[57] Other statutes, like Washington, limit notification to the area of threat posed by the offender. In some states, officials notify individuals or institutions that may be the most likely targets of the offenders. For example, schools and day care facilities may be notified if a child molester lives in the area. Past victims and landlords may also be notified.[58] Generally speaking, active systems implement community notification on a "need to know" basis (i.e., only those at risk are notified).

3. Communitywide Notification. Sometimes, however, authorities notify the entire community of the offender's presence. The method and scope of the notification varies. It may include publication of the offender's picture and other relevant information in a newspaper that has a broad audience, or the police may canvass a neighborhood, telling people or leaving flyers. Many people will be told that a sex offender lives in their neighborhood whether they want to know it or not and whether they are likely victims or not.

CONSTITUTIONAL CHALLENGES

Numerous constitutional challenges have been made to registration and notification laws. The courts have rejected most of them, although some courts have ordered changes made in how these laws are implemented.

Cruel and Unusual Punishment

The Eighth Amendment to the United States Constitution prohibits the government from inflicting "cruel and unusual punishments."[59] Because of the serious harm suffered by those subject to registration and notification, convicted sex offenders have claimed that these laws inflict cruel and unusual punishment on them, thereby violating this constitutional prohibition.[60]

The Eighth Amendment applies only to "punishments." Courts have generally concluded that the purpose of registration and notification laws is not to punish offenders, but rather to prevent crime and to provide law enforcement with regulatory tools for investigating future sex crimes. Thus, courts have almost unanimously concluded that these laws are "civil" rather than "punitive" in purpose and effect and do not violate the Eighth

---

[57] Finn, *supra* note 23, at 9.
[58] *See* Scholle, *supra* note 9.
[59] U.S. Const. amend. VIII.
[60] *See, e.g.*, Roe v. Farwell, 999 F. Supp. 174 (D. Mass. 1998); Doe v. Kelley, 961 F. Supp. 1105, 1112 (W.D. Mich. 1997); State v. Scott, 961 P.2d 667; 676 (Kan. 1998); Doe v. Poritz, 662 A.2d 367, 405 (N.J. 1995).

Amendment.[61] Even assuming these laws are punitive, courts have determined that any punitive aspect of registration or notification is constitutionally proportionate to the nature of the sex offenses and thus not excessive.

Ex Post Facto

Article I of the United States Constitution prohibits states from passing *"ex post facto"* laws[62] that punish people for conduct that occurred *before* the law prohibiting the conduct was passed. This prohibition ensures that people know in advance what conduct is criminal and what penalties they face if they commit those crimes.

Registration Laws

Many registration laws apply to sex offenders convicted before these laws were enacted, thus retroactively requiring them to register. Offenders who committed their qualifying sex crimes before these laws went into effect resisted registering, claiming that these laws inflicted additional punishment on them *after* they were convicted and punished, thereby violating the Constitution's *ex post facto* prohibition.

The United States Supreme Court has explained that the prohibition against *ex post facto* laws forbids "any law which imposes a punishment for an act which was not punishable at the time it was committed; or imposes additional punishment to that then prescribed."[63] Just as in the Eighth Amendment context, the key question here is whether registration or notification laws constitute "punishment" and are therefore subject to the *ex post facto* prohibition. The courts have almost always rejected these attacks, concluding that these laws are "civil" rather than "punitive."[64]

Notification Laws

Courts have been slightly more willing to entertain *ex post facto* challenges to broad notification laws because these laws expose offenders to

---

[61] *See* Scott, 961 P.2d 667 (discussing cases and articles concerning Eighth Amendment challenges to registration and notification laws, and holding that Kansas' version of those laws does not constitute cruel and unusual punishment); *see also* Licia A. Esposito, Annotation, *State Statutes or Ordinances Requiring Persons Previously Convicted of Crime to Register With Authorities*, 36 A.L.R. 5th 161, at § 5 (1996) (summarizing cases).

[62] U.S. CONST. art. I, § 9, cl. 2.

[63] Weaver v. Graham, 450 U.S. 24, 28 (1981).

[64] *See, e.g.*, Russell v. Gregoire, 124 F.3d 1079 (9th Cir. 1997), *cert. denied*, 523 U.S. 1007 (1998); Stearns v. Gregoire, 523 U.S. 1007 (1998); Doe v. Pataki, 120 F.3d 1263 (2d Cir. 1997), *cert. denied.*, 522 U.S. 1122 (1998); E.B. v. Verniero, 119 F.3d 1077 (3d Cir. 1997), *cert. denied.*, 522 U.S. 1109 (1998). Stephen R. McAllister, *"Neighbors Beware": The Constitutionality of State Sex Offender Registration and Community Notification Laws*, 29 TEX. TECH L. REV. 97, 109 n.67 (1998).

community stigma and other harms. For instance, while upholding their state's registration law, Alaska, Louisiana, and Kansas courts have found that extensive public notification provisions, when applied to sex offenders convicted *before* notification laws were passed, violate the *ex post facto* prohibition.[65] As one court noted, "Public dissemination provisions, which would subject the registrants to public stigma and ostracism that would affect both their personal and professional lives, impose[s] an affirmative disability or restraint, showing a punitive effect."[66]

Despite occasional contrary decisions, the clear trend has been for courts to reject *ex post facto* challenges to both registration and notification laws. Instead, courts accept the states' position that these laws are regulatory in nature and that any public stigma, ostracism, or vigilantism are incidental to their operation, or arise not from registration and notification but from the fact of the offenders' "underlying criminal convictions."[67]

Double Jeopardy

The Fifth Amendment of the Constitution directs that no person shall be "subject for the same offence to be twice put in jeopardy of life or limb."[68] The United States Supreme Court has interpreted this clause as "serv[ing] the function of preventing both successive punishments and . . . successive prosecutions."[69]

In challenges similar to those launched under the Eighth Amendment or the *ex post facto* clause, offenders have argued that registration and notification provisions, when imposed on offenders who have already completed their sentences, amount to successive, and therefore unconstitutional, punishments. Once again, the key question is whether registration and notification laws constitute punishment. Consistent with the case trends in the other constitutional challenges, courts have invariably concluded that these laws are regulatory, not punitive, and therefore do not violate the constitutional prohibition against double jeopardy.[70]

---

[65] *See, e.g.,* State v. Babin, 637 So. 2d 814 (La. Ct. App. 1994); Rowe v. Burton, 884 F. Supp. 1372 (D. Alaska 1994); State v. Myers, 923 P.2d 1024 (1996).

[66] Myers, 923 P.2d 1024, 1039 (1996).

[67] *See, e.g.,* Collie v. State, 710 So. 2d 1000 (Fla. Ct. App. 1998); State v. Cook, 700 N.E.2d 570 (Ohio 1998); Parolee S.V. v. Calabrese, 246 A.D.2d 655 (N.Y. App. Div. 1998); Commonwealth v. Mountain, 711 A.2d 473 (Penn. 1998); Dep't of Pub. Safety v. County of Maricopa, 949 P.2d 983 (Ariz. Ct. App. 1997); Doe v. Pataki, 120 F.3d 1263 (2nd Cir. 1997); Artway v. Attorney Gen. of N.J., 81 F.3d 1235 (3rd Cir. 1996). *See generally* Wayne A. Logan, *The Ex Post Facto Clause and the Jurisprudence of Punishment,* 35 Am. Crim. L. Rev. 1261 (1998).

[68] U. S. Const. amend. V.

[69] United States v. Ursery, 518 U.S. 267, 273 (1996).

[70] *See, e.g.,* Collie v. State, 710 S.2d 1000 (Fla. Ct. App. 1998); Artway v. Attorney Gen. of N.J., 81 F.3d 1235 (3rd Cir. 1996).

Equal Protection

The Fourteenth Amendment to the United States Constitution prohibits states from denying "to any person within its jurisdiction the equal protection of the laws."[71] Thus, a state may not treat one class of people differently from another class without a legally acceptable rationale. This is not a command that all people be treated alike but, rather, "a direction that all persons *similarly situated* should be treated alike."[72]

Sex offenders subject to registration and notification have objected that they are being unconstitutionally differentiated from other similarly situated offenders, such as drug offenders, burglars, or murderers, when they alone are forced to comply with these laws. This argument has been readily rejected on grounds that "protecting the public from recidivistic sex offenders is a legitimate state interest," which will justify differentiating sex offenders from other types of offenders.[73]

Procedural Due Process

The Fourteenth Amendment to the United States Constitution also prohibits states from "depriv[ing] any person of life, liberty, or property, without due process of law."[74] Under this provision, an individual is often (though not always) entitled to notice of the proposed government action, a hearing before a neutral decision maker, the right to present evidence and to cross-examine the government's evidence, and the assistance of a lawyer.

Whether sex offenders have been provided constitutionally adequate due process when a state agency determines which offenders will be considered at high risk of reoffending and subject to extensive public notification is a close question. Most courts have held that an individual does not have a "liberty interest" in his reputation that is protected by the Constitution. Thus, they conclude that the government does not have to provide procedural due process to sex offenders.[75]

A minority of courts, however, does require the state to provide these protections. For example, the New Jersey Supreme Court has agreed that "under both the Federal and State Constitutions, the Registration and Notification Laws implicate protectible liberty interests in privacy and reputation, and therefore trigger the right to due process."[76] Thus, the state must

---

[71] U.S. CONST. amend. XIV, § 1.
[72] City of Cleburne v. Cleburne Living Ctr., 473 U.S. 432, 439 (1985).
[73] Doe v. Poritz, 662 A.2d 367, 414 (N.J. 1995). *See generally* McAllister, *supra* note 64.
[74] U.S. CONST. amend. XIV, § 1.
[75] McAllister, *supra* note 64. *See also* Logan, *supra* note 39.
[76] Doe v. Poritz, 662 A.2d 367, 420 (N.J. 1995).

provide notice and an opportunity to be heard before an offender is classified as a moderate or high-risk offender subject to the state's broader notification provisions.[77] The courts of Oregon and Massachusetts have reached similar conclusions.[78]

Other Constitutional Provisions

Registration and notification statutes raise other constitutional concerns. These include challenges that such statutes are vague or overbroad,[79] that judges' failure to warn offenders that they would have to register if convicted rendered guilty pleas "unknowing" and thus invalid,[80] and that requirements that offenders submit to mug photographs, fingerprinting, and DNA testing violated the Fourth Amendment's guarantee against "unreasonable searches and seizures."[81] Most of them have been rejected.[82]

Constitutional Limits?

Unconstitutional Punishment

If registration and notification requirements are too onerous and impose a significant economic hardship on registrants, courts could decide they are unconstitutional. In 2001, the United States Federal Court of Appeals for the Ninth Circuit held that the Alaska Sex Offender Registration Act went too far and, in its effect, was additional punishment rather than reasonable regulation. Consequently, the court struck down the law because it violated the *ex post facto* clause of the Constitution.[83]

The Alaska law required almost all sex offenders, including those convicted before its enactment, to reregister in person with the police four times a year for at least 15 years, and in some cases for the rest of their lives. Unlike most other state laws that only required re-registration if the

---

[77] *Id.* at 421.

[78] Noble v. Bd. of Parole, 964 P.2d 990 (Or. 1998); Doe v. Sex Offender Registry Bd., 697 N.E.2d 512 (Mass. 1998).

[79] *See, e.g.,* State v. Patterson, 963 P.2d 436, 439 (Kan. 1998) and State v. Fortman (1998) WL 135811, at *8 (Ohio Ct. App. March 27, 1998).

[80] *See, e.g.,* Benitez v. State, 667 So.2d 476 (Fla. Ct. App. 1996) (holding that obligations under registration act were merely collateral consequence of guilty plea, and therefore district court not required to advise defendant that his plea would result in him being subjected to act).

[81] *See, e.g.,* Doe v. Poritz, 662 A.2d 367 (N.J. 1995) (rejecting Fourth Amendment challenge to registration requirements).

[82] *See, e.g.,* State v. Patterson, 963 P.2d 436, 440 (Kan. 1998) (finding that statute imposing registration and notification duties on offenders who committed nonsex crimes that were "sexually motivated" was not impermissibly vague or overbroad, but noting "we do have some concern over the possibility that this statute could be extended beyond reason"); State v. Fortman, 1998 WL 135811 (Ohio Ct. App., March 27, 1998) (unpublished opinion rejecting vagueness attack on registration and notification laws).

[83] Doe v. Otte, 259 F.3d 979 (9th Cir. 2001), *cert. granted,* 534 U.S. 1126 (2002).

offender moved or important information had changed, sex offenders in Alaska had to appear at the police station even if there was no change in the information already provided to the police.[84] Moreover, this information was made available on the Internet, literally making it available to the world.[85]

The court concluded that requiring someone to go to the police station four times a year was similar to being sentenced to probation or other postrelease police supervision. It also determined that providing Internet access to this information subjected offenders to community "obloquy and scorn," making it very difficult for them to hold a job or find housing.[86] Consequently, the court held "that the *Ex Post Facto* Clause limits . . . application [of the Alaska Sex Offender Registration Act] to those sex offenders whose crimes were committed *after* its enactment."[87] Thus, sex offenders convicted *before* this law was enacted do not have to comply with its stringent registration procedures. Those convicted after its enactment must comply with it or challenge the Alaska law on other constitutional grounds.

This case logic strongly suggested that the Constitution does not give legislatures a blank check in enacting registration and notification laws. Sex offenders could be required to provide police with information they reasonably need to prevent or investigate sex crimes, but they cannot be summoned periodically to the police station if the police already have all the information they need.

Moreover, the opinion suggested that information provided by offenders can be given only to those who have a "need to know" it. These people should include public safety officials and those who may be at risk of victimization. But it is difficult to see why *everyone*, anywhere in the world, needs to know the conviction record of a sex offender in Alaska and therefore should have access to it. Ready accessibility of this information should not be confused with universal access.

A Denial of Due Process

In 2001, the United States Federal Court of Appeals for the Second Circuit ruled that Connecticut's sex offender registration law was unconstitutional.[88] Connecticut listed all convicted sex offenders in a public registry

---

[84] Registrants had to be photographed, provide fingerprints, and give their date of birth, address, place of employment, and information about their conviction, including the crime, date, and place of conviction. *Id.* at 984. *See also* ALASKA STAT. § 12.63.010 (Michie 2000).

[85] *Otte,* 259 F.3d at 984.

[86] *Id.* at 987–88.

[87] *Id.* at 995 (emphasis added).

[88] Doe v. Dep't of Pub. Safety, 271 F.3d 38 (2d Cir. 2001), *cert. granted,* 535 U.S. 1077 (2002), *rev'd,* 538 U.S. 1 (2003).

accessible to anyone, without any attempt to determine which offenders were dangerous and which were not. The federal court determined that, in the public's mind, *all* offenders on this list were dangerous. Consequently, it held that this scheme violated an individual's Fourteenth Amendment right to procedural due process because offenders were not given an individual hearing to determine whether "they are particularly likely to be currently dangerous before being labeled as such."[89] The court required the state to provide each offender a chance to dispute the "false stigma" of being placed on a list, which, by its very nature, strongly suggests that they are dangerous.[90]

The Supreme Court Upholds Both the Alaska and Connecticut Laws

In March 2003, the United States Supreme Court reversed both decisions, upholding both the Alaska and Connecticut registration and notification laws. The Court decided that the Alaska law did not impose punishment on sex offenders; therefore, it did not violate the *ex post facto* clause of the Constitution. In *Smith v. Doe*[91] a majority of the justices decided that the primary purpose of the Alaska law was to protect the public from sex offenders. Although this purpose was also consistent with the goal of the criminal justice system, the legislature intended to create a civil regulatory scheme that would notify the public that convicted sex offenders live or work nearby. The Court also rejected claims that the Alaska notification scheme was "punishment" because it publicized the crime and associated the individual's name with the crime, sometimes for life. The Court said:

> Punishments such as whipping, pillory, and branding inflicted physical pain and staged a direct confrontation between the offender and the public. Even punishments that lacked the corporal component, such as public shaming, humiliation, and banishment, involved more than the dissemination of information. They either held the person up before his fellow citizens for face-to-face shaming or expelled him from the community. [Citations omitted.] By contrast, the stigma of Alaska's Megan's Law results not from public display for ridicule or shaming but from the dissemination of accurate information about a criminal record, most of which is already public. Our system does not treat dissemination of truthful information in furtherance of a legitimate governmental objective as punishment.[92]

Worldwide Internet access did not trouble the Court either, because "Widespread public access is necessary for the efficacy of the scheme and the

---

[89] *Id.* at 62. The court also concluded that Connecticut's registration statute was onerous because it required some offenders to register every 90 days, to notify authorities of "regular" travel into another state, and/or to supply a blood sample and photograph every 5 years. *Id.* at 57.
[90] *Id.* at 62.
[91] 538 U.S. 84 (2003).
[92] *Id.* at 98.

attendant humiliation is but a collateral consequence of a valid regulation."[93] Nor did the Alaska law impose a form of probation or supervised release on sex offenders. The law imposed no physical restraint on sex offenders. They were free to live and work wherever they chose without supervision. (And, it turns out, sex offenders did not have to update their registration information in person.) Nor is there any substantial evidence that registration and notification made sex offenders unable to obtain employment or housing. Any "painful impact" on sex offenders resulted not from registration and notification, but "from the fact of conviction, already a matter of public record."[94]

Finally, the Court agreed that a legislature might conclude that a single sex offense provides evidence of a "substantial risk of recidivism" and that sex offenders are, therefore, a dangerous class of people. Consequently, individual risk assessments to determine dangerousness are not constitutionally required.[95] Moreover, because the Alaska law only imposes the minor condition of registration on sex offenders, the "State can dispense with individual predictions of dangerousness and allow the public to assess the risk on the basis of accurate, nonprivate information about the registrants' convictions without violating the prohibitions of the *Ex Post Facto* Clause."[96]

In the companion case involving the Connecticut law, a unanimous Court concluded that individuals required to register as sex offenders solely because of a single conviction of a sex crime did not have a procedural due process right to a hearing on whether they were dangerous.[97] The Court decided that the Connecticut law's obligation to register is not based on a finding of current dangerousness, and thus the law does not use a finding of dangerousness to stigmatize any individual on the list. Instead, the registration scheme is based solely on the fact of conviction. Thus, even if a sex offender could show that he was not dangerous, he would still have to register.[98]

Sweeping State Power

These two cases just discussed confer enormous power on states to require sex offenders—and other offenders, if they choose—to register with the police. The state can constantly monitor where they live and work for

---

[93] *Id.* at 99.
[94] *Id.* at 101.
[95] *Id.* at 103.
[96] *Id.* at 104.
[97] 538 U.S. 1 (2003).
[98] Two months after this decision, the Iowa Supreme Court decided that public dissemination of information about sex offenders exposed them to community stigma and, therefore, they had a due process right to an individual hearing on the risk assessment used to determine the extent to which the state made public disclosures about them. Brummer v. Iowa Dep't of Corr., 661 N.W.2d 167 (Iowa 2003).

many years, even a lifetime. Extensive personal information about these offenders can be provided to neighborhoods, towns, states, countries, and even the world. The individual is not entitled to a hearing to demonstrate that he is no longer a danger to the community if the law only uses the fact of a conviction to require registration. In short, once convicted of a sex crime, a person's life is now an "open book," with his past criminal history and present life circumstances available for anyone to read. It is extremely unlikely that any constitutional challenge will succeed in limiting the state's unfettered authority to keep track of convicted sex offenders and to tell the community about them.

IMPLEMENTATION AND COSTS

Implementing registration and notification laws is expensive and time consuming. Implementation costs begin with collecting registration information, escalate with actually notifying the community, and continue with litigation challenges and compliance efforts. The costs are never-ending.

Under the Jacob Wetterling Act, offenders must register for at least 10 years and, in many cases, for life. The Act also obligates federal states to verify and update each offender's address *at least* annually, and in the case of certain violent sex offenders, *every 90 days*.[99] Every day, new offenders are being released from prisons and jails, adding hosts of new registrants to the rolls.

Implementing Registration Laws

First, state departments of correction must compile a list of sex offenders required to register prior to their release and then forward it to the relevant registration agency.[100] Probation officers must gather this information for offenders on probation.[101] For offenders released from both custody and supervision before the registration laws were passed, the financial burden of collection may fall on the local sheriff's department.[102]

---

[99] 42 U.S.C. § 14071(3) (2004).

[100] See, e.g., OKLA. STAT. ANN. tit. 57, § 584(E) (West 2004) (obligating state department of corrections to maintain a file of all sex offender registrations and forward lists of offenders to all municipal police and county sheriff departments in which released offenders reside).

[101] See, e.g., CALIF. PENAL CODE § 290(c) (West 2004) (obligating probation officers to collect information and forward to the Department of Justice as well as to the appropriate local law enforcement agency where the offender expects to reside).

[102] See, e.g., WASH. REV. CODE ANN. § 9A44.130 (West 2004) (obligating offenders to report to and register with sheriff of resident county; however, specifically not requiring sheriff to actively determine whether offenders are living in sheriff's county of jurisdiction).

States that include DNA samples in registration information must hire employees properly trained and licensed to collect blood samples and also pay laboratory costs for the preservation or testing of the samples.[103] Oklahoma recoups some of these expenses by requiring some offenders to pay a $15.00 DNA testing fee.[104]

States must also "promptly" forward required information (and all subsequent updates of that information) to the Federal Bureau of Investigation, complying with guidelines issued by the United States Attorney General for participating in the National Sex Offender Registry.[105]

Some state laws require a registered sex offender to *confirm* his address every 90 days.[106] Should any offender change his residence within a state, he is required to notify the appropriate agency of this change.[107]

Implementing Notification Laws

States incur further costs in conducting community notification. The Jacob Wetterling Act allows the states to determine how they will disseminate information about offenders. Washington State uses numerous methods, which vary from county to county, such as mailing bulletins to residents, leaving flyers at residences, sending flyers home from schools with children, conducting door-to-door visits with residents, conducting informal conversations with schools and community groups, and issuing press releases.[108]

Police in Mesa, Arizona, decided to spend their limited resources on enforcing compliance with the registration laws instead of providing personalized notification to the public. In 2001, the police stopped going door to door to tell neighbors when sex offenders had moved into a neighborhood, because they estimated that this personalized approach cost about $1,310 on average for each notification. Instead, they decided to mail flyers. Police officers now spend more time arresting sex offenders who have not registered as required by law.[109]

---

[103] *See* OKLA. STAT. ANN. tit. 57, § 588 (West 2004) (setting forth requirements for obtaining DNA samples from offenders subject to registration).
[104] § 588.
[105] 42 U.S.C. § 14071(b)(2) (2004).
[106] *See* Artway v. Attorney Gen., 81 F.3d 1235, 1243 (3d Cir. 1996) (describing the requirements in the New Jersey statute).
[107] 42 U.S.C. § 14071(b)(4) (2004).
[108] Finn, *supra* note 23, at 18 (appendix chart setting forth details of Washington state notification procedures by county).
[109] Garin Groff, *Mesa Police Take New Tack in Monitoring Sex Offenders*, MESA TRIBUNE (Ariz.), Nov. 4, 2001.

Educating the Public

Laudably, many states have taken on the additional duty of educating the public about the purposes and potential abuses of notification.[110] These states must also train their notifying agencies in how to promote community responsibility, prevent a false sense of security, and conversely, to prevent an inflated sense of fear and vigilantism.

New Burdens Without New Resources

Even supporters of notification and education complain that it is "very time consuming and burdensome."[111] New Jersey, which had 4,392 registered sex offenders as of August 1997, reported spending approximately $2 million implementing its registration and notification programs in 1997.[112]

A 1996 National Institute of Justice telephone survey of eight notifying states revealed only two, Washington and New Jersey, that were providing additional funding for notification.[113] Even with additional resources, the job may be overwhelming. In 1996, one New Jersey prosecutor reported that her office had made community notifications in only 70 of the backlog of 184 offenders living in her jurisdiction.[114]

Critics within law enforcement have noted that fulfilling notification requirements without additional funding diverts both funding and staffing resources, which might be better spent monitoring the offender or on other unrelated law enforcement tasks.[115] A survey of local law enforcement agencies in Wisconsin revealed that many police departments were concerned about the additional use of manpower required to provide community notification.[116] One quarter complained that the laws "created a strain on departmental resources."[117] Local agencies considered notification duties to be an unfunded mandate by the state.[118]

---

[110] See Finn, *supra* note 23, at 8, for a description of how New Jersey prosecutors fulfill their duty under that state's guidelines to train and educate community organizations.

[111] Id. at 14.

[112] National Criminal Justice Ass'n, U.S. Dep't of Justice, *Sex Offender Community Notification October 1997 Policy Report* 19 (1997).

[113] Finn, *supra* note 23, at 11.

[114] Id. at 14.

[115] Id. at 11 (the voluminous task of data collection would include, and not be limited to, the following: (1) the cost of tracking each sexual offender; (2) costs associated with community education; (3) costs associated with notification that is fulfilled by the county officials; (4) Web site maintenance; (5) prosecution of noncompliance).

[116] Zevitz & Farkas, *supra* note 24.

[117] Id. at 5.

[118] Id.

Computing Costs for Registration and Notification Laws

Determining how much money is actually spent statewide or nationally on registration and notification is very difficult. New Jersey, for example, implements the registration and notification duties on a county level. Any estimate requires data from each county prosecutor for both registration and notification costs; this information is not collected. Not surprisingly, there are no sound studies available to accurately determine these costs.[119]

Iowa has a staff of at least seven people in its Division of Criminal Investigation that operates and maintains the state registry for sex offenders. This group's responsibilities include completing sex offender risk assessments, notifying the public when necessary, and investigating cases of noncompliance.[120] The Dallas Police Department established a special unit to enforce compliance. It found and arrested many sex offenders who had not registered as required.[121]

Compliance by Offenders

To comply with the Jacob Wetterling Act, each state must impose criminal penalties on an offender who fails to fulfill his or her registration duties. In turn, this requirement places an additional burden on parole officers, police, and prosecutors to monitor and prosecute registration violations. Compliance efforts are most likely to be effective when a sex offender is initially released from prison, because authorities can require him to tell them where he will live after his release. After an offender is living in the community, however, compliance efforts are more problematic because it is much harder to trace individuals in our mobile society.

Reported compliance rates vary considerably. Washington State has reported that by 1996, approximately 84% of the 11,802 offenders required to register had complied.[122] On the other hand, Iowa estimates that 40% of its sex offenders have not registered,[123] whereas in Tennessee 28% of offenders move without registering again.[124] In California at the end of 2002, more than 33,000 convicted sex offenders did not check in with the police, and the state had lost track of 44% of them.[125] Michigan claims 82% of its sex offenders complied with the registration law in 2003, but acknowledges that it does not know the whereabouts of more than 1,300 sex offenders.[126]

---

[119] Scholle, *supra* note 9.
[120] Id.
[121] B. Walsh, *SOAP Cleaning Up in Dallas*, 43 DALLAS POLICE NEWS 1 (1998).
[122] Scott Matson & Roxanne Lieb, *Community Notification in Washington State: 1996 Survey of Law Enforcement* 2 (1996).
[123] Scholle, *supra* not 9.
[124] Id.
[125] Naseem Stecker, *Sex Offender Registry Raises Complex Legal Issues*, MICH. B. J., Feb. 2003, at 36.
[126] Id.

Others reported that compliance rates are problematic because they are based on the number of registered offenders and the number of those who absconded. These "rates" do not take into consideration the movement of an offender to a new state, the different registration requirements from state to state, or simple bureaucratic mistakes. Nor can they be verified by the state agencies responsible for maintaining offender registration.[127] Thus, these statistics may give a false sense of security or alarm to the public.

Enforcing compliance has costs. In Washington State, 106 offenders were convicted of the felony "failure to register" offense between 1990 and 1996.[128] Iowa has conducted a sweep in Des Moines and arrested 25 sex offenders who did not register.[129]

Litigation Costs

There have been numerous legal challenges to these laws. Many were brought by sex offenders convicted before the laws were passed.[130] Other offenders have attacked the procedures used to classify them or the scope of notification. Thus, states have had to bear the costs of responding to these legal challenges. New Jersey reported spending $4 million in 1997 just to defend against legal challenges to the registration and notification laws.[131] These costs should decrease as courts resolve these legal challenges.

State Liability

The majority of registration and notification statutes provide immunity from civil suits, and apparently no civil suits brought against any state agencies either by victims of crimes committed by released offenders or by offenders subject to notification have been reported or have been reported in offenders' case reports.[132] However, successful lawsuits have reportedly been brought by victims attacked by sex offenders who did not register even though required to do so by law. In January 2001, Washington State agreed to pay $8.8 million to settle two lawsuits involving women who were attacked by Gary Wayne Puckett, a convicted sex offender who had failed to register as a sex offender as required by law. The lawsuit claimed that the state had not realized Mr. Puckett was required to register as a sex offender and that

---

[127] See, e.g., http://wwwlklaaskids.org/st-kan.htm (Reporting a compliance rate of 93.3% based on a number of 1,820 registered and 140 of those absconded. The office of the Kansas State Bureau of Investigations could not substantiate this number).

[128] Matson & Lieb, supra note 122, at 2.

[129] Scholle, supra note 9.

[130] See this chapter, supra.

[131] National Criminal Justice Ass'n, supra note 112, at 49.

[132] See Finn, supra note 23, at 14–15. The Jacob Wetterling Act also provides immunity for state officials for "good faith conduct." 42 U.S.C.A. § 10471(e) (West 2004).

he had not registered. Consequently, the state had not supervised him adequately after his release.[133]

PRACTICAL EFFECTS OF REGISTRATION AND NOTIFICATION

The effects of registration and notification laws have been much debated. Because these laws have been in effect for a relatively short time, few meaningful empirical studies corroborating either their claimed positive or negative effects have been done. Consequently, much of the evidence on their impact is anecdotal or plain conjecture. Nonetheless, the available evidence is useful for conducting a preliminary evaluation of these laws.

Contribution to Law Enforcement and Reduction of Recidivism

Because Washington State boasts the oldest community notification law, research on the impact of its laws is particularly useful. One study in that state compared a sample of 90 offenders subject to community notification with 90 offenders not subject to it. It concluded that the offenders subject to notification were arrested sooner if they reoffended than offenders not subject to it.[134] However, the percentage of offenders who reoffended after 4.5 years was similar for each group. This finding suggests that notification does not *prevent* crime but may aid in the *investigation* of crime.[135]

Although speculating that these offenders might have been "watched more closely" and that "increased attention results in earlier detection," the study in fact did not determine how or why these arrests were made. Without this information, it is impossible to know whether police access to registration information, community vigilance in response to notification, or any one of many other possible reasons lead to the arrest of these sex offenders.[136]

Even this latter conclusion must remain tentative, however. It is also plausible that community notification, by disrupting the employment and housing of sex offenders and denying them a supportive environment in which to become law-abiding citizens, increases the risk of their reoffending.[137] Having a job and housing can provide a regular routine for sex

---

[133] Mike Barker, *$8.8 Million Settlement Reached With Victims of Released Offender*, SEATTLE POST-INTELLIGENCER, Jan. 2001, at B1.

[134] Finn, *supra* note 23, at 11 (summarizing D.D. Schram & D.D. Milloy, Wash. State Ins. for Public Policy, *Community Notification: A Study of Offender Characteristics and Recidivism*, (1995)); Center for Sex Offender Management, *An Overview of Sex Offender Community Notification Practices: Policy Implications and Promising Approaches* (1997), *available at* http://www.csom.org/pubs/notify.pdf (last visited Feb. 13, 2004).

[135] *Id.*

[136] Logan, *supra* note 24.

[137] *See supra* note 28 and accompanying text.

offenders, and support groups can more readily monitor an offender's daily behavior. Being jobless and homeless can also increase stress for some offenders. In any event, the inadequate design of the Washington study and the extremely small number of participants simply do not allow researchers to draw any firm conclusions about the effect of notification on deterrence or crime solution.

A comprehensive review of the literature, which included the Washington State study, concluded, "There is no empirical evidence that notification is achieving its stated objectives of increasing public safety and assisting law enforcement with sex offender investigation."[138] As of now, the claim that community notification effectively accomplishes its purposes remains unsubstantiated.

Nonetheless, law enforcement personnel believe that registration and notification laws help them apprehend offenders.[139] Some anecdotal evidence exists in support of claims that registration and public notification aid in crime prevention.[140] If done correctly, notification can also serve as an opportunity to implement community-policing strategies that have proven to deter and solve crime.[141]

Most law enforcement agencies in Wisconsin reported in 1998 that the registration provisions increased information sharing about sex offenders among agencies. Almost half of the agencies also believed that registration would assist in future investigations and enhanced surveillance of sex offenders.[142]

Sense of Community Safety

Self-Help

Notification should give interested parents and others an opportunity to take some self-help measures that may be effective in preventing more sex crimes. Parents might watch their children more carefully, limit where they play, and keep a watchful eye on registered sex offenders. Although effective crime prevention is the primary goal of these laws, there is as yet no sound research on whether they work.

---

[138] See Finn, *supra* note 23, at 23.
[139] See *id*. at 2.
[140] See http://caag.state.ca.us/megan/stories.htm (updated May 1998). For instance, the California Attorney General hosts a Web site titled "How California's Megan's Law Has Kept Citizens Safer," featuring examples of individuals who used the state sex offender database to learn the criminal histories of offenders in their communities. In one example, a woman's recognition of a man who often played with children in the community pool apparently led to his arrest for violating his probation and a new offense of child molestation.
[141] Lucy Berliner, *Victim and Citizen Perspectives on Sexual Offender Policy*, ANNALS OF THE N.Y. ACAD. OF SCI. 464 (2003).
[142] Zevitz & Farkas, *supra* note 24, at 6.

Feeling Safe

These laws may also contribute to a psychologically valuable sense of community safety and individual control over a potential hazard in the local environment.[143] Psychological studies on "information control" suggest that individuals who have information about potential stressful situations or events are more confident in their ability to manage them.[144]

Some researchers have concluded that community reactions to public notification meetings were "generally positive."[145] Most attendees supported community notification, but had negative feelings toward the offender and the fact that he would be living in their community. However, the researchers' conclusion was based primarily on the informal assessments of audience reaction by law enforcement officials who were conducting the meetings.[146] Better empirical studies present a different picture. A comprehensive survey in Wisconsin in 1998 revealed that many citizens who attended notification meetings left feeling "more concerned than before."[147] Thus, community notification may do more harm than good in reassuring the community that it is a safer place to live as a result of the notification.

Many citizens attended notification meetings to learn as much useful information as possible about protecting themselves and their children against dangerous sex offenders. It appears that well-run notification meetings can accomplish that goal.[148] However, many attendees want to blame officials for placing sex offenders in their communities and to try to prevent that from happening. Not unexpectedly, they were disappointed in the meetings.[149]

Parents who did not take precautions after attending these meetings and whose child was sexually victimized by someone known to them through notification may feel intense guilt because of their failure to act on the information and prevent this criminal act against someone in their care.[150] Police and prosecutors, who otherwise may feel helpless to prevent future sex crimes, may take satisfaction in providing concrete and useful information to a community to prevent them.[151]

---

[143] Bruce J. Winick, *Sexually Violent Predator and Sex Offender Registration and Community Notification Laws: A Therapeutic Jurisprudence Analysis of Sex Offender Law in the 1990s*, 4 PSYCHOL. PUB. POL'Y & L. 505, at notes 188–189 (1998).

[144] *Id.* at 553.

[145] Matson & Lieb, *supra* note 122.

[146] Richard G. Zevitz & Mary Ann Farkas, *Sex Offender Community Notification: Managing High Risk Criminals or Exacting Further Vengeance?* 18 BEHAV. SCI. & L. 375, 378 (2000).

[147] Zevitz & Farkas, *supra* note 24, at 3.

[148] *Id.*

[149] *Id.*

[150] Winick, *supra* note 143, at 554.

[151] *Id.* at 553.

Notification, however, is usually a one-time event, especially when handled by the police or the offender. Consequently, the beneficial impact on public safety is likely to dissipate with the passage of time.

Inaccurate Information

Of course, an enhanced sense of safety assumes that correct information is provided about all (or at least most) of the dangerous sex offenders living in the community. For many reasons, this is probably not the case. It is very unlikely that all dangerous sex offenders are registered, that the information is correct for many sex offenders who have registered, that accurate determinations of dangerousness and nondangerousness have been made, and that effective notification has been made to everyone who may be at risk.

Missing the Target Area

A registered sex offender subjected to community notification may commit a serious crime in another county or state. Registration may misdirect the investigation because police are more likely to initially investigate registered sex offenders who live in the area in which the crime was committed. If so, registration could, at least momentarily, waste valuable time and energy. Moreover, some of the information contained in a state or national registry may be of minimal assistance to police in investigations, though DNA, fingerprints, and other evidence allowing physical identification should be useful to them in solving the crime. Of course, notification will not have been useful to community prevention, because offenders who commit sex crimes outside the area of notification will be unknown to the neighborhood.

False Sense of Security

Unfortunately, these laws may create a false sense of security, because the majority of sex crimes are committed not by strangers, but by family members and friends.[152] When community residents are distracted from this reality by warnings about the "dangerous stranger" down the street, they may not be as watchful for potential sex offenses committed by family members or others in their social circle.[153]

---

[152] See Joel B. Rudin, Megan's Law: Can It Stop Sexual Predators and at What Cost to Constitutional Rights? 11 CRIM. JUST. 3, 8 (1996); see also Eric Lotke, Politics and Irrelevance: Community Notification Statutes, FED. SENTENCING REP., Sept./Oct. 1997 (noting that "90% of rape victims under 12 years old knew their attackers").

[153] M.J. Simon, Matching Legal Policies With Known Offenders in Bruce J. Winick & John Q. La Fond (eds.), PROTECTING SOCIETY FROM SEXUALLY DANGEROUS OFFENDERS: LAW, JUSTICE, AND THERAPY, American Psychological Association, 2003.

Fear

States like Connecticut, which allow public access to information provided by *all* sex offenders, without any attempt to differentiate relative dangerousness among these offenders, may create the false impression that all sex offenders are dangerous, thereby significantly overstating the risk to the community. Moreover, such indiscriminate warnings do not allow people to focus on the most dangerous offenders.

Some notification methods may also create intense fear and anxiety in the community, particularly if they are done frequently and involve a large number of individuals.[154] Although no research has been conducted on this question, it is likely that too many notifications may trigger a "fatigue effect" in which parents stop listening to the warnings.[155]

Certain notification methods may induce unnecessary fear in a community. Some states have distributed flyers that look like "wanted posters" from the Old West. They have declared, for instance, that a released offender "has sadistic and deviant sexual fantasies which include torture, sexual assault, human sacrifice, bondage and the murder of young children," and "is viewed as an extremely dangerous untreated sex offender with a very high probability for reoffense."[156] This type of notice invites vigilantism because it, in effect, tells the community that there is nothing more the *police* can do to prevent the offender from committing another heinous crimes.

States can also be criticized for leaving provocative flyers on residents' front doors where the residents' children may find them, or even worse, sending such flyers home from schools with the children,[157] directly exposing them to warnings of danger their parents may prefer to share with their young ones in a more sensitive manner, if at all.

Educating the Public

One answer to the dual problems of complacency and fear is better community education. One Seattle police officer has reported that during community meetings he emphasizes "residents are more likely to be abused by an unregistered relative than by a stranger."[158] This sort of education may help minimize these problems. However, as a practical matter, it is

---

[154] Winick, *supra* note 143, at 554.

[155] *See* Logan, *supra* note 24 (*citing* David Chanen, *An Unwelcome Mat for Sex Offenders*, STAR-TRIBUNE (Minneapolis-St. Paul), May 13, 1999, at 1B (noting same)); Mary H. Gottfreid, *Sex Offenders Live in Poorer Areas*, PIONEER PRESS (St. Paul), Mar. 8, 2002, at A1 (same).

[156] Snohomish County Sheriff's Office Community Notification Bulletin re: Joseph Gallardo (July 7, 1993); *see also* John Arthur Wilson, *Gallardo's Story*, SEATTLE WKLY., July 28, 1993.

[157] *See* Nicole Koch, *Butler Co. Parents Told to Be Alert*, THE WICHITA EAGLE, Nov. 1, 1998 (describing police bulletin about recently released "high-risk" sex offender; bulletin was sent home with small-town Kansas grade school students).

[158] Finn, *supra* note 23, at 13.

unlikely that agencies in heavily populated areas will have the financial resources, adequate staffing, or time to educate the public while also carrying out their notification duties.

The Probable Future

Eventually, it is very likely that most people will simply stop paying attention to a constant stream of public notifications, especially if, as one would expect, most sex offenders, including those identified as at high risk of reoffending, live in the community without reoffending. Eventually, community notification will probably become mere background noise in our modern and complex lives.

Vigilantism

Notification laws have resulted in acts of vigilantism against both released offenders and their families.[159] These acts include destroying personal property, gunshots fired into a residence, and physical beatings and threats.[160] Other incidents of vigilantism have included assaults on offenders, the firebombing of a released offender's car on a busy street in California, the decapitation of an offender's dog in Washington State, public protests outside of the homes of offenders and their families, the throwing of rocks or eggs at offenders and their houses, verbal harassment, and the loss or denial of jobs and eviction from rental units.[161]

These terrorist attacks can be extremely serious. In Washington State, the police posted notices in a neighborhood warning that Joseph Gallardo, who was soon to be released from prison, was "an extremely dangerous, untreated sex offender with a very high probability for re-offense."[162] In the early morning hours of his release date, unknown criminals burned his family house to the ground.[163] Fearing that his life was in danger, Gallardo fled to his brother's home in a small town in New Mexico.[164] In less than a week, local residents drove Gallardo and his brother out of town with death threats and public protests.[165]

The few attempts to quantify how many acts of vigilantism have been committed against sex offenders suggest that most of these offenders are not

---

[159] See id. at 6; Alex B. Eyssen, Does Community Notification for Sex Offenders Violate the Eighth Amendment Prohibition Against Cruel and Unusual Punishment? A Focus on Vigilantism Resulting From "Megan's Law," 33 ST. MARY's L.J. 101 (2001).
[160] http://online.statemanjournal.com/sp_section_article.cfm?I+19416&s=1129.
[161] See Matson & Lieb, supra note 122, at 15; Jan Hoffman, Calls Climb for Notification on Releasing Sex Offenders, N.Y. TIMES, Aug. 4, 1994; Rudin, supra note 152, at 9.
[162] Wilson, supra note 156.
[163] Id.
[164] Id.
[165] Id.

victims of this misbehavior.[166] One limited 1995 survey in Oregon indicated that fewer than 10% of sex offenders are targets.[167] A Washington State survey of law enforcement conducted in 1996 indicated that, since the state's community notification law went into effect in 1990, only 33 incidents of harassment occurred, a rate of 3.5%.[168] Nonetheless, these data probably understate the extent of vigilantism victimization, because it is likely that many sex offender victims do not report these incidents to the police.

The victims of vigilantism have not been limited to offenders and their immediate families. In Kansas, a family unwittingly moved into the former residence of an offender and was mistakenly targeted by neighbors, who were not aware that the offender, who had registered as living at that address, had moved.[169] Local children teased the innocent family's daughters, and rocks were thrown at their home.[170] In New Jersey, an innocent apartment resident barely escaped harm from five gunshots fired through his bedroom windows and walls late one night; the shots were apparently intended for the registered offender living in the basement apartment of the same building.[171] And in Texas, a mentally retarded refugee, while playing with neighborhood children, was viciously attacked by four men, who mistakenly believed he was a pedophile because he lived at an address where a sex offender had once lived.[172]

Impact on Registrants

Increased Public Safety

These laws may impose more accountability on registrants and make them more aware that they are being monitored. If true, registrants may be more law abiding, and sexual recidivism should decrease. Unfortunately, many registrants do not believe these laws will have any deterrent effect on them.[173]

Harming Rehabilitation

On the other hand, these laws, especially if community notification is given, may make it more difficult for sex offenders to obtain housing and

---

[166] See Finn, *supra* note 23, at 19 and authorities cited therein.
[167] Oregon Dept. of Corrections, *Sex Offender Notification in Oregon* (1995) (prepared for the 1995 Legislature).
[168] See Matson & Lieb, *supra* note 122.
[169] *Family Becomes Victims of Sex-Offender List*, THE NEWS TRIBUNE (Tacoma, WA.), May 4, 1997, at A14.
[170] *Id.*
[171] Robert Hanley, *Shots Fired at the House of a Rapist Out on Parole*, N.Y. TIMES, June 17, 1998, at A24.
[172] See Eyssen, *supra* note 159.
[173] Logan, *supra* note 24 (*citing* Zevitz & Farkas, *supra* note 146).

employment and to maintain their families and friends, who can be important components of a community support group that help the offender not to reoffend. All but 1 of 30 offenders in Wisconsin subjected to extensive community notification stated in a 1998 survey that notification had adversely affected their transition from prison to the community. They often cited loss of employment, exclusion from residence, and the breakup of personal relationships as consequences of the notification.[174]

Difficulty in Obtaining Housing

Parole and probation officers agree that these laws make it very difficult for sex offenders to arrange for apartments or homes to live in. Sometimes just the fact of notification creates the problem. In the 1998 Wisconsin survey, 66% of officials who specifically supervise high-risk sex offenders reported difficulty in obtaining housing for individuals subject to notification.[175] Some released sex offenders in Wisconsin who were subject to extensive notification had to live in minimum-security or correctional centers because they could not find housing in the community.[176]

Sometimes, registration laws themselves or related laws specifically limit housing opportunities for convicted sex offenders. At least 13 states have statutes that limit housing options for convicted sex offenders released from prison.[177] An Iowa law, for example, imposes residency restrictions that prohibit registered sex offenders from residing "within two thousand feet of ... a[n] ... elementary or secondary school or a child care facility."[178] This statute effectively excludes released sex offenders from residing in about 30% of the towns in Iowa. As a practical matter, these restrictions exacerbate the problem of finding housing for registered sex offenders generally.[179] Already, police and corrections officers complain of overpopulation of halfway houses and prisons due to delayed placement of sex offenders in the community.

For treated sex offenders who have been released from prison custody (either for completing a sentence or being paroled to community

---

[174] Zevitz & Farkas, *supra* note 24, at 9.

[175] *Id.* at 8.

[176] *Id.* at 9–10.

[177] Doe v. Miller, 2004 WL 232749, *3 (S. Dist. Iowa, Feb. 9, 2004), n.2 (citing states that restrict by statute where convicted sex offenders may live. These states include Alabama, Arkansas, California, Florida, Georgia, Illinois, Iowa, Kentucky, Louisiana, Ohio, Oklahoma, Oregon, and Tennessee. *See also Sex Offenders in Iowa Fight Housing Restriction, at* http://www.cnn.com/2003/US/Central/12/14/sex.offender.challenge.ap/ (last visited Jan. 28, 2004).

[178] Iowa Code § 692A.2A(2) (2003). The law requires any sex offender who committed an offense against a minor to reside according to these restrictions, even if the offense is not a crime in Iowa, and even if the offense was committed in another state or as a minor. *See* Doe v. Miller, 216 F.R.D. 462 (S.D. Iowa 2003).

[179] *See Sex Offenders in Iowa Fight Housing Restriction, supra* note 177.

supervision), remaining confined in already overcrowded prisons can undermine their successful reintegration into communities. Numerous critics point out that the current overcrowded condition of the prison system in the United States has serious negative consequences for prisoners, including violence among inmates and increased risk of recidivism after prisoners are released.[180] Making sex offenders stay longer than necessary in such surroundings makes no sense.

Legal Challenges to Housing Limitations

Given current punitive public attitudes about sex offenders, especially as reflected in variations of Megan's Law throughout the states, the chances that released sex offenders can obtain legal recourse or protection might appear to be slim to none.[181] For example, California law precludes registered sex offenders from bringing a cause of action against lessors or renters of residential property who disclose to potential lessees and tenants the existence of the database indicating proximity of sex offender residents to the property.[182] Some legal scholars have suggested that discrimination against released sex offenders in renting housing to them might be a violation of federal housing law, because it is discrimination based on a "personal handicap." However, federal statutory language provides no such classification for sex offenders. Thus, this argument appears relatively weak and has yet to be tested before the courts.[183]

Nonetheless, the problem of discrimination in housing for sex offenders is serious and is just beginning to be litigated, with surprising results. A group of sex offenders represented by the Iowa Civil Liberties Union filed a class action lawsuit in federal district court challenging the constitutionality of Iowa's sex offender residency law, which prevented everyone convicted of a sex offense against a minor from living within 2,000 feet of a an

---

[180] See J.C. Oleson, *The Punitive Coma*, 90 CAL. L. REV. 829, 850-53 (2002). See also Heidi Lee Cain, *Housing Our Criminals: Finding Housing for the Ex-Offender in the Twenty-First Century*, 33 GOLDEN GATE U. L. REV. 131 (2003) (discussing findings from a study conducted in Britain showing a correlation between available housing and recidivism).

[181] See, e.g., CONN. GEN. STAT. §§ 54-251, 54-252, 54-254 (West 2001). By 1996, the federal government and every state had enacted some variation of Megan's Law. The Supreme Court recently upheld the constitutionality of sex offender registry laws in a pair of cases, Conn. Dep't of Pub. Safety v. Doe, 538 U.S. 1 (2003) (upholding registry law under a procedural due process challenge under the Fourteenth Amendment) and Smith v. Doe, 538 U.S. 84 (2003) (upholding registry law under an *ex post facto* challenge).

[182] CAL. CIV. CODE § 2079.10a(b) (West 2004). See, e.g., Shelley Ross Saxer, *"Am I My Brother's Keeper?" Requiring Landowner Disclosure of the Presence of Sex Offenders and Other Criminal Activity*, 80 NEB. L. REV. 522 (2001).

[183] See Brian E. Davis, Comment, *The State Giveth and the Court Taketh Away: Preserving the Municipality's Ability to Zone for Group Homes Under the Fair Housing Amendments Act of 1988*, 59 U. PITT. L. REV. 193 (1997).

elementary or secondary school or a day care center.[184] Initially, the court granted a temporary restraining order enjoining prosecutors from enforcing the Iowa housing restriction.[185] The court found that the displacement of sex offenders by the enforcement of the statute would result in irreparable harm to them.[186] The judge was clearly influenced by the circumstances of individual plaintiffs. One plaintiff was still residing in a correctional facility because the Iowa statute prevented him from living with his mother. Another plaintiff had received parole but was still incarcerated four months later because, under the law, virtually no alternative residence was available for his family in Des Moines. Another was forced to rent an apartment shortly after purchasing and moving into a house at an address that originally had been cleared by the Des Moines police department.

In February 2004, the court struck down the Iowa law as unconstitutional, holding that it violated the *ex post facto* clause, Fourteenth Amendment rights to substantive and procedural due process and Fifth Amendment.[187] The court was influenced by the law's practical effect. Although not literally "banishing" sex offenders from living in Iowa, it prevented all of them of them from living in many smaller towns and cities and severely limited housing in big cities to expensive developments, industrial areas, or the outskirts. Many sex offenders had to stay in prison rather than live with their families. The state presented no evidence that the law actually protects children. In fact, the one study conducted on this type of law concluded that there was "no evidence ... that residential proximity to schools or parks affects [sexual] reoffense."[188] An expert presented by the state indicated the law could be counterproductive, denying sex offenders the right to live with families who often were the only people who would help them get back on their feet. In addition, the law did not allow individualized determinations of dangerousness. The evidence in this case plainly demonstrated that these laws impede successful rehabilitation of sex offenders without making our communities safer.

Other Adverse Impacts

Innocent victims and increased recidivism. In a 1998 Wisconsin survey, 70 percent of the 30 sex offenders interviewed reported "being humiliated in their daily lives, ostracized by neighbors and lifetime acquaintances, and

---

[184] *See* Doe v. Miller, No. 3:03-CV-90067, (S.D. Iowa June 24, 2003) (complaint filed by Iowa Civil Liberties Union), *available at* http://www.iowaclu.org/pdf/residency_complaint.pdf (last visited Feb. 7, 2004).
[185] *See* Doe v. Miller, 216 F.R.D. 462 (S.D. Iowa 2003). This case also certified a class of sex offenders in the state of Iowa.
[186] *Id.* at 468–69.
[187] Doe v. Miller, 2004 WL 232749 (S.D. Iowa 2004).
[188] *Id.* at 30 (S.D. Iowa).

harassed or threatened by nearby residents or strangers."[189] Two thirds also described how notification had harmed their family members, including parents, brothers and sisters, and their children.[190] Surprisingly, offenders were often concerned that notification would harm their victims.[191]

Targets of serious vigilantism have little choice but to flee, which disrupts their attempts to create a stable work and home life and a support group to help keep them from reoffending. (Some commentators have called this the "displacement effect."[192]) These experiences not only impede efforts to rehabilitate sex offenders and to reintegrate them into the community,[193] they also give offenders ample incentive to violate registration laws in the future. Some may seek out states with limited or no notification provisions. Forced into a defensive posture within the community, offenders are less able to reintegrate. Some critics warn "the added stress of notification may even increase the risk of re-offending."[194] A sex offender in Corpus Christi, Texas, ordered by a judge to post warning signs and bumper stickers, attempted suicide.[195]

Offenders believe these laws will increase, not decrease, sexual recidivism.[196] Children of sex offenders may also be subject to ridicule and harassment as a result of these laws. The worst outcome would be for sex offenders to go "underground" and to hide their past.

Refusing to plead guilty to sex offenses. Many sex offenders are refusing to plead guilty to sex offenses because of the serious ramifications of conviction, including registration and notification laws, as well as sexual predator commitment laws.[197] This refusal can result in more trials or guilty pleas to nonsex offenses. Both results can interfere with rehabilitation, reinforcing defendant denials and failure to accept responsibility for their crimes.[198]

---

[189] Zevitz & Farkas, *supra* note 24, at 9.

[190] *Id.*

[191] *Id.*

[192] S. Pullen & K. English, *Law Enforcement Registration and Community Notification, in* K. English et al. (eds.) MANAGING ADULT SEX OFFENDERS: A CONTAINMENT APPROACH (prepared for the U.S. Dep't of Justice, National Institute of Justice Lexington Kentucky: American Probation and Parole Association) (K. English et al., eds., 1996). Jenny A. Montana, Note, *An Ineffective Weapon in the Fight Against Child Abuse: New Jersey's Meagan Law*, 3 J. L. & POL. 569 (1995); Sex Offender Supervision Network, *Sex Offender Community Notification in Oregon*; Abril R. Bedarf, *Examining Sex Offender Community Notification Laws*; Bonnie Steinbock, *A Policy Perspective: New Jersey's Megan's Law: Community Notification of the Release of Sex Offenders*, 14(2) CRIM. JUST. ETHICS, June 22, 1995, at 4–9.

[193] Bedarf, *supra* note 192; Steinbock, *supra* note 192; Montana, *supra* note 192.

[194] *See* Finn, *supra* note 23, at 14.

[195] Milloy, *supra* note 46.

[196] Logan, *supra* note 24 (*citing* Zevitz & Farkas, *supra* note 24).

[197] *See* chapter 5, which describes and analyzes sexual predator commitment laws in detail.

[198] *See, e.g.,* Jeffrey A. Klotz et al., *Cognitive Restructuring Through Law: A Therapeutic Jurisprudence Approach to Sex Offenders and the Plea Process*, 15 U. PUGET SOUND L. REV. 579 (1992); Robert M. Wettstein, *A Psychiatric Perspective on Washington's Sexually Violent Predator Statute*, 15 U. PUGET SOUND L. REV. 597 (1992).

Future Research

Professor Wayne Logan has thoughtfully suggested other research questions that need answers.[199] Do these laws encourage sex offenders to think of themselves as immutable sex offenders who cannot change their behavior, thus increasing their risk of committing more sex crimes? If so, then these laws may actually increase sex offending in some cases. Will these laws encourage sex offenders to commit crimes outside of their area of notification? If true, then they will not deter crime; they will only displace it and perhaps make detection and solution more difficult. Will the laws discourage sex offenders in prison from engaging in treatment for fear that officials will use information obtained from offenders to make registration and notification more burdensome for them? If so, then these laws may decrease prisoner-initiated efforts at rehabilitation and crime reduction.

Managing Sex Offenders in the Community

Many reports by law enforcement personnel indicate that notification laws are very useful aids in managing sex offenders in the community. Police and parole officers have used the threat of community notification to motivate sex offenders to seek treatment, adhere to the terms of their parole or probation, find a job, or otherwise demonstrate that they are not dangerous.[200] Of course, this is an inappropriate use of the law unless the offender's behavior is truly relevant to risk evaluation and warrants community notification.

Diverting Scarce Resources

These laws are labor and time intensive. More than a decade after their enactment, there is still no evidence showing that they make our communities any safer. The scarce resources consumed by laws passed by politicians to show that they were "doing something" could be used to support strategies that are more effective in preventing future sex crimes.[201]

RECOMMENDATIONS

We need to rethink our current all-encompassing federal and state system of sex offender registration and community notification. These laws need to be changed dramatically.

---

[199] Logan, *supra* note 24.
[200] *See* Finn, *supra* note 23, at 16.
[201] *See* chapter 5.

The System Sweeps Too Broadly

The system sweeps far more broadly than is necessary or can possibly be justified to protect the public. In short, these laws are overinclusive. They require far too many sex offenders who are *not dangerous* to register, thereby distracting us from offenders who do pose a high risk for committing more sex crimes.

If we insist on having them, registration laws should focus only on those sex offenders who are at very high risk of reoffending. As noted in chapter 2, we know who they are.[202] Focusing on high-risk offenders will allow communities to compile a compact list of dangerous sex offenders and allow the police to concentrate their monitoring and investigative efforts on these individuals.

No real law enforcement benefit exists in registering virtually every single sex offender. Most sex offenders are not dangerous and are unlikely to commit another sex crime.[203] Often, registration laws include minor sex offenders who have committed a single, less serious sex crime.[204] Requiring registration of sex offenders who commit crimes within the family may also discourage the reporting and prosecution of those crimes.[205] Many sex offenders who were required to register had committed their crimes before theses laws were passed and have been living safely in the community for a long time, with families and jobs.[206] There is no need to disrupt their lives.

The Laws Are Too Expensive

Registration and notification laws are costly and can require significant use of police resources that could be used more effectively to protect the public against all criminals, including sex offenders. The number of people subject to registration is growing fast, and compliance is likely to diminish

---

[202] R. Karl Hanson, *What Do We Know About Sex Offender Risk Assessment?* 4 PSYCHOL. PUB. POL'Y & L. 50, 67 (1998).

[203] *See* chapter 2.

[204] *See, e.g.*, State v. Bani, 36 P.3d 1255 (2001) (Hawaii Supreme Court held that offender who pleaded no contest to fourth-degree sexual assault after twice grabbing the buttocks of a 17-year-old girl while drunk was denied due process under the state constitution when he was not afforded a meaningful opportunity to avoid community notification under the state's "Megan's Law" by demonstrating that he does not represent a threat to the community).

[205] Berliner, *supra* note 2, at 1213 (children do not always report the crimes because, in part, they do not want punishment or incarceration for their offenders).

[206] *See, e.g.*, Doe v. Poritz, 662 A.2d 335, *aff'd. as mod.*, 662 A.2d 367 (1995) (Doe, convicted sex offender, had completed sentence and parole, had participated in treatment while in prison, and was living and working in the community, in anonymity and without reoffense, when state passed registration law requiring community notification; Doe's *ex post facto* challenge was unsuccessful.).

over time.[207] Arguably, those sex offenders most likely to reoffend are also those most likely not to register. Even registered sex offenders who do commit crimes may commit them far from where they live. If so, then registration may not provide assistance to police to investigate those sex crimes. It may even lead to innocent suspects.

Universal Disclosure Harms Public Safety

States should not publicly disclose the names of all registered sex offenders as a matter of course, as Connecticut does. Instead, they should use the most accurate methods available to screen registered sex offenders to determine whether they are currently dangerous. As we saw in chapter 2, actuarial instruments are available that allow public officials to assess sexual dangerousness quickly with both moderate accuracy and moderate cost.[208]

Releasing the names of sex offenders who do not pose any significant risk of reoffending serves no valid state interest. Instead, it only makes the offender an object of public scorn, encouraging others to shun him and deny him housing and a job, and in extreme cases, subjecting him to vigilantism.[209] No good purpose is served in putting barriers in the way of nondangerous sex offenders who want to reintegrate themselves into the community.

In addition, universal disclosure probably endangers the public by overwarning about all sex offenders without distinguishing serious risk from minimal risk. A rational and effective warning system would notify the public only about sex offenders who are dangerous; otherwise, the public is not given any real help in sorting out significant risk from insignificant risk.

Current Risk Assessment Is Inaccurate

State registration and notification laws that classify the relative dangerousness of sex offenders by the crime of conviction use clearly inaccurate prediction methodology.[210] Although limited in important ways, actuarial tools are the best available means of identifying which sex offenders are members of a group likely to reoffend.[211] Using a categorical approach, like crime of conviction, will inevitably result in too many mistakes being made.

---

[207] See supra 12–13 and accompanying text.
[208] See chapter 2.
[209] See supra notes 173–195 and accompanying text.
[210] See, e.g., CAL. PENAL CODE § 290(a)(2)(A) (West Supp. 2002); N.J. STAT. ANN. § 2C:7-2 (West Supp. 2002); N.Y. CORRECT. LAW § 168-a (McKinney 2002).
[211] See chapter 2.

These include predicting dangerousness when the person is unlikely to reoffend and predicting safety when the individual is at greater risk of reoffending. Misinforming the public in this way defeats the whole purpose of notification laws and may create more risk to public safety.

Even when states use more objective tools to assess risk, they often include other variables in individual cases to adjust their risk assessment. Some experts argue that this is less accurate than using purely objective variables.[212] To compound the problem, many of the individuals involved in this system are simply not qualified by education or experience to make these determinations. Nor seemingly is there any attempt to assess the accuracy of their risk assessment decisions over time.

Accurate Information Is Needed

Individual determinations of risk are no better than the information they are based on. Although there is no research on this point, providing an opportunity for sex offenders to review and challenge that information would help ensure that accurate information underlies these important decisions. Public safety is not enhanced if erroneous information is used to make risk assessments.

Fairness Is Needed

If the government uses state-of-the-art techniques for assessing risk, then there should be no need to automatically provide every sex offender with an individual hearing. Providing hearings to all sex offenders would be too costly. The government's initial determination of sexual risk should be presumed accurate.

However, sex offenders who believe the government has erred in how it conducted their risk assessment, or that they are not dangerous and can provide relevant evidence supporting their claim, should be entitled to a judicial hearing before their names are broadcast publicly. These hearings would enhance the accuracy of risk assessments and allow decision makers to take into account important new information, such as successful participation in a prison treatment program, that may strongly suggest the individual is not likely to reoffend. Hearings would also create incentives for sex offenders to take meaningful steps to decrease their risk and also enhance the accuracy of these determinations.[213] Both nondangerous offenders and

---

[212] See Winick, supra note 143.
[213] Id.

the public have the same interest in limiting public disclosure to those offenders who really do pose a significant risk of reoffending.

The Efficacy of the Laws Is Uncertain

We simply do not know whether registration or notification reduces sex offending. We do know that these laws are overinclusive, expensive, time consuming, and often inaccurate. If we keep these laws, it is imperative that researchers determine whether they work as intended and whether they are cost-effective.[214]

The Registration Laws Have Therapeutic Potential

Registration and notification laws should be used as a therapeutic tool to increase incentives for offenders to change positively and thereby decrease their risk of reoffending. Professor Bruce Winick has argued forcefully that these laws can and should be used as an ongoing tool for reducing risk to the community.[215] By not providing incentives for safety, the laws may cause sex offenders to be discouraged from taking positive steps, such as participating in a community treatment program, to reduce their risk of reoffending.[216] Moreover, notification laws may disrupt offenders' efforts to become law-abiding members of the community by causing them to lose their jobs and homes and the support of family and friends who could help keep them from reoffending. Currently, many state systems do not provide this essential flexibility.

Notification Should Be Done on a "Need to Know" Basis

There are legitimate situations in which notification is necessary to protect safety. In such instances, a simple rationale should control the extent of such disclosure. Only those institutions and individuals who need to know this information in order to take necessary cautionary measures should be told. For example, day care operators may need to know to prevent a convicted pedophile from securing employment. No one can seriously argue that anyone in the state, or in the world for that matter, should be able to obtain this information *without a good reason* simply by accessing a Web site.[217]

---

[214] Logan, *supra* note 24.
[215] *See* Winick, *supra* note 143.
[216] *Id.*
[217] *See* n. 56 and Web sites indicated therein.

The Community Has a Responsibility to Avoid Vigilantism

There is absolutely no excuse for the acts of vigilantism that notification laws invite.[218] Notification laws can create even more crime for police to investigate, burdening already limited public safety resources. Some forms of notification may encourage this terrorism. Use of "Wanted" poster formats is irresponsible because they suggest the released sex offender is an "outlaw" without any right to his safety. Notifications should be done in a standardized form that provides necessary and useful information, not inflammatory invitations to citizens to take the law into their own hands.

Any notification should be accompanied by educational efforts to remind the community of their responsibility to obey the law. Indeed, a more effective form of community notification would enlist the community together with the offender to form a mutual support and monitoring group to help restore the offender to the community by helping him with his efforts at relapse prevention, cognitive restructuring, and victim empathy.[219] Restorative justice has much to teach all of us about how an offender may publicly reenter a community in ways that benefit his victim, the community, and the offender.[220]

Is Community Notification a Public Safety Measure or an Invitation for a Posse?

Most important, the logic of community notification is, at one level, simply bizarre. Community notification laws were enacted to provide individual citizens with information about very dangerous sex offenders living nearby so that citizens could take necessary precautions to prevent them from committing another serious sex crime.

Think about this. The government is telling people that it cannot protect them from a person the government considers very dangerous and that every person is now responsible for his or her own and loved ones' safety. That is truly remarkable. If the person really *is* that dangerous, then he should be subject to intensive control while living in the community. Simply casting an extremely dangerous sex offender adrift in society with a "warning label" attached is irresponsible. Government owes it to its citizens to take effective steps to manage the risk posed by this person. These measures could include intensive parole and community containment measures, which are discussed in chapter 7. Surely, the government's fundamental responsibil-

---

[218] See Eyssen, *supra* note 159.
[219] See chapter 3.
[220] See, e.g., Lois Presser & Elaine Gunnison, *Strange Bedfellows: Is Sex Offender Notification a Form of Community Justice?*, 45 CRIME & DELINQ. 299 (1999).

ity is to provide community protection. It should not be allowed to jettison this basic responsibility so easily.

Summary

Universal registration and broad community notification laws enacted during the 1990s may give the community a sense of increased security. However, in their present form, these laws are expensive and likely to be ineffective. They may also make us less safe. It is time to change them so they really do protect the community.

5

SEXUALLY VIOLENT PREDATOR LAWS

In 1987, Earl Shriner, who had an IQ of 67 and a childhood history of being physically and sexually abused, was released from prison in Washington State, despite dire warnings, based on his bizarre prison drawings of torture machines and threats of killing children, that he was a walking time bomb who would sexually mutilate and murder young children.[1] But Shriner had served his full 10-year prison term for assault and abduction of two young girls, his only conviction, and could no longer be held in the criminal justice system. Just before his release, public officials tried to civilly commit him as mentally ill and dangerous to others. The court declined, concluding that Shriner, although dangerous, was not mentally ill. Now, there was nothing public officials could do to protect the community from this peril. Shriner was released from prison without supervision.

Almost 2 years after his release, Shriner sexually mutilated a 6-year-old boy, raped him, and left him to die. Luckily, the little boy lived. The public was outraged. Driven by this and other sexual murders committed by convicted sex offenders, and goaded by talk radio shows, victims' rights groups and others demanded that the governor and legislature do whatever was necessary to protect the public from dangerous sex offenders.[2]

---

[1] David Boerner, *Confronting Violence: In the Act and in the Word*, 15 U. PUGET SOUND L. REV. 525 (1992).

[2] Stuart Scheingold & Toska Olson, *The Politics of Sexual Psychopathy: Washington State's Sexual Predator Legislation*, 15 U. PUGET SOUND L. REV. 809 (1992).

Governor Booth Gardner quickly appointed a task force (Task Force) to review Washington laws, talk to victims' families, consult with experts, and prepare recommendations for law reform that would protect the public against predatory sex offenders. Most important, the law had to promise that people like Earl Shriner would never again be released from prison to commit another heinous sex crime.[3]

The Task Force drafted a novel law, the Sexually Violent Predator (SVP) statute, that did just that. It allowed the state to confine dangerous sex offenders when they could no longer be confined in the criminal justice system. The prosecutor had to prove that the individual had been convicted of a qualifying sex crime and suffered from a "mental abnormality"[4] or "personality disorder"[5] that made him likely to commit another sex crime against a stranger.[6]

THE INVENTION OF THE SEXUALLY VIOLENT PREDATOR LAW

The SVP statute was drafted because the Task Force realized that the current law had gaps in it that allowed dangerous people to go free.

Criminal Law

Criminal law generally punishes people for crimes they have *already committed* by imposing a sentence, frequently requiring incarceration for a specified period of time. The *ex post facto* clause of the Constitution[7] prohibits extending someone's prison term *after* conviction and punishment. Thus,

---

[3] For an excellent description of these events, *see* Boerner, *supra* note 1.

[4] The Washington SVP law defines *mental abnormality* as a "congenital or acquired condition affecting the emotional or volitional capacity which predisposes the person to the commission of criminal sexual acts in a degree constituting such person a menace to the health and safety of others." WASH. REV. CODE § 71.09.020(8) (2003). This definitional language borrowed heavily from the old Washington statutory definition of *sexual psychopath*. WASH. REV. CODE § 71.06.010 (1989), which had been repealed. *See generally* Boerner, *supra* note 1.

[5] The Washington SVP law does not define *personality disorder*. However, it is a medically recognized diagnosis. AMERICAN PSYCHIATRIC ASSOCIATION, THE DIAGNOSTIC AND STATISTICAL MANUAL OF MENTAL DISORDERS (4th ed., text revision 2000) (hereinafter *DSM–IV–TR*) lists 11 specific types of personality disorder and one not otherwise specified. *Id.* at 685. Invariably, the specific type of personality disorder diagnosis given to SVPs is *antisocial personality disorder*. The *DSM–IV–TR* describes this disorder as follows: "[t]he essential feature of Antisocial Personality Disorder is a pervasive pattern of disregard for, and violation of, the rights of others that begins in childhood or early adolescence and continues into adulthood." *Id.* at 701. The specific diagnostic criteria listed for this disorder include criminal behavior, deceitfulness, impulsivity, irritability or aggressiveness, reckless disregard for the safety of others, consistent irresponsibility, and lack of remorse. *Id.* at 706. Commonly, a history of criminal arrests and convictions is a primary basis for diagnosing this disorder.

[6] WASH. REV. CODE § 71.09.010-115 (2003).

[7] U.S. CONST. art. I, § 10; *see also* Collins v. Youngblood, 497 U.S. 37 (1990).

once an offender has served his full sentence, he must be released. With these constitutional mandates in mind, the Task Force began its review of Washington law.

It found that Washington had very recently reformed its criminal law by eliminating *indeterminate sentencing,* which had allowed judges to give a convicted criminal an indefinite sentence, subject to a maximum term. A parole board could release an offender before he had served his maximum sentence if it determined he was not likely to reoffend. Most offenders so released were placed on parole and were supervised in the community. In its place, the legislature had adopted *determinate sentencing.* Under this system, offenders served a fixed sentence and then had to be released without any community supervision even if considered dangerous. Making matters worse, Washington also set relatively short sentences for serious sex crimes.[8] The Task Force feared that many dangerous sex offenders would have to be released without any supervision after serving relatively short prison terms. In view of recent events and public outcry, this was absolutely unacceptable.

Civil Commitment

Every state has passed a law that gives courts authority to order the involuntary commitment of a person who is mentally ill and dangerous to a psychiatric hospital.[9] The purpose of this civil commitment was to *prevent* the person from harming himself or others. Although commitment was usually for a limited time, it could be indeterminate. However, the state's power was limited. It had no authority to commit someone who was dangerous but *not* mentally ill.[10]

By 1987, most states, including Washington,[11] had reformed their civil commitment laws to allow hospitalization for a limited time of people with serious mental disorders whose recent behavior indicated they were dangerous to themselves or others.[12] Although indeterminate in theory, most patients were released in a relatively short time. From the Task Force's perspective, short-term confinement of sexually dangerous offenders was simply out of the question. Moreover, most sex offenders did not suffer from a mental disorder.

---

[8] At about the same time, several other states, including Minnesota and Wisconsin, had also enacted a similar determinate sentencing system to replace an indeterminate scheme. They, too, set relatively short sentences for sex crimes. John Q. La Fond, *Washington's Sexually Violent Predator Law: A Deliberate Misuse of the Therapeutic State for Social Control*, 15 U. PUGET SOUND L. REV. 655 (1992).

[9] *See generally* JOHN Q. LA FOND & MARY L. DURHAM, BACK TO THE ASYLUM: THE FUTURE OF MENTAL HEALTH LAW AND POLICY IN THE UNITED STATES (1992).

[10] Addington v. Texas, 441 U.S. 418 (1979).

[11] La Fond, *supra* note 8.

[12] *See generally* MICHAEL L. PERLIN, MENTAL DISABILITY LAW: CIVIL AND CRIMINAL, 1989; SAMUEL JAN BRAKEL ET AL., THE MENTALLY DISABLED AND THE LAW (3d ed. 1985).

Like many other states, Washington had in the past used the state's civil commitment authority to civilly commit sex offenders as "sexual psychopaths" to secure therapeutic facilities for control and treatment. But, as we shall soon see, Washington, together with most other states, had repealed its sexual psychopath statute in 1984 and since then had relied exclusively on its criminal justice system to confine dangerous sex offenders.

Preventive Detention

Preventive detention was a third option the Task Force considered. Some states and the federal government used this alternative to confine dangerous persons who were *not* mentally ill to prevent them from harming others. However, the Constitution strictly limits the use of preventive detention for short-term confinement only.[13] Everyone on the Task Force agreed that the government could not use preventive detention to confine dangerous sex offenders *indefinitely* after their release from prison.[14] Any such law would surely be struck down as unconstitutional.

The Solution

The Task Force concluded that a new law was needed that allowed the government to indefinitely confine dangerous sex offenders about to be released from prison who did not suffer from a mental disorder and could not be committed under the state's general commitment law. The Task Force created just such a law: the sexually violent predator law.[15] This statute allowed the state to commit sex offenders who were about to be released from prison or had already been released from prison. SVPs would be confined indefinitely in secure institutions until they were safe to be released. The Task Force considered the SVP law a "stop gap" measure that would be used until longer criminal sentences for sex crimes could take effect, thereby eliminating the need for this law.

The SVP law enacted by the Washington legislature was clear in describing the group it was targeting:

> The legislature finds that a small but extremely dangerous group of sexually violent predators exist who do *not* have a mental disease or defect that renders them appropriate for the existing civil commitment law ... In contrast ... sexually violent predators generally have *anti-*

---

[13] United States v. Salerno, 481 U.S. 739 (1987).

[14] La Fond, *supra* note 8.

[15] *See* WASH. REV. CODE § 71.09.010-115 (2003). This was the first sexual predator law in the country. Most states used this law as the model for drafting their own laws.

social personality features which are *unamenable to existing mental illness treatment modalities* and those *features* render them likely to engage in future sexual behavior.[16]

Since Washington's SVP law went into effect in 1990, 15 other states have enacted similar laws.[17] The District of Columbia has an old law similar to the SVP law, but it is almost never used. Texas enacted its own version of the SVP law: It only allows *outpatient* commitment. Sex offenders in Texas are not committed to secure mental health facilities; instead, they are closely monitored in the community.[18]

Pennsylvania has enacted an SVP statute for juvenile sex offenders found to be "sexually violent delinquent children."[19] These are individuals who, "due to a mental abnormality or personality disorder, have serious difficulty in controlling sexually violent behavior and thereby pose a danger to the public."[20] It authorizes a court to commit juvenile sex offenders who satisfy the statutory definition for an initial 1-year commitment for involuntary treatment. This initial commitment can be renewed for subsequent 1-year periods.[21]

To understand how SVP laws differ from the old sexual psychopath laws, it is necessary to describe the psychopath statutes briefly.

SEXUAL PSYCHOPATH LAWS

Illinois enacted the first sexual psychopath law in 1938.[22] By the early 1970s, more than half of the states had enacted them. Instead of sending sex offenders to prison, these laws allowed prosecutors to civilly commit sex offenders who had been charged with or convicted of a sexual offense, confining them as "sexual psychopaths" to a mental health facility where experts would treat them. The offenders would be released when they were cured and no longer sexually dangerous.

---

[16] WASH. REV. CODE, § 71.09.010 (2003) (emphasis added).

[17] W. Lawrence Fitch & Debra A. Hammen, *The New Generation of Sex Offender Commitment Laws: Which States Have Them and How Do They Work?* in PROTECTING SOCIETY FROM SEXUALLY DANGEROUS OFFENDERS: LAW, JUSTICE, AND THERAPY (Bruce J. Winick & John Q. La Fond eds., 2003).

[18] John Q. La Fond, *Outpatient Commitment's New Frontier: Sexual Predators,* 9 PSYCHOL. PUB. POL'Y & L. 159 (2003); *see also* TEX. CODE ANN. § 841.081 (Vernon Supp. 2002). (SVP is to be committed for outpatient treatment and supervision.)

[19] 42 Pa. C.S.A. § 6401 et. seq.

[20] 42 Pa. C.S.A. § 6401.

[21] 42 Pa. C.S.A. § 6403.

[22] *See generally* SAMUAL JAN BRAKEL ET AL., THE MENTALLY DISABLED AND THE LAW (3d ed. 1985).

Mental Disorder and Treatment

Sexual psychopath laws assumed that many sex offenders suffered from a mental disorder that made them more likely to commit sex crimes and that mental health professionals (MHPs) could identify these individuals. Not only could MHPs accurately predict which sex offenders were dangerous; they could also effectively treat and cure them and determine when they were safe to be released.[23]

This therapeutic approach, which stressed treatment rather than punishment, was consistent with the emphasis on rehabilitation that dominated the criminal justice system during the 1950s and 1960s.[24] Much criminal behavior, especially sexual offending, was seen as caused by illness. Experts could identify and cure those sex offenders who suffered from a psychological disorder, allowing their release into society as safe and productive members. The best interests of the patient and the community would be served.[25]

Repeal of Psychopath Laws

By the mid-1980s, however, most states had repealed their sexual psychopath laws, or simply did not use them. As Brakel put it:

> Growing awareness that there is no specific group of individuals who can be labeled as sexual psychopaths by acceptable medical standards and that there are no proven treatments for such offenders has led such professional groups as the Group for the Advancement of Psychiatry, the President's Commission on Mental Health, and, most recently, the American Bar Association Committee on Criminal Justice Mental Health Standards to urge that these laws be repealed.[26]

A major review of the treatment research literature for sex offenders published in 1989 confirmed this pervasive skepticism. It concluded that there was "no evidence establishing that treatment effectively reduces sex offense recidivism." [27]

There were other reasons why these laws were repealed. Some evidence suggested that serious sex offenders who were committed to treatment programs often served less time than if they had been sent to prison.[28] Critics

---

[23] See ABA Criminal Justice Mental Health Standards 7-8.1 (1989).

[24] Francis A. Allen, *Criminal Justice, Legal Values, and the Rehabilitative Ideal*, 50 J. Crim. L., Criminology & Police Sci. 226 (1959).

[25] See La Fond, *supra* note 8.

[26] Brakel et al., *supra* note 22.

[27] See Lita Furby et al., *Sex Offender Recidivism: A Review*, 105 Psychol. Bull. 3, 25 (1989).

[28] The American Bar Association commented, "Some legislatures came to feel that offenders were being released prematurely under such [sexual psychopath] statutes, with consequent danger to public safety." ABA Criminal Justice Mental Health Standards, 7-8.1, at 459 (1989).

believed that sex offenders manipulated these programs, using them to avoid prison. They also felt that these laws undermined personal responsibility and denigrated the harm done to victims. In 1981, California abolished its sex offender psychopath program. The legislature declared, "In repealing the mentally disordered sex offender commitment, the Legislature recognizes and declares that the commission of sex offenses is not itself the product of mental disease."[29] Washington abolished its sexual psychopath law in late 1984[30] and instead provided treatment on a voluntary and limited basis to sex offenders in prison.

The clear trend in the late 1970s and 1980s was to convict and punish sex offenders as morally responsible persons, send them to prison, and provide treatment there to those prisoners who wanted it. Civil commitment was simply not considered an appropriate strategy for protecting the community or for treating sex offenders.[31]

THE DIFFERENCE BETWEEN SEXUAL PSYCHOPATH AND SEXUAL PREDATOR LAWS

SVP laws differed from the discarded psychopath laws in several important ways. First, they exhibited an unusual, clinically contradictory "punish first, treat later" attitude. These laws also glossed over the requirement that the offender have a genuine mental disorder before he or she be committed to treatment. They also did not require recent evidence of dangerousness before committing SVPs. And, perhaps most important to actual effectiveness, the laws did not deal with intrafamily offenders.

Punish First, Treat Later

Unlike psychopath laws, which required the government to *choose* between punishment or treatment, a sex offender *must* serve his full prison term before he can be committed as a predator. Treatment is often delayed until many years after the individual has committed his sex crimes.

---

[29] 1981 CAL. STAT. ch. 928, § 4 at 3485. At the same time, however, the California legislature called for a small research program with a valid experimental design to determine if treatment is effective in reducing sex offender recidivism. This legislation led to California's ground-breaking Sex Offender Treatment and Evaluation Project.
[30] WASH. REV. CODE § 71.06 (2002), (*repealed prospectively by* 1984 Wash. Laws 209) (codified at WASH. REV. CODE § 71.06.005 (2003)).
[31] La Fond, *supra* note 8.

Mental Disorder Not Required

Unlike most sexual psychopath laws,[32] the government did not have to prove the offender suffered from a medically recognized mental illness. It need only prove the person suffered from a *mental abnormality* (a phrase that has no common or authoritative definition generally understood by mental health professionals) or a *personality disorder*. This latter term is a recognized mental disorder contained in the *Diagnostic and Statistical Manual of Disorders*,[33] the common "dictionary" of mental illnesses used by mental health professionals and courts alike. However, the type of personality disorder most commonly used in SVP trials is *antisocial personality disorder*, which is a diagnosis that is usually based on the individual's criminal history.[34]

No Recent Evidence of Dangerousness Required

Most sexual psychopath laws required the government to charge or convict an individual of a sex crime before it could seek civil commitment of the offender. This would ensure that the government had *recent* evidence indicating the offender was sexually dangerous. Under SVP laws, the government does not have to prove deteriorating mental condition or any recent criminal conduct or inappropriate behavior that manifests sexual dangerousness before seeking possible lifetime confinement.

Family and Familiar Offenders Excluded

Sexual psychopath laws had often been used to commit intrafamily offenders, including individuals who had committed incest. This made sense because, as we saw in chapter 1, most sex crimes are committed against victims known to the offender.[35] Nonetheless, the Washington SVP law applied only to sex offenders who had committed sex crimes against "strangers or persons with whom they established a relationship" in order to victimize the individual.[36] It could not be used against offenders who had committed sex crimes against family members or victims known to them (e.g., "date

---

[32] *See* 725 Ill. Comp. Stat. 205/0.01 (1992 and Supp. 2002). Under the Illinois Sexually Dangerous Persons Act, a "sexually dangerous person" is defined as one who suffers from a mental disorder. *Id.* at § 1.01.

[33] *DSM–IV–TR, supra* note 11, at 685–729.

[34] Id. at 701–06 (criminal conduct is one of several diagnostic criteria; it would not, standing alone, necessarily give rise to a clinical diagnosis of antisocial personality disorder—a point that might be overlooked in the legal system).

[35] *See* chapter 1.

[36] *See, e.g.*, Wash. Rev. Code § 71.09.092(9) (2002). This latter phrase was intended to include offenders, like Boy Scout leaders or members of the clergy, who established a relationship with victims in order to have access to their victims and opportunities to commit sex crimes against them.

rape"). The Task Force was concerned that family members might not report sex crimes committed by other family members or cooperate with the prosecutor if conviction could lead to lifetime commitment of a family member who was a sex offender.

HOW DO SVP LAWS WORK?

SVP laws enact a process whereby offenders who have already served their time are run through another trial. Here they face the likely possibility of further incarceration, this time in a secure mental health facility, and unlike the prison term, this incarceration may last indefinitely. I examine this legal process in this section.

Screening

Because SVP laws can be used only on sex offenders who have served their full prison sentence, state agencies must screen the records of every sex offender scheduled to be released from prison in the near future. Agencies must compile complete records, including out-of-state convictions, and screen them to identify individuals who might qualify as an SVP.[37] The names and records of individuals selected as potential SVPs are then forwarded to prosecutors, who decide whether to file an SVP petition. Some states, like Washington, have kept referrals to prosecutors fairly low, sending about 20 cases a year to prosecutors out of 2,000 cases reviewed by the End of Sentence Referral Subcommittee.[38] Other states, like Florida, have an extremely high referral rate. In the first 6 months after its SVP law went into effect, Florida referred 2,631 cases for possible SVP filing. By January 2002, that number had ballooned to 9,307.[39]

Probable-Cause Hearing

If a prosecutor files a petition seeking commitment of a sex offender under the SVP law, a probable-cause hearing will be held. A judge must decide whether credible evidence exists that could lead a reasonable person to believe the offender is an SVP. In some states, like California, these

---

[37] John Q. La Fond, *The Costs of Enacting a Sexual Predator Law*, 4 PSYCHOL. PUB. POL'Y & L. 468 (1998).
[38] D. SCHRAM & C.D. MILLOY, SEXUALLY VIOLENT PREDATORS AND CIVIL COMMITMENT: A STUDY OF THE CHARACTERISTICS AND RECIDIVISM OF SEX OFFENDERS CONSIDERED FOR CIVIL COMMITMENT BUT FOR WHOM PROCEEDINGS WERE DECLINED (Document Number 98-02-1001). (Washington Institute for Public Policy, February 1998).
[39] Fitch & Hammen, *supra* note 17.

hearings are time consuming and expensive, sometimes lasting several days. If conducted properly, probable-cause hearings can screen out offenders who should not be committed as SVPs. California eliminates about 20% of its cases at the probable-cause hearing. In other states, like Washington, these hearings are perfunctory; judges almost always find probable cause, and there is no effective screening at this stage.[40]

Evaluation

Once probable cause is found, the offender is placed in a secure institution where MHPs, either employed permanently or specially hired by the government to conduct these evaluations, determine whether the individual meets the SVP definition. In some states, like California, these evaluations are conducted before the probable-cause hearing. In other states, like Washington, these evaluations are conducted after the probable-cause hearing. In many states, offenders languish in these institutions for many months, and sometimes for years, before these evaluations are actually conducted. If found to be an SVP by government MHPs, the defense counsel will arrange for an independent evaluation by an MHP of his or her choosing.[41] If the offender is indigent, the state pays for this evaluation.

Trials

In most cases, a trial will be held to determine whether the individual will be committed as an SVP. In many states, either party may request a jury; prosecutors almost always do because juries are more likely to commit than judges. A trial can take several days and, in some cases, weeks. Prosecutors often put past victims on the stand who relive their terrible ordeals, as well as one or more MHPs, who testify that, in their opinion, the defendant is an SVP. Defense lawyers also present an MHP, who, on the basis of his or her evaluation, has concluded that the defendant is not an SVP. Defense lawyers consider these cases much like death penalty cases, because a positive finding often results in their client's being committed to secure institutions for many years. As a result, most defense lawyers litigate these cases very aggressively.

---

[40] John Q. La Fond, *The Costs of Enacting a Sexual Predator Law and Recommendations for Keeping Them From Skyrocketing, in* PROTECTING SOCIETY FROM SEXUALLY DANGEROUS OFFENDERS: LAW, JUSTICE, AND THERAPY (Bruce J. Winick & John Q. La Fond eds., 2003). *See also* La Fond, *supra* note 37.

[41] For a thorough explanation of how a MHP should conduct an SVP evaluation, *see* Roy Lacoursiere, *Evaluating Offenders Under a Sexually Violent Predator Law: The Practical Practice, in* 4 PROTECTING SOCIETY FROM DANGEROUS SEX OFFENDERS: LAW, JUSTICE, AND THERAPY (Bruce J. Winick & John Q. La Fond eds., 2003).

Release

In most states, commitment is for an indefinite period, although in California commitment is only for a 2-year period, which can be renewed.[42] An SVP can be released only if he is found "safe" to live in the community. State hospital staff generally do not have authority to release SVPs, either on conditional release to the community or on final release. Instead, prosecutors can ask for a judicial hearing, usually requesting a jury to determine whether the offender is "safe" to be released. Often juries will conclude that the individual is still "likely to reoffend," and release is denied. The defendant can also seek his release from a court. Usually, a second jury trial (usually at the prosecutor's request) will be held.

Conditional Release

SVPs who progress satisfactorily in treatment are released to the community under strict monitoring. (Such placement is often called an *outpatient commitment* or an *LRA* for placement in the "least restrictive alternative.") This placement allows the offender to implement strategies to avoid sexual offending that he has learned and also allows MHPs to conduct more realistic risk assessments, because the offender is living in the real world rather than in a secure institution.[43]

Final Release

Some SVPs eventually obtain their complete release from all state control. Most often, this occurs after they have been placed on an LRA (sometimes called *community release, conditional release,* or *outpatient commitment*) and have demonstrated that they pose a reduced danger to the community.

THE ARGUMENTS FOR SVP LAWS

Supporters claim that the SVP law fills a hole in society's legal protective system. No society can tolerate unleashing extremely dangerous sex offenders to find more victims. The state simply must have legal authority to protect the community.

---

[42] Roxanne Lieb, *State Policy Perspectives on Sexual Predator Laws, in* PROTECTING SOCIETY FROM DANGEROUS SEX OFFENDERS: LAW, JUSTICE, AND THERAPY (Bruce J. Winick & John Q. La Fond eds., 2003).

[43] *See* La Fond, *supra* note 8, at app. A (report of Dr. Vernon Quinsey).

Sick and Dangerous

Proponents believe that a number of sex offenders do, in fact, suffer from a serious mental condition that makes them very likely to commit another sex crime. In their view, SVP laws are a legitimate exercise of the state's civil-commitment authority to hospitalize people with mental illness who, as a result of their illness, pose a serious threat of harm to others.

New Expertise, Accurate Predictions, and Effective Treatment

Some MHPs are confident that they can accurately identify these mentally disturbed and dangerous sex offenders. Experts who treat sex offenders also believe that, despite disappointing results in the past, they now have better treatment approaches that can change sex offenders' attitudes and behaviors and reduce sexual recidivism.[44]

Increased Public Safety

Prosecutors and police support the law as an effective way to keep dangerous sex offenders off the streets.[45] They believe that these laws prevent many terrible sex crimes from being committed. Prosecutors are also confident that SVP laws will be applied only in the most serious cases.

Generous Due Process

Supporters believe these laws are narrowly drawn and would provide ample procedural due process protection to individuals whom the state sought to commit as SVPs, including the right to a jury trial. Indigent defendants (and most defendants would be indigent because they would have just finished serving prison terms) would be provided, at government expense, with a lawyer to represent them and a mental health expert to evaluate them and to assist their attorney in presenting their case. Thus, fact-finding would be fair and accurate.

Protecting Future Victims

Victims' rights groups are very active and extremely effective in supporting passage of these laws. They will not accept that the law is powerless to prevent more tragic cases like that of Earl Shriner. The media also supports

---

[44] See chapter 3 for a thorough discussion of sex offender treatment.
[45] See, e.g., Norm Maleng, The Community Protection Act and the Sexually Violent Predators Statute, 15 U. PUGET SOUND L. REV. 821 (1992).

SVP laws. And no legislator in his or her right mind will oppose passage of an SVP law.[46] All of these groups are confident that SVP laws will prevent future sex crimes, thereby protecting future victims.

THE ARGUMENTS AGAINST SVP LAWS

In this section, I detail arguments made by opponents of SVP laws, including the complaints of such disparate voices as civil libertarians, the American Psychiatric Association, plaintiffs in various court cases, and others opposed to the legislation.

Preventive Detention, Not Treatment

Civil libertarians are outraged. In their view, an SVP law is simply a form of preventive detention masquerading as involuntary treatment. Using a sham civil commitment scheme to extend prison terms on a selective basis is a deliberate misuse of the state's authority to involuntarily hospitalize people who really are mentally ill and dangerous to themselves or to others.[47] Other scholars argue that these laws blur the line between criminal punishment and civil commitment and threaten basic justice, bona fide therapy, and constitutional values.[48]

Detachment From the Medical Treatment Model

The American Psychiatric Association is critical of these new laws. In its view, most sex offenders do not have a mental illness. Yet the laws' definitions, crafted by legislatures, sweep too broadly, using terms that are not recognized as genuine mental disorders by authoritative medical texts or mental health associations. Necessarily, MHPs, who evaluate individuals and testify in court, must construct their own definitions. Consequently, they are unlikely to reach consistent and accurate results when evaluating thousands of prospective SVPs. In sum, the American Psychiatric Association argues that SVP laws are a misuse of psychiatry and involuntary civil

---

[46]For an interesting analysis of the politics surrounding enactment of the first SVP law in the nation, see Scheingold & Olson, *supra* note 2.

[47]La Fond, *supra* note 8. *See also* Peter C. Erlinder, *Minnesota's Gulag: Involuntary Treatment for the "Politically Ill,"* 19 Wm. Mitchell L. Rev. 99 (1993).

[48]Stephen J. Morse, *Bad or Mad?: Sex Offenders and Social Control,* in Protecting Society From Sexually Violent Offenders: Law, Justice, and Therapy (Bruce J. Winick & John Q. La Fond eds., 2003).

commitment for social control of dangerous people rather than for providing necessary mental health treatment to people who are severely disabled.[49]

The Slippery Slope

SVP laws also rely on "personality disorder" as a diagnosis that qualifies an individual as an SVP. "Antisocial personality" is a subcategory of personality disorder and is the diagnosis most commonly used to commit people as predators. Unfortunately, a diagnosis of antisocial personality disorder may be based on a history of criminal conduct and other antisocial behavior.[50] Not surprisingly, anywhere from 25% to 50% of the adult prison population qualifies for this diagnosis.[51] If a diagnosis of antisocial personality disorder justifies civil commitment of sex offenders, it could also justify the civil commitment of many other kinds of criminals, such as wife batterers, pyromaniacs, and drug users.[52] There is no logical stopping point for this steep "slippery slope."

Impossible to Determine Volitional Impairment

In *Kansas v. Crane*,[53] the Supreme Court required the government to prove in an SVP trial that a defendant's mental condition significantly impaired his ability to control his sexual behavior. Yet there is virtually unanimous consensus that MHPs cannot determine when an individual has significant difficulty controlling his behavior. In 1982–1983, both the American Bar Association[54] and the American Psychiatric Association[55] recommended eliminating the volitional prong of the American Law Institute (ALI) insanity defense, because experts simply could not make this determination. As the association said, "The line between an irresistible impulse and an impulse not resisted is probably no sharper than that line

---

[49] AM. PSYCHIATRIC ASSOC., DANGEROUS SEX OFFENDERS, A TASK FORCE REPORT OF THE AMERICAN PSYCHIATRIC ASSOCIATION (1999).

[50] *DSM–IV–TR*, *supra* note 11, at 701–06.

[51] AM. PSYCHIATRIC ASSOC., A TASK FORCE REPORT ON SEXUALLY DANGEROUS OFFENDERS (Draft) 107 (Dec. 12, 1996) (concluding that approximately one third to one half of inmates currently in correctional institutions in the United States qualify for a diagnosis of antisocial personality disorder). *See also* P. Moran, *The Epidemiology of Antisocial Personality Disorder*, 34 Soc. PSYCHIATRY & PSYCHIATRIC EPIDEMIOLOGY 213, 234 (1999) (noting that 40–60% of the male prison population is diagnosable with antisocial personality disorder).

[52] *See, e.g.*, Mary Lynn Krongard, A Population at Risk: Civil Commitment of Substance Abusers After Kansas v. Hendricks, 90 CAL. L. REV. 111 (2002).

[53] Kansas v. Crane, 534 U.S. 407 (2002).

[54] AMERICAN BAR ASSOCIATION, ABA CRIMINAL JUSTICE MENTAL HEALTH STANDARDS, STANDARD 7-6.1 (First Tentative Draft)(1983).

[55] AMERICAN PSYCHIATRIC ASSOCIATION, AMERICAN PSYCHIATRIC ASSOCIATION STATEMENT ON THE INSANITY DEFENSE (1982).

between twilight and dusk."[56] As a result of this unanimous national consensus, Congress in 1984 changed the federal insanity defense to eliminate the volitional prong, as have at least eight states since then. Simply put, experts cannot tell whether an individual is unable or simply unwilling to control sexual behavior.

Tautological Definitions

The primary evidence of "mental abnormality" or "antisocial personality disorder," "volitional impairment," and "dangerousness" is the commission of past sex crimes. The SVP law creates an inescapable tautology: People who commit sex crimes are sick, they cannot control their sexual conduct, and they are "likely" to reoffend. Therefore, they must be committed indefinitely for control and treatment.

Irresistible Political Pressure

In theory, SVP laws were designed to commit only the most dangerous sex offenders who could not be controlled by any other mechanism. Even staunch supporters, however, admit that there "will be substantial political pressures on corrections departments to refer low-risk offenders for commitment, and on attorneys general and prosecutors to file commitment petitions to avoid public displeasure if a nonreferred offender is released and commits a new offense."[57]

Questioning the New Expertise

Some critics are skeptical that sex offenders can be treated effectively. If treatment is not available, then the SVP laws will simply result in warehousing hundreds, and eventually thousands, of men indefinitely without any hope of improvement or release.

Defense Lawyers

Defense lawyers argue that SVP laws, although seemingly providing significant procedural due process, make it virtually impossible for a convicted sex offender to prevail in a commitment hearing. Most defense lawyers are willing to stipulate to the defendant's criminal record. Yet, most

---

[56] *Id.* at 11. However, for an excellent analysis of the contributions psychiatry can make to resolving the issue of volitional capacity under sexual predator laws, *see* Bradley D. Grinage, *Volitional Impairment and the Sexually Violent Predator*, 48 J. FORENSIC SCI. 1, 1–8 (2003).

[57] Lucy Berliner, *Sex Offenders: Policy and Practice*, 92 Nw. U. L. REV. 1203, 1222 (1998).

prosecutors still insist on presenting the defendant's entire criminal history by putting their victims on the stand and having them retell their painful stories. Predictably, juries are inflamed by this heart-rending testimony and will not take responsibility for releasing someone who may commit another serious sex crime. Instead, they will err on the side of safety and vote to commit. For defense counsel, trying an SVP case is a nightmare right out of Kafka.[58]

THE CONSTITUTIONALITY OF SVP LAWS

Constitutional challenges were launched against SVP laws in several states, including Washington and Kansas. The Washington State Supreme Court upheld the Washington law,[59] but a federal district court struck it down as unconstitutional.[60] The Kansas State Supreme Court concluded that an almost identical version of the SVP law was unconstitutional.[61] Clearly, the United States Supreme Court would have to give the final answer to the question of whether SVP laws were constitutional and could be used to confine selected sex offenders beyond their prison terms.

The *Hendricks* Case

In 1997, the Supreme Court, in a close 5–4 decision, upheld the Kansas SVP law as constitutional.[62] In the *Hendricks* case, the majority concluded that legislatures have broad authority to define which class of dangerous people should be civilly committed to protect the community because they suffer from some mental condition that impairs their ability to control their behavior.[63] It did not have to limit civil commitment to people suffering from those mental disabilities that are recognized by psychiatrists, psychologists, and other mental health professionals. Thus, mental illness is a *political*

---

[58] Robert C. Boruchowitz, *Sexual Predator Law—The Nightmare in the Halls of Justice*, 15 U. PUGET SOUND L. REV. 827 (1992).

[59] *In re* Personal Restraint of Young, 857 P.2d 989 (Wash. 1993).

[60] Young v. Weston, 898 F. Supp. 744 (W.D. Wash. 1995).

[61] Kansas v. Hendricks, 521 U.S. 346 (1997).

[62] *Id.*

[63] For a thorough analysis of the *Hendricks* case, *see* Stephen J. Morse, *Fear of Danger, Flight From Culpability*, 4 PSYCHOL. PUB. POL'Y & L. 250 (1998); Stephen R. McAllister, *Sex Offenders and Mental Illness: A Lesson in Federalism and the Separation of Powers*, 4 PSYCHOL. PUB. POL'Y & L. 268 (1998); Eric S. Janus, *Hendricks and the Moral Terrain of Police Power Civil Commitment*, 4 PSYCHOL. PUB. POL'Y & L. 297 (1998); Robert F. Schopp, *Civil Commitment and Sexual Predators: Competence and Condemnation*, 4 PSYCHOL. PUB. POL'Y & L. 323 (1998); and John Kip Cornwell, *Understanding the Role of the Police and Parens Patriae Powers in Involuntary Civil Commitment Before and After Hendricks*. 4 PSYCHOL. PUB. POL'Y & L. 377 (1998). *See also* Eric S. Janus & Wayne A. Logan, *Substantive Due Process and the Involuntary Confinement of Sexually Violent Predators*, 35 Conn. L. Rev. 319 (2003).

decision, not a medical decision, and elected state officials have broad authority to decide who can be civilly committed.

The Court also concluded that the law was not punitive in purpose or effect and, therefore, did not violate either the *ex post facto* or double jeopardy provisions of the U.S. Constitution. The majority accepted the assertion by Kansas, made in oral argument for the first time, that it would provide mental health treatment to sex offenders committed as SVPs.

The minority agreed with the majority on this score. However, four justices considered the law to be punitive because it required sex offenders to be fully punished *before* they could be committed for treatment and because the Kansas SVP law did not allow a sex offender to be placed in an LRA if that would accomplish the government's purpose in protecting the community.[64]

The *Crane* Case

In 2002, the Supreme Court revisited the *Hendricks* decision in *Kansas v. Crane*.[65] The Court again upheld the Kansas SVP law, but limited its application. The six-justice majority further explained the earlier *Hendricks* decision by requiring the prosecution to prove that the mental condition caused the offender to have "serious difficulty in controlling [his sexual] behavior."[66] This requirement that there be a significant causal connection between the offender's mental condition and the resulting impairment in his sexual volitional control was designed to distinguish SVPs from most other sex offenders, who should be dealt with by the criminal justice system because they are capable of controlling their sexual desires and therefore considered responsible for their choices and deserve punishment.

The Impact of *Hendricks* and *Crane*

Hendricks gave constitutional approval to all state SVP laws already enacted and also gave a constitutional green light to any state that wanted to enact an SVP law. Thus, states could use civil commitment to keep dangerous sex offenders from being released from prison or to return them to prison after their release.

In theory, the *Crane* decision should reduce the number of sex offenders who can be committed as SVPs. The government must now prove that a sex offender suffers from a mental condition that makes it very difficult for him to obey the law against committing sex crimes. Experts must be able

---

[64] *Hendricks*, 521 U.S. at 385–89 (Breyer, J., dissenting).
[65] Kansas v. Crane, 534 U.S. 407 (2002).
[66] *Id.* at 870–71.

to explain to judges and juries how this condition interferes with normal choices that people make about having sex. One would expect that the number of incarcerated sex offenders selected for either clinical evaluation or probable-cause hearings would decline. Also, the number of individuals actually committed as SVPs should decrease, and more SVPs committed before the *Crane* decision should be released.

After this case, some state supreme courts, like Missouri,[67] required that all SVP trials that were held before the *Crane* case was decided must be retried because the government had not established this lack of control in those trials. Most other state supreme courts, however, held that in proving the statutory elements of a mental condition that makes the individual likely to reoffend, the government had necessarily established that the individual had serious difficulty in controlling his sexual conduct.[68] In their view, the *Crane* decision added nothing new to their SVP laws or what the government must prove.

Although firm conclusions cannot yet be drawn from the available research, anecdotal evidence suggests that the *Crane* decision is having little impact. Defense lawyers report that some MHPs testifying for the government tell the jury that any sex offender diagnosed with a "mental abnormality" or "personality disorder" that makes him "likely to reoffend," by definition, has difficulty in controlling his sexual conduct. We will simply have to see whether the rate of referrals, the number of probable-cause hearings, the number of SVP trials being held, and—most important—the number of sex offenders committed as SVPs decline at all in the future or seem to remain about the same as before *Crane*.

THE EMPIRICAL CONSEQUENCES OF ENACTING AN SVP LAW

How Many SVPs Are Committed?

The first SVP law went into effect in 1990 in Washington State. A national survey conducted in the summer of 2002 revealed that 2,478 men (and several women and juveniles) were confined in SVP facilities; 1,632 had been committed as sexual predators, and 846 were confined and awaiting trial.[69] California had the most SVPs in confinement with 509, whereas

---

[67] Thomas v. State, 74 S.W.3d 789 (Mo. 2002).
[68] *See* State v. Laxton, 647 N.W.2d 784, 792-94 (2002), *In re* Clair Luckabaugh, 568 S.E.2d 338, 348–49 (2002), and *Westerheide v. State*, 831 So. 2d 93, 106–08 (2002).
[69] W. Lawrence Fitch, *Sexual Offender Commitment in the United States: Legislative and Policy Concerns*, 989 N.Y. ACAD. SCI. 489, 492 (2003).

Florida had 404, Wisconsin 246, and New Jersey 223.[70] Of course, these numbers have increased since the survey. If history holds true, most of those individuals awaiting trial will be committed. Clearly, SVPs are a growth industry.

How Many SVPs *Will Be* Committed?

Most states are committing more offenders as SVPs than they initially expected. Florida initially estimated in December 1999 that it would have 614 offenders committed as SVPs by 2009. In early 2002, it raised that estimate, projecting that it would have between 1,000 and 1,200 individuals committed by the end of 2010.[71] California estimates that it will have a maximum SVP population committed to institutions of 1,500. Minnesota hopes to cap its SVP population at 350, whereas Wisconsin expects a maximum SVP population of 600.[72]

Although there are numerous variables that can affect how many people will be committed as SVPs,[73] it is very likely that the number will increase for at least a decade. Most states have assumed that longer prison sentences will solve the problem and, in time, most dangerous sex offenders will remain confined in the prison system. However, most states face at least another decade, if not more, of sex offenders being scheduled for release after they have served their fixed sentence. An SVP law is the only available means for keeping them in confinement.

And as we will see now, very few SVPs are being released from institutions on outpatient commitment. Consequently, the number of SVPs in confinement is likely to swell. Simply put, no one really knows how large the SVP population will eventually be.[74]

How Many SVPs Have Been Given Conditional Release?

Most states are releasing many fewer SVPs to conditional release in the community than they initially expected. The 2002 survey reported that only 96 SVPs had been placed in an LRA or community placement.[75] As

---

[70] *Id.* As of summer 2003, some other states reported as follows: Massachusetts (260), Minnesota (190), DC (9), Arizona (93), Illinois (185), Iowa (46), Kansas (78), Missouri (62), North Dakota (9), South Carolina (58), and Washington (164). Minnesota, Illinois, and DC included sex offenders committed under older sex offender commitment statutes.

[71] La Fond, *supra* note 40.

[72] *Id.*

[73] *Id.*

[74] *Id.*

[75] These states reported as follows: Arizona (36), Washington (9), Illinois (3), Kansas (3), and New Jersey (2). Fitch, *supra* note 69, at 492.

of September 2003, this number had been reported to be 86.[76] Thus, an extremely small percentage of SVPs have been conditionally released to the community.

Wisconsin, which passed its law in 1994, has placed more SVPs on conditional release than any other state. As of September 2003, it had released 32 SVPs to the community who were subject to ongoing supervision. This number accounted for about one third of all SVPs placed on community release in the country. The state's relatively high conditional release rate is due, in large measure, to the Department of Health and Family Services' decision to recommend conditional release for those SVPs whose needs and risks can be managed in the community, even if they have not completed treatment or have refused it altogether while committed.[77] (Once this state's high release rate became public, some legislators immediately proposed changing the law to make release of SVPs more difficult.[78]) Although Wisconsin has been aggressive in providing community release, it has also been aggressive in recommitting SVPs who violate the conditions of their release. Wisconsin has returned to secure institutions about half of those put in the community on conditional release.

There are many reasons why states are not placing SVPs on LRAs. Most states have not built LRA facilities or established systematic LRA programs designed to allow community placement of SVPs. Constructing LRA facilities is expensive, and they too must be staffed. Communities fiercely resist having them located in their midst.[79] Site requirements can be self-contradictory, requiring access to treatment providers, educational opportunities, and employment, while also insisting that LRA facilities not be close to schools, residential neighborhoods, or potential victims.[80] It is no surprise that without LRA facilities and programs in place, SVPs are having difficulty in obtaining an LRA placement. Washington State, almost 13 years after enacting the first SVP law, finally constructed its first LRA facility to house predators granted conditional release. It did so only after ordered to by a federal judge.[81] Many people, including some victims' rights groups, oppose virtually all such releases; in their view, the whole point of an SVP law is to confine sex offenders as long as possible.

---

[76] Jessica McBride & Reid J. Epstein, *State Tops in Release of Sexual Predators*, MILWAUKEE SENTINEL, Sept. 22, 2003 (*citing* H. Lawrence Fitch, Forensic Services Director, Maryland Department of Hygiene).

[77] *Id.*

[78] Jessica McBride & Reid J. Epstein, *Tougher Sexual Predator Law Sought. Changes Would Make It Harder to Release Inmates*, MILWAUKEE SENTINEL, Sept. 25, 2003.

[79] *See* La Fond, *supra* note 18.

[80] La Fond, *supra* note 40.

[81] Turay v. Weston, No. C91-664WD (W.D. Wash. 1994).

Treatment is taking a lot of time, even when states have actually established professionally appropriate treatment programs. Many state officials report that they expect most SVPs will be in treatment for 4 to 5 years before they will be considered ready for conditional release.[82] Thus, many SVPs will not even be considered for conditional release for several years after their initial commitment. Whether it really takes this long for effective treatment is not known. State officials argue that SVPs are the "worst of the worse" and that treatment should take a long time.[83] On the other hand, strong evidence exists that state officials sometimes use this argument to justify extended confinement even though offenders have successfully completed the institutional treatment program.[84] Interestingly, California's SVP law only authorizes commitment for 2 years at a time; yet it also reports an average treatment time of 4 to 5 years.[85] It had placed very few SVPs on conditional release as of 2003. Minnesota's treatment program had a meltdown in 2003. All three psychologists with a PhD quit, as did five other licensed clinical psychologists.[86] This unfortunate development cannot further treatment goals.

In many states, a large number of SVPs are not participating in treatment. In California, 80% of the 480 offenders confined in the SVP program were not participating in treatment as of March 7, 2003.[87] In Minnesota, only 40% had submitted to treatment as of August 2003.[88] Many offenders awaiting trial will not participate on the advice of their lawyers, who fear that statements obtained in therapy will be used at their clients' trials to commit them as SVPs. Many individuals already committed as SVPs do not believe that they will ever be released, because so few SVPs have been placed on conditional release so far. Not surprisingly, they see no point in participating.[89] It is extremely unusual for staff to recommend community placement for any SVP who has not completed the institutional treatment program.

Some states, like California, have had extreme difficulty in locating landlords willing to rent apartments to SVPs on conditional release. More

---

[82] Freddie Yap, *Treatment for Sexual Criminals Debated. ASH Abuzz as Two Are Poised for Release*. San Luis Obispo Tribune, March 7, 2003, *available at* 2003 WL 4116610.

[83] Rachel Stassen-Berger, *State Sex Offender Program Invites Scrutiny*, St. Paul Pioneer Press, Aug. 10, 2003.

[84] *See supra* notes 98–103 and accompanying text.

[85] Yap, *supra* note 82.

[86] Rachel Stassen-Berger, *Commissioner Reassesses Request for Sex Offender List*, St. Paul Pioneer Press, July 26, 2003.

[87] Yap, *supra* note 82.

[88] Stassen-Berger, *supra* note 83.

[89] *Id.* (quoting Rich McDeid, a sex offender committed under Minnesota's SVP law as follows: "I think the general sense here is that no one is ever going to be released.").

than 100 landlords refused to rent a house as a residence for California's first predator in an LRA, so the state had to house him in a trailer on state-owned land near Soledad prison.[90] Without conditional release facilities of their own, states that rely on private property owners have a convenient excuse for their inability to place SVPs on conditional release in the community. In addition, many states will not pay for treatment in an LRA or will only pay for part of it.[91] If the offender is unable to pay for his own treatment in the community, then his chances of obtaining an LRA are minimal. Locating MHPs willing to treat SVPs in the community can also be difficult.

Prosecutors often resist release into an LRA. State officials are concerned about the political backlash and potential state liability if a sex offender commits another serious sex crime while on an LRA.[92] Politics can also play an important role. In 2003, the Governor of Minnesota issued an executive order barring state officials from releasing sexually dangerous persons into communities unless the law required it or a court had ordered release.[93] He did this after newspaper reports indicated that the state planned to move some SVPs from secure treatment facilities to less restrictive community placements. Lawyer and psychologist Warren Maas, a critic of the Minnesota program, believes that sex offenders are "just as unpopular as terrorists." He considers the state's program to be a hypocritical form of preventive detention, concluding, "They clearly have no intention of voluntarily releasing anyone, no matter how well they do in treatment and how far they have progressed in treatment."[94]

Ironically, none of the SVPs released into community placements had reoffended as of October 2003. Reportedly, Washington State had released six men from its McNeil Island LRA facility as of July 2003, and none of them had offended as of then. Arizona had released 37 patients on conditional release without any of them committing another crime.[95] This indicates that treatment combined with aggressive community monitoring of sex offenders, including recommitment of SVPs who violate the conditions of their release, can keep them from committing more sex crimes.[96]

---

[90] Greg Moran, *Public Incensed as Sex Offender Goes Free. State Rethinks How to Confine Predator*, San Diego Union-Tribune, Aug. 17, 2003.

[91] John Kip Cornwell, *Sex Predators and the Right to Treatment in the Community*, Address at Association for the Treatment of Sexual Abusers 22nd Annual Research and Treatment Conference, St. Louis, MO. (Oct. 10, 2003).

[92] *See* La Fond, *supra* note 18.

[93] Bill Salisbury, *Governor's Office: Order Requires Legal Means to Release Sexual Predators*, St. Paul Pioneer Press, July 11, 2003.

[94] Stassen-Berger, *supra* note 83.

[95] Jonathan Martin, *Rapist Breaks Release Conditions; No New Crimes, But Violations, Tracked by Satellite Return Him to Custody*, Seattle Times, Oct. 9, 2003; Jonathan Martin, *What Do We Do With John Mathers? He Is a Child Molester and Rapist. He's Spent Nearly 40 Years Behind Bars. Now the State Is Willing to Pay More Than $700,000 to Find Him a New Life*, Seattle-Times, July 27, 2003.

[96] Martin, *supra* note 95.

How Many SVPs Have Been Given Unconditional Release?

Very few SVPs have been given their final discharge. Wisconsin also leads in this category; as of September 2003, it had discharged seven men without supervision.[97] In Washington State, where the first SVP law was implemented in 1990, not a *single* SVP had been given a final release as of October 2002. That is simply amazing. No expert ever thought that it would take over a decade to treat every single offender committed as an SVP.

Politics and SVP Laws: The *Ghilotti* Case

The case of Patrick Ghilotti, the "Lincoln Avenue" rapist in California, is a sensational example of how traumatic the proposed release of a sexual predator can be. Ghilotti, who was convicted of raping four Marin County women and admitted raping at least six others, was committed to the California SVP program in 1997 after he had finished serving his prison sentence.[98] After his initial 2-year commitment under the California SVP statute, Ghilotti agreed to another 2-year commitment.

During this time, he completed the SVP treatment program at Atascadero State Hospital and became the first SVP in California eligible for final release.[99] At the end of this second commitment, three independent mental health experts personally evaluated him and concluded that Ghilotti no longer met the statutory criteria for commitment and should be given his final, unconditional release. Refusing to accept these unanimous recommendations, the director of the California Department of Mental Health filed his own petition seeking to have Ghilotti committed for another 2-year term even though the California law did not authorize his action. A spokeswoman for Governor Gray Davis, who was running for reelection in a hotly contested race at the time, said "Obviously, the governor's office took a strong interest in the case . . . We did not pressure, but worked constructively with the Department of Mental Health."[100]

After a trial judge held that the director was not authorized to file a petition on his own initiative without affirmative evaluations of the offender by at least two mental health professionals, the State appealed to the California Supreme Court. In April 2002, in a 5–2 decision, the California Supreme

---

[97] McBride & Epstein, *supra* note 76.

[98] Chuck Squatriglia, *State Justice Blocks Release of Rapist*, S. F. CHRON., Dec. 1, 2001, at A13, *available at* 2001 WL 3421214.

[99] Harriet Chiang, *Ruling May Slow Release of Rapists/Court Says Judge Can Evaluate Risk*, S. F. CHRON., Apr. 26, 2002 at A1, *available at* 2002 WL 4018919.

[100] Pamela J. Podger, *Serial Rapist to Stay Confined Until Justices Rule/State Supreme Court to Hear Arguments on Violent Sexual Predator Law in February*, S. F. CHRON., Dec. 13, 2001, at A1, *available at* 2001 WL 3422296.

Court ruled that the state's SVP law did not authorize the director to file a petition unless two mental health professionals had in fact filed reports concluding the individual was an SVP. However, the court virtually invited the director to have two mental health professionals on his staff conduct new evaluations; if they were to conclude that Ghilotti was an SVP, then a new petition seeking his commitment could be filed.

The court also ruled that the evaluators do not have to conclude that there is more than a 50% chance that someone would commit a sex crime to consider him an SVP. Instead, they need only find that he "presents a substantial danger—that is a serious and well-founded risk—of reoffending. . . ."[101] This decision to lower the standard of dangerousness was contrary to the result reached by courts in six other states, which had interpreted virtually identical language in their respective SVP laws to require the state to prove that the offender was "more likely than not" to commit another sex crime in order to commit someone as an SVP.[102] Three of the justices on the California Supreme Court had to be approved for retention by the voters in November 2002.[103]

COSTS OF IMPLEMENTING AN SVP LAW

States must pay a stiff price for passing an SVP law because they are extremely expensive to operate. In 2003, states reported per capita treatment costs ranging from $47,555 in Florida to $138,8412 in North Dakota. A good rule of thumb is that it costs about $100,000 per person to keep someone committed in an institution for a year as an SVP. These costs do not include the capital expense of building or renovating facilities to house SVPs. In addition, states must pay associated expenses of a commitment system, such as compiling records for sex offenders about to be released from prison, screening those records, conducting pretrial evaluations, representing the prosecution and the defendant in probable-cause hearings and in trials and appeals, establishing a community release program, and other associated costs.[104] One state official in Washington State estimated that court and litigation costs average about $35,000 per patient per year. Minnesota officials have estimated that the cost of a single commitment proceeding costs about $100,000 for attorneys and experts alone. This estimate does not include other court costs.[105]

---

[101] People v. Ghilotti, 44 P. 3d 949 (2002).
[102] Id. (Wedegar, J., dissenting).
[103] Bob Egelko, *Sexual-Predator Case a Risk for Justices/Political Futures at Stake in Ruling by High Court*, S. F. Chron., Dec. 16, 2001, at A11, *available at* 2001 WL 3422620.
[104] La Fond, *supra* note 40.
[105] Fitch, *supra* note 69, at 493.

Security and Therapy

SVP laws are costly because they require the state to provide a facility that is both *secure* and *therapeutic*. Thus, states are, in effect, running *both* a prison *and* a hospital.

New Facilities

Because SVPs comprise a unique class of mentally disordered and dangerous patients, they cannot be housed with convicted prisoners or with patients civilly committed under a state's general commitment law. Consequently, states must either build new facilities or renovate other facilities to house and treat them separately from other patients. California expects that it will cost approximately $365 million to build a new facility for SVPs, which is expected to house 1,500 patients and open in 2005.[106] Washington State expects to spend at least $81 million to build a new facility to house 400 SVPs.[107] Florida Governor Jeb Bush canceled plans to build a new SVP facility because it would be too expensive. Two of Minnesota's facilities were full in 2003. With a shortage of beds, the state faced having to build new facilities or expand old ones.[108]

Hiring and Training More Staff

States must also hire new staff and train them to treat sex offenders. There are simply not many qualified mental health professionals to staff these facilities. Both Washington State and Florida moved their major SVP facility a considerable distance. In both cases, over half of the staff quit and the state had to hire and train more staff.

Right to Treatment

Individuals civilly committed as SVPs have both a constitutional and statutory right to treatment.[109] The government must provide a safe, humane, and therapeutic environment. It must also staff its facilities with qualified mental health professionals knowledgeable in treating sex offenders. MHPs must develop treatment programs that comply with professionally accepted

---

[106] Alan Garthright, *Other Molesters to Follow DeVries*, S. F. CHRONICLE, Aug. 17, 2003.
[107] La Fond, *supra* note 40.
[108] J. Marcotty, *Panel Raps Program for Sex Offenders; Fewer Restrictions Urged for Some of the Patients*, STAR-TRIBUNE (MINNEAPOLIS), Sept. 19, 2003.
[109] Turay v. Weston, No. C91-664WD (W.D. Wash. 1994); *see* La Fond, *supra* note 18.

standards.[110] They must also prepare an individual treatment plan for each SVP that sets treatment goals and measures of progress toward those goals for each patient.

Washington State lost a lawsuit claiming that it was not providing constitutionally required treatment. As a result, it had to spend millions of dollars upgrading its program and has been subject to an injunction since 1994.[111] As of September 2003, it had accumulated fines in excess of $8 million that it would have to pay if it did not locate a community 12-bed halfway house for SVPs as ordered by a federal court.[112] In June 2004, a Seattle judge ruled that Washington was finally in substantial compliance with the court order and set aside nearly $11 million in fines.[113] Right-to-treatment lawsuits have been filed in several other states, including California.[114]

Community Release

States must also establish a community placement program. This may require constructing a separate facility with its own staff, often in the face of fierce community opposition. Washington State reportedly spends nearly $60 million a year to operate an LRA facility on McNeil Island. Although it has 24 beds, only 4 SVPs lived there in 2004.[115] The costs of placing an individual in a community LRA vary widely. In 2003, reported costs in Washington State generally ranged from $25,000 to $400,000, though individual costs can be astronomical. Washington, reportedly, spent $740,000 on placing one SVP on conditional release for 1 year in 2003. These costs include having at least one guard accompany the offender any time he leaves McNeil Island (where one LRA facility is located), while he wears a Global Positioning Satellite Tracking device.[116]

Many SVPs on conditional release, though not all, are also taking drugs designed to reduce their sex drive.[117] These drugs are expensive. Kansas reported that it spends $100,000 annually for "transitional services" for SVPs in the community. Illinois reported an average of $80,000 for each of its

---

[110] Various professional associations, such as the Association for the Treatment of Sexual Abusers (ATSA) have established standards for practice and hold training conferences. ATSA 19th Annual 2000 Research and Treatment Conference: Putting It Together—The Art of Integrating Research and Practice, Nov. 1–4, 2000, San Diego, CA.

[111] La Fond, *supra* note 40.

[112] Garthright, *supra* note 106.

[113] Adam Lynn, DSHS in compliance, judge says, NEWS TRIBUNE (Tacoma), June 15, 2004.

[114] La Fond, *supra* note 18.

[115] Adam Lynn, DSHS in compliance, judge says, NEWS TRIBUNE (Tacoma), June 15, 2004.

[116] Martin, *supra* note 95.

[117] *See* chapter 6 for a discussion of these drugs.

five patients in the community.[118] California expects to spend $180,000 per year on placing its first SVP in the community; this compares with $28,500 for the average prison inmate.[119] Although expensive at the outset, the costs of placing SVPs into community LRAs should decline as economies of scale are reached, state facilities are established, and the monitoring of individuals who show progress is reduced. Eventually, it should be less expensive to place SVPs into LRAs than to keep them confined in institutions.[120]

Women and Adolescent SVPs

Although almost all SVPs are men, a few are women or juveniles. Women cannot be placed in treatment with male sex offenders because there is a serious risk that the women will be harmed psychologically and physically. The same is true for adolescents. Thus, states, like Washington and California, must establish separate treatment programs for women and juveniles or contract with other states to provide these services. Because it is difficult to achieve economies of scale, the per capita cost for providing institutional treatment for these individuals is very high.

A 2003 court decision from Missouri may prove to be extremely important in reining in the costs states incur in committing and treating female SVPs. The court, in *In re Coffel*,[121] reversed the civil commitment of a woman under Missouri's SVP law because, currently, no empirical evidence exists to justify its application to women. The court noted that virtually all of the available research concerning sexual recidivism was based on studies of *male* sex offenders. Yet most experts agree that men and women commit sex crimes for different reasons. Not surprisingly, researchers have yet to identify the factors associated with female sexual reoffending or to develop actuarial tools for predicting the likelihood that a particular female sex offender will commit another sex crime, and women have a very low rate of sex offending in any event. Consequently, there is simply insufficient empirical evidence on female sex offenders that any expert could use to reliably predict Angela Coffel's likelihood of sexual reoffending. Without such information, predictions of sexual dangerousness involving women do not rest on expertise based on scientific research or generally accepted in the psychological community. As a result, predictions of sexual dangerousness are no more accurate than flipping a coin. Whether other state courts will reach

---

[118] Fitch, *supra* note 68, at 493.
[119] Garthright, *supra* note 106.
[120] *See* La Fond, *supra* note 18.
[121] 117 S. W. 3d 116 (Mo. Ct. App. 2003).

the same conclusions and effectively limit the use of SVP laws to male sex offenders remains to be seen.

Diverting Scarce Resources

Directors of state mental health programs are very concerned that SVP programs will consume an inordinate share of limited state funding available for people with mental illness.[122] Minnesota now spends most of the funding available to provide mental health services in the criminal justice system on its SVP program.[123]

WHAT SHOULD WE DO WITH SVP LAWS?

There are two options on what can be done with existing SVP laws: abolition or reform.

Abolition

A good case can be made for abolishing SVP laws on the basis of two arguments: It is too easy to commit offenders, and it is all but impossible to gain release once committed.

Too Easy to Commit

These laws are not a legitimate and bona fide form of civil commitment. SVP laws do not identify a group of sex offenders who suffer from a recognized mental disorder that seriously interferes with their ability to obey the law. Mental health experts are unable to tell us definitively why sex offenders commit sex crimes.[124] One statutory definition of mental pathology, *mental abnormality*, has no authoritatively recognized meaning to MHPs. The other, *personality disorder*, has a very broad meaning that could include most sex offenders because of its subcategory, *antisocial personality disorder*. Nor can MHPs shed much light on whether someone has serious difficulty in controlling his sexual behavior.[125] In practice then, the prosecutor simply uses a defendant's criminal history to prove mental pathology, volitional impairment, and dangerousness.

---

[122] Fitch & Hammen, *supra* note 17.
[123] Eric S. Janus, *Sexual Predator Commitment Laws: Lessons for Law and the Behavioral Sciences*, 18 BEHAV. SCI. L. 5, 18 (2000).
[124] See chapter 1.
[125] See *supra* notes 53–56.

Impossible to Release

Once committed as an SVP, it is almost impossible to be released. Very few SVPs have been placed in outpatient commitment, and even fewer have been given their final release. This is not surprising. In fact, it is difficult for experts to determine when an SVP is unlikely to reoffend if released, for a number of reasons.

First, we simply do not know for certain whether treatment is effective in reducing sexual recidivism.[126] Thus, even if a state has provided constitutionally required treatment and the offender has sincerely participated in treatment and successfully completed it, we do not know for certain whether he has a lower risk of reoffending. Second, experts have not yet developed proven techniques for determining when a sex offender has changed for the better and is ready for release. Predictions of sexual dangerousness are based primarily on fixed or static facts that do not change.[127] Predictions of sexual safety are based primarily on dynamic factors that can change, such as modified attitudes toward victims and successful mastery and use of relapse prevention strategies. Experts have not yet identified which of these changeable variables reliably predict lessened sexual dangerousness, nor have they developed instruments like the actuarial instruments used to predict sexual dangerousness[128] to identify sex offenders who have lessened sexual dangerousness. In short, experts are better at predicting sexual dangerousness than at predicting sexual safety.[129] Finally, the significant procedural due process protections provided in SVP trials do not appear to work very well. In particular, juries will usually err on the side of safety and commit rather than release a convicted sex offender.[130]

Reforming SVP Laws

Although these laws should be repealed as soon as feasible, it is clear that a number of states will keep their SVP laws in force because of intense public pressure. Even then, important changes should be made in SVP laws.

Use the Medical Model of Diagnosis

An authentic scheme for civil commitment based on mental illness should be limited to those who suffer from a medically recognized mental

---

[126] *See* chapter 3

[127] *See* chapter 2.

[128] *See* chapter 2.

[129] For a thorough discussion of these issues, *see* John Q. La Fond & Bruce J. Winick, *A Therapeutic Jurisprudence Approach to Managing Sex Offender Risk: A Proposal for Sex Offender Reentry Courts*, 989 N.Y. ACAD. OF SCI. ANNALS 337 (2003).

[130] *See* La Fond, *supra* note 18.

disorder. Authoritative mental health organizations and texts do recognize a limited number of mental disorders, called *paraphilias*, that are based on sexually deviant desires and behaviors.[131] Many mental health experts argue that, in most cases, only sex offenders who suffer from a paraphilia should be subject to commitment under these laws.[132] SVP commitment should be limited to those who suffer from a recognized mental disorder.[133] Legislators should not have carte blanche power under our constitutional system of ordered liberty to designate a pattern of criminal offending as a mental illness without any scientific or medical basis.[134]

Require Two Convictions and Screen Better

Because most SVP laws require only a *single* conviction to qualify as an SVP, they subject far too many sex offenders to indefinite commitment. At the very least, these laws should require conviction of at least two qualifying offenses.

In addition, states must do a better job of screening records to determine which offenders should be identified as potential SVPs. At the very least, state-of-the-art actuarial instruments should be used to identify that group of sex offenders who truly do have a high risk of committing more sex crimes.

Limit Authority to File SVP Petitions

Most SVPs confer final authority to file on local prosecuting attorneys, most of whom are elected officials. The pressure on prosecutors to file SVP petitions whenever there is any possibility of a sex offender committing another crime is immense. It is always easier for an elected prosecutor to protect himself from voter reprisals by filing. Only MHPs who are experienced in diagnosing and treating sex offenders and truly independent of the prosecutor should be involved in the filing decision. A good argument can be made that no SVP petition should be filed unless these experts concur. A decision to file is tantamount to a decision to commit in most states.

Take Probable Cause Seriously

Judges must take the probable-cause hearing seriously, especially because many people languish in jails or prison for months and sometimes

---

[131] According to the American Psychiatric Association, the essential features of paraphilia are "recurrent, intense sexually arousing fantasies, sexual urges, or behaviors generally involving 1) nonhuman objects, 2) the suffering or humiliation of oneself or one's partner, or 3) children or other nonconsenting persons that occur over a period of at least 6 months. . . ." *See DSM–IV–TR, supra* note 11, at 566.

[132] *See, e.g.,* Judith V. Becker & William D. Murphy, *What We Know and Do Not Know About Assessing and Treating Sex Offenders*, 4 PSYCHOL. PUB. POL'Y & L. 116 (1998).

[133] For example, some individuals with brain damage or developmental disabilities may suffer from a recognized mental disorder that qualifies them for involuntary civil commitment under an SVP law.

[134] *See, e.g.,* Morse, *supra* note 63 and Janus, *supra* note 63.

years before they actually go to trial. Evaluations by state MHPs should be conducted *before* the probable-cause hearing. Some of these evaluations will be negative, thus eliminating the need to proceed any further in those cases. At the hearing, judges should probe the opinion of the state expert's diagnosis and its impact on the individual's ability to control his sexual behavior. If there is not sufficient evidence that the offender suffers from a qualifying mental condition that significantly interferes with his volitional control, the petition should be dismissed with prejudice. Only California seemingly eliminates a significant number of SVP cases at the probable-cause stage. Other states should learn from California.

Ensure a Speedy Trial

Pressure should be put on both prosecutors and defense counsel to bring these cases to trial within a reasonable time. On the filing of the petition, the Washington SVP law requires that the probable-cause hearing be held within 72 hours of taking the individual into custody and that the trial be held within 45 days of the probable-cause hearing.[135] The 45-day time limit is almost *never* met. No wonder some people do not go to trial until years after they were initially committed.

Limit Right to Jury Trial to Defendants

In many states, prosecutors can also request a jury trial, and they usually do, because they realize that a jury is more likely than a judge to commit someone as an SVP. Juries will invariably "play it safe" and commit rather than release a convicted sex offender.[136] Judges have more experience in making this type of decision and can better determine whether the prosecution has proven its case. Thus, only a defendant should be entitled to choose a trial before a judge or a jury; this is a right granted to defendants in many general civil commitment statutes.[137]

Provide Finality

Because commitment is a civil case and not a criminal case, there is no double jeopardy protection against a prosecutor retrying a case that he or she has lost. This allows prosecutors, literally, to keep trying until they finally win. If mental health experts conclude that an offender is not an SVP, some prosecutors feel free to "shop around" until they find some who

---

[135] Wash. Rev. Code § 71.09.040-050 (2002).
[136] La Fond, *supra* note 40.
[137] *See, e.g.,* Wash. Rev. Code § 71.09.050 (2002).

will.[138] If a jury has not committed someone after the government has had its "best shot," he should be released immediately.

Allow Outpatient Commitment at Outset

The law should allow a judge or jury to conclude that someone is an SVP, but in appropriate cases to also determine that he should be committed at the outset as an outpatient rather than placed in an institution. Without this option, juries have only two stark choices: commit or release. Understandably, juries and even judges are prone to err on the side of safety and commit sex offenders rather than release them. As detailed in chapter 7, effective risk-management strategies, including an aggressive community containment program, can control sex offenders who are living in the community, thereby reducing significantly their risk of reoffending. Outpatient commitment, eventually, should be less expensive than institutional confinement, while also allowing the level of control to be increased or decreased as officials learn more about how the offender is behaving.[139]

Limit the Terms of Commitment

Only California limits the term of commitment to 2 years. This term can be, and has been, renewed if necessary. Without a limited term, there is no pressure on institutional treatment teams to provide intensive treatment. Without some hope of release in the foreseeable future, there is no incentive for many SVPs to participate in treatment—and too many do not.[140]

Finally, without an explicit expectation of when most, although not all, SVPs should be ready for outpatient commitment, the number of SVPs in state institutions will grow, costs will increase dramatically, and any realistic hope of providing effective treatment may disappear. Some states reportedly are developing presumptive or average time periods for SVP commitment. At the end of this period, most SVPs would normally be expected to be placed on outpatient commitment or released. This is a welcome development.

Allow Staff to Release

Most SVP laws allow prosecutors to oppose a staff decision to release SVPs, even though staff members are the experts and have worked intensively with the offender. In some states, like Washington, prosecutors have

---

[138] *See supra* notes 98–103 and accompanying text.

[139] *See* chapter 7 for a more extensive discussion of how various risk management strategies could be implemented to protect the community.

[140] *See* La Fond, *supra* note 40 (describing how some SVPs are refusing to participate in treatment and how some SVPs are considered "untreatable."). *See also supra* notes 86–88 and accompanying text.

objected to the conditional release of almost every SVP, even though these individuals would be subject to outpatient commitment and control. Political pressure should not short-circuit a statute whose purpose, in theory, is to treat people and, after successful completion of treatment, to allow them to resume their lives in the community.

Insulate the System From Political Interference

The political pressure not to release SVPs into the community, even with aggressive supervision, is intense. The political pressure not to give them their final release, with or without supervision, is irresistible. Even courts, the mainstay of our constitutional system, seem unable to stand up to this pressure.[141] SVP laws must be revised to prevent another *Ghilotti* case.[142] In that case, the California Supreme Court virtually invited the government to use its own employees rather than independent evaluators to file recommitment petitions.[143] The SVP commitment system must be allowed to function without political interference. Otherwise, the public should be prepared to pay for warehousing a growing number of sex offenders at budget-busting costs and to fight ongoing right-to-treatment lawsuits.[144]

THE FUTURE OF SVP LAWS

After an initial spurt of SVP legislation, enthusiasm for these laws has dwindled. This is not surprising, for several reasons. First, these laws were passed as a stop-gap measure to keep dangerous sex offenders from being released after they have served their prison terms. For the most part, only states that had enacted determinate sentencing, had set relatively short sentences for serious sex crimes, and had abolished parole needed these laws to keep these men confined past their sentences. Many states, including those with SVP laws, have set much longer sentences for sex crimes and have also enacted mandatory minimum sentences for them. Many states have also passed "three-strike" laws that impose lifetime sentences on serious repeat criminals, including sex offenders.[145] Simply put, with harsher criminal

---

[141] John Q. La Fond, *Can Therapeutic Jurisprudence Remain Normatively Neutral?, Sexual Predator Laws: Their Impact on Participants and Policy*, 41 ARIZ. L. REV. 375 (1999).

[142] *See supra* notes 98–103 and accompanying text.

[143] People v. Ghilotti, 44 P.3d 949, n.7 (2002) ("We observe that nothing in the SVPA appears to preclude the use of Department employees, including staff psychologists and psychiatrists directly involved in the treatment of an already committed person, as the initial designated evaluators under section 6601, subdivision (d).").

[144] *See supra* notes 62–64 and accompanying text.

[145] *See* chapters 1 and 8 for a discussion of these laws.

sentencing in place, there will—eventually—be no need for SVP laws to provide a "back-stop" for inadequate sentencing laws.[146]

Second, these laws are extremely expensive and consume enormous financial, executive, and judicial resources. States that enact an SVP law can expect at least three generations of litigation.[147] The first generation will include legal challenges to the implementation of these laws, including procedural and evidentiary issues that state courts will have to resolve. The second generation will include challenges to the conditions of confinement and right to treatment lawsuits. SVPs will sue to make sure that the state provides treatment required by the Constitution and by the SVP statute. As we have seen, these costs are immense. Finally, a third generation of lawsuits will seek release of SVPs, many of whom will stay in SVP facilities for most of their lives, requiring more medical services as they age.[148] Simply put, SVP laws create "black holes" that burn through cash almost as fast as failing Internet companies.

Third, policymakers will, one hopes, recognize that other strategies for protecting the community against dangerous sex offenders are far superior and cost much less. These measures include long prison sentences for repeat violent sex offenders and risk-management strategies that protect the community while creating incentives for sex offenders to live safely in the community.[149]

A BETTER SOLUTION:
A "DANGEROUS SEX OFFENDER" SENTENCE

The real purpose of SVP laws is to keep very dangerous sex offenders in confinement so they cannot commit new sex crimes. Although SVP laws have the formal appearance of being civil commitment laws designed to withstand constitutional attacks, the essential element of proof presented by the government in SVP cases is that the individual is sexually dangerous. That is why the government presents evidence of his past sex crimes and introduces expert opinions that, because of his criminal history, the offender is dangerous and likely to commit another sex crime if released. The criminal justice system is more than capable of keeping extremely dangerous sex offenders confined for as long as they are dangerous, and at much less expense than SVP laws.

---

[146] Lieb, *supra* note 42.

[147] La Fond, *supra* note 40; *see also* La Fond, *supra* note 37; A.J. Harris, A Prospective Analysis of Sexually Violent Predator Civil Commitment Policies (2004) (Unpublished dissertation, New York University)

[148] La Fond, *supra* note 37.

[149] *See* chapter 8.

The Problem: Determinate Sentencing

During the past two decades, many states enacted determinate sentencing laws, specifying a limited range of sentences on the basis of the offender's criminal history and the crime for which he was convicted. Several factors influenced this movement. Some critics complained (with some justification) that criminal sentencing was racially biased. Sending someone considered dangerous to prison to protect society was too open-ended in the absence of any demonstrated expertise to predict dangerousness[150] or to rehabilitate him. Determinate sentencing could eliminate or severely limit the exercise of this bias under the guise of predicting dangerousness and would also acknowledge the absence of rehabilitative expertise.[151]

Others no longer believed in rehabilitation as a sound penological goal. In their view, criminals deserved to be punished for their crimes.[152] Many legal scholars supported the shift to determinate sentences by arguing that the primary purpose of punishment is retribution, paying the offender back for the harm he has done. In their view, there was no proof that either specific or general deterrence worked, and there was certainly no proof that offenders could be rehabilitated.[153] Thus, indeterminate sentences to reform the individual and to release him when he was successfully rehabilitated were no longer necessary. Even liberals worried that indeterminate sentences for rehabilitation were being abused.[154] As a result, many states enacted determinate sentences that do not currently provide sufficiently long sentences for dangerous sex offenders.[155]

The Solution: The "Sexually Dangerous Offender" Sentence

States with inadequate criminal sentences for very dangerous sex offenders should enact a "Sexually Dangerous Offender" sentencing law. Under this law, prosecutors could, after the second conviction of a serious sex crime, move to have the offender sentenced to an indeterminate term in addition to the normal punishment provided under the state's sentencing

---

[150] See Bruce J. Ennis & Thomas R. Litwack, *Psychiatry and the Presumption of Expertise: Flipping Coins in the Courtroom*, 62 CALIF. L. REV. 693 (1974) (setting forth a devastating critique of the claim that experts can predict dangerous behavior accurately and reliably).

[151] AMERICAN FRIENDS SERVICE COMMITTEE, STRUGGLE FOR JUSTICE: A REPORT ON CRIME AND PUNISHMENT IN AMERICA (1971); JAMES Q. WILSON, THINKING ABOUT CRIME (1975); ANDREW VON HIRSCH, COMMITTEE FOR THE STUDY OF INCARCERATION, DOING JUSTICE: THE CHOICE OF PUNISHMENTS (1976).

[152] ERNEST VAN DEN HAAG, PUNISHING CRIMINALS, CONCERNING A VERY OLD AND PAINFUL QUESTION (1975).

[153] Id.

[154] N.N. KITTRIE, THE RIGHT TO BE DIFFERENT: DEVIANCE AND ENFORCED THERAPY (1971).

[155] For a more thorough discussion of this changing ideology, see generally La Fond & Durham, *supra* note 9.

laws. This law should be constitutional so long as appropriate procedural due process, including the right to contest the state's evidence, to present evidence with the assistance of counsel and his expert, is provided to the defendant[156] and a jury makes this finding.[157]

The prosecution would have to present evidence at this special hearing that the defendant is a "sexually dangerous offender" because he has an enduring propensity to commit serious sex crimes and is more likely than not to do so if released into the community.[158] This hearing would focus solely on the offender's current sexual dangerousness. It would not try to "diagnose" the offender, nor would it require a finding that the offender has substantial difficulty in "controlling" his sexual conduct.

These findings are consistent with the expertise currently available. As mentioned in chapter 1, experts, using actuarial instruments that have been scientifically validated, can now identify a group of sex offenders who pose a serious risk of reoffending. As Hanson has noted, we can now identify a small subgroup of sex offenders whose rate of committing another sexual offense can be conservatively estimated at 50% and reasonably estimated at 80%.[159] Offenders at the high end of this predicted dangerousness should be sentenced to an indeterminate sentence under this proposed law. Experts can establish a proven, objective basis for concluding that the offender poses a very high risk of committing another sex crime. This should limit the inappropriate role that racial or class bias has too often played in our criminal justice system.

The evidence admissible at this sentencing hearing is very similar to the evidence currently presented at SVP trials. The prosecution should be able to present the offender's full criminal record. There is, however, no need to present live testimony from past victims. This evidence does not

---

[156] Specht v. Patterson, 386 U.S. 605 (1967) (holding that Colorado's Sex Offenders Act, which allowed the judge to sentence a convicted sex offender to a possible indeterminate life sentence if he found the offender "constitutes a threat of bodily harm to members of the public or is an habitual offender and mentally ill" violated procedural due process because the law did not afford a defendant a meaningful hearing at which he could contest the state's evidence and present his own evidence with the assistance of counsel.).

[157] Apprendi v. New Jersey, 530 U.S. 466, 490 (2000) (holding that a jury must find beyond a reasonable doubt any fact that extends a criminal sentence beyond that authorized by the statute). See also Ring v. Arizona, 122 S. Ct. 2428 (2002) (statute violates Sixth Amendment where, once jury found defendant guilty of first degree murder, the statute required the judge to determine presence or absence of aggravating factors necessary for the imposition of the death penalty; if the state makes an increase in defendant's authorized punishment contingent upon a finding of fact, that fact must be made by a jury beyond a reasonable doubt).

[158] At least six states with SVP laws currently require the jury to find that an SVP is "more likely than not" to commit another qualifying sex crime in order to commit him as an SVP. Some set an even higher standard. People v. Ghilotti, 27 Cal. 4th 888, 931 (2002) (Werdergar, J., concurring).

[159] R. Karl Hanson, *What Do We Know About Sex Offender Risk Assessment?*, 4 PSYCHOL. PUB. POL'Y & L. 50 (1998).

materially assist either the expert in formulating his or her opinion on sexual dangerousness or the trier of fact in determining the offender's past criminal record. Nor would experts consider it particularly useful in assessing the risk posed by the offender. Simply put, most of the evidence that prosecutors use at SVP trials to civilly commit someone years after he has served his criminal sentence is already available for use for sentencing the offender at his criminal trial.

Release

As discussed in chapter 2, there is also some modest basis for believing that treatment for sex offenders may reduce sexual recidivism. Sex offender treatment should be provided in prison for offenders sentenced under this provision because treatment offered soon after conviction is much more effective than treatment delayed until the end of an offender's prison term.[160] The offender must serve the normal sentence provided for under state law.

In addition, he would be confined for an indeterminate period thereafter. Prison treatment authorities would, if appropriate in light of the offender's progress in treatment, be able to recommend his release, one hopes to an aggressive community supervision program like those described in chapter 7. If a judge agreed with the treatment staff's recommendation, the offender would be released. This approach would provide strong incentives for convicted sex offenders to participate fully and sincerely in prison treatment programs.[161] It would also allow the state to confine these criminals for as long as they remain dangerous to the community. Sex offenders sentenced under this law who did not participate in treatment would be confined for life or, more likely, until their advancing age made reoffense unlikely.

The Canadian Experience

Canada has recently amended its criminal code to include indefinite sentencing provisions for sex offenders deemed to be "dangerous offenders." This group includes offenders who have (a) been convicted of statutorily specified sex offenses and (b) demonstrated a failure to control their sexual impulses in *any* sexual matter, not just the offense of conviction, thereby posing a likelihood of injury to others. The prosecution may submit its application for "dangerous offender" status either before the defendant is

---

[160] Robert M. Wettstein, A *Psychiatric Perspective on Washington's Sexually Violent Predators Statute*, 15 U. PUGET SOUND L. REV. 597 (1992).
[161] La Fond & Winick, *supra* note 129.

sentenced or within 6 months afterward. After this application is filed, the court appoints an expert to conduct a psychological assessment. If the court finds the defendant to be a "dangerous offender," it is *required* to impose an indefinite sentence, and the defendant must serve a minimum of 7 years before he will be eligible for parole.[162] Although Canada's "dangerous of-fender" provisions, which went into effect in 1997, are a powerful tool to protect the public against sexual violence, they have been rarely invoked since that time. This parsimonious use suggests that an indeterminate sen-tence based on dangerousness should be used only in extraordinary cases.

Canada has also enacted "long-term offender" provisions, which apply to those sexual offenders who do not satisfy "dangerous offender" criteria but who are, nonetheless, perceived as a significant risk to public safety. The prosecution must establish that there is both a "substantial risk" that the person will reoffend *and* a reasonable possibility that such risk could eventually be controlled in the community. An assessment of the defendant by a court-appointed expert assists the judge in making this determination. If the court concludes that the individual is a "long-term offender," the court must, in addition to the sentence for the crime of conviction, impose an additional period of supervision for up to 10 years.[163]

The Benefits

In addition to avoiding the subterfuge and hypocrisy of SVP laws and their extraordinary expense, this special sentencing law meets the problem head on. It confines very dangerous sex offenders for as long as necessary to prevent them from committing another sex crime. Using the criminal justice system in this way also satisfies basic principles of legality and notice, informing offenders in advance that if they commit serious sex crimes and are found to be dangerous, they may be punished indefinitely. It also avoids the unnecessary and inept use of "three-strike" laws that do not use state-of-the-art methods for predicting dangerousness and, as a result, overpre-dict it.[164]

---

[162] Dangerous Offenders and Long-Term Offenders Act, Criminal Code, Part XXIV, R.S.C. ch. C-46 § 753 et seq. (1985, amended 1997 ch. 17 § 4) (Can.).

[163] Id. For an in-depth discussion of Canada's long-term and dangerous sex offender provisions, *see* Yukimi Henry, *Psychiatric Gating: Questioning the Civil Committal of Convicted Sex Offenders*, 59 U. TORONTO FAC. L. REV. 229 (2001) and Isabel Grant, *Legislating Public Safety: The Business of Risk*, 3 CAN. CRIM. L. REV. 177 (1998). Canada has considered and rejected the idea of enacting civil commitment legislation aimed at sex offenders, on the basis of a task force finding that such a statute would pose serious constitutional problems and would be costly, unwieldy, and probably ineffective. *See* Henry, *supra*.

[164] *See supra* chapter 7.

SUMMARY

SVP laws are fatally flawed—morally, economically, and practically. They corrupt concepts of responsibility and illness, allow preventive detention under the guise of treatment, and drain scarce resources away from law-abiding citizens who are truly mentally ill and desperately need mental health services. These laws, at best, are only a bandage solution to a fundamental structural problem in the criminal justice system. Because they are so extraordinarily expensive, and will become even more expensive, they can hope to control only a relatively small number of sex offenders. SVP laws should be repealed as soon as possible. Instead, states should spend more money on keeping very dangerous sex offenders locked up longer and on providing effective risk-management programs to monitor many more sex offenders living in the community.[165]

The criminal justice system can protect society against very dangerous sex offenders more effectively and at much less cost. There is no good reason why policymakers should not use it to do the job.

---

[165] *Id.*

6

SHOULD SEX OFFENDERS BE CASTRATED?

During the 1990s, state lawmakers insisted that the government take even more drastic steps to prevent sexual recidivism. Legislators wanted the government to use drugs to change a sex offender's basic human biology. The drugs would eliminate or reduce his sex drive and thereby dramatically change his sexual behavior. The media quickly dubbed it "chemical castration." The logic was simple: A sex offender who does not have a sex drive will not commit more sex crimes.

Many states considered passing legislation that would allow states to use drugs to eliminate or significantly reduce offenders' sex drive.[1] As of 2002, five states had actually passed these so-called "chemical castration" laws, but others may follow. California was first in 1996,[2] with Montana,[3] Florida,[4] and Texas[5] enacting their own chemical castration laws in 1997. In 1999, Oregon enacted a law that requires some sex offenders to be

---

[1] For a canvass of states that have considered enacting chemical castration laws, see Robert D. Miller, *Forced Administration of Sex-Drive Reducing Medications to Sex Offenders: Treatment or Punishment?*, 4 PSYCHOL. PUB. POL'Y & L. 175 (1998).
[2] CAL. PENAL CODE § 645 (West 2004).
[3] MONT. CODE ANN. § 45-5-512 (2003).
[4] FLA. STAT. ANN. § 794.0235 (West 2003).
[5] TEX. GOV'T CODE ANN. § 501.601 (Vernon 2003).

chemically castrated on their release from prison.[6] In addition, California is insisting that some sex offenders committed under its SVP law[7] take these drugs as a condition of being released from a secure institution to placement in a community release program.[8]

As discussed in chapter 3, some research suggests that surgical castration may be effective in reducing sexual recidivism.[9] Drugs may also have the same effect.[10] Nonetheless, state action that physically or chemically changes an individual's human biology raises profound moral, constitutional, and ethical questions. Can the state use physical or chemical castration to punish sex offenders, or does castration violate the Eighth Amendment's ban on "cruel and unusual punishment"? Does this physical or chemical intrusion violate a person's constitutional rights to bodily integrity and to procreate? Does it make a difference whether the state chemically castrates sex offenders to treat them? Should sex offenders be allowed to choose surgical castration to avoid prison or get out of prison sooner? Or is biological reengineering induced by the state contrary to basic American values and therefore unacceptable, even if the individual consents?

In this chapter, I examine recent state laws that require or allow the state to alter the biology of sex offenders by giving them drugs that reduce the body's production or use of testosterone. I also analyze whether sex offenders can be surgically castrated to avoid prison or reduce their sentences. Then, I explore whether the Constitution allows these drastic measures. Finally, I consider whether society should use this radical strategy to reduce sexual recidivism.

TYPES OF CASTRATION

Castration to reduce sexual recidivism, whether by surgery or by drugs, is based on certain assumptions. Policymakers assume that eliminating or suppressing the production or uptake of testosterone will suppress an offender's deviant sexual fantasies and sex drive. In turn, this will stop his paraphilic criminal behavior. Simply put, the individual will no longer want to engage in illegal sexual conduct.

---

[6] OR. REV. STAT. § 144.625 (2001). *See* Carole M. Wong, *Chemical Castration: Oregon's Innovative Approach to Sex Offender Rehabilitation, or Unconstitutional Punishment?* 80 OR. L. REV. 267 (2001).
[7] See chapter 5 for a thorough discussion of sexually violent predator (SVP) laws.
[8] People v. Ghilotti, 44 P.3d 949 (Cal. 2002). *See also* Pamela J. Podger, *Marin D.A. Files to Detain Rapist at Atascadero, Patrick Ghilotti Due for Release*, S. F. CHRON., Nov. 29, 2001, at A23, *available at* 2001 WL 3421008.
[9] See chapter 3.
[10] AM. PSYCHIATRIC ASS'N, DANGEROUS SEX OFFENDERS: A TASK FORCE REPORT OF THE AMERICAN PSYCHIATRIC ASSOCIATION (1999).

Surgical Castration

In this procedure, surgeons physically remove a man's testicles from his scrotum. The primary effect is to reduce the production of the male hormone testosterone and thereby eliminate or diminish sex drive. The surgery, called an *orchiectomy*, is seemingly "not particularly painful and has few side effects."[11] It is, however, irreversible. It is currently an accepted medical procedure in the United States for the treatment of testicular and prostrate cancer.[12] Surgical castration has also been used, primarily in Europe, to treat sex offenders, although its use there has declined significantly over recent decades.

Surgical castration does not necessarily eliminate sexual desire or prevent sexual functioning. Two small studies indicate that a significant percentage of castrated men, ranging from 40% to 50%, continued to have intercourse within 3 to 7 years of the operation. A larger study found the following:

> Libido and sexual activity among the offenders was practically extinct within 6 months of castration for over seventy-five percent of castrates; libido and sexual activity were possible with intense stimulation for about fifteen percent of castrates, while about ten percent of the castrates had reduced levels of libido and sexual activity.[13]

However, taking testosterone readily reverses the effects of surgical castration.[14] Male sex offenders without testes can usually restore sexual desire and function simply by taking drugs.

Surgical removal of the testes does have side effects, which can include the following:

> ... changes in metabolic processes, loss of protein, augmentation of pituitary functions, augmentation of keratin found in urine, lowering of the hemoglobin percentage, changes in fat distribution in the body,

---

[11] J. Michael Bailey & Aaron S. Greenberg, *The Science and Ethics of Castration: Lessons From the Morse Case*, 92 Nw. U. L. Rev. 1225, 1238 (1998). Side effects may include: "changes in metabolic processes, loss of protein, augmentation of pituitary functions, augmentation of keratin found in urine, lowering of the hemoglobin percentage, changes in fat distribution in the body, diminution of the calcium content of bones after a period of time, hot flashes and sweating, and diminishment of beard and body hair." William Winslade et al., *Castrating Pedophiles Convicted of Sex Offenses Against Children: New Treatment or Old Punishment?*, 51 SMU L. Rev. 349 at 371 (1998) *citing* G.K. Stürup, *Treatment of Sexual Offenders in Herstedvester, Denmark, the Rapists*, 204 Acta Psychiatry Scandanavia 14 (1968). Psychological side effects may include "depressive reactions, suicidal tendencies, emotional lability, and indifference to life." Winslade et al. at 371 *citing* Reinhard Wille & Klaus M. Beier, *Castration in Germany*, 2 Annals Sex Res. 103 (1989). Winslade et al. noted that, "these mental effects are very much in dispute." Winslade et al. at 371. In one study, the most common complaint of those who had surgical castration was the stigma of empty scrota. Implants are now available to address this concern. Bailey & Greenberg, at 1235.
[12] Winslade et al., *supra* note 11, at 349.
[13] *Id.* at 370.
[14] *Id.*

diminution of the calcium content of bones after a period of time, hot flashes and sweating, and diminishment of beard and body hair.[15]

Men who have been castrated can also suffer from adverse psychological distress, including depression, suicidal tendencies, emotional lability, and indifference to life.[16]

One influential professional organization, the Association for the Treatment of Sex Offenders (ATSA), opposes the use of surgical castration of sex offenders. Its position paper, *Anti-Androgen Therapy and Surgical Castration*, states, "ATSA is opposed to surgical castration procedures based on the availability of anti-androgen medications which can achieve the same, if not better, results."[17]

Chemical Castration

Drugs can also reduce the production of testosterone or prevent the uptake of testosterone by androgen receptors located throughout the body, which convert the testosterone into male sexual drive. These chemicals can have the same effect as surgical castration in reducing male sexual urges. Depending on dose, it may cause decreases in erections, ejaculations, and the production of sperm. These drugs also suppress or eliminate sexual fantasies[18] and may reduce aggression generally, including sexual aggression.[19]

The primary drug used currently to suppress the production of testosterone is medroxyprogesteron acetate (MPA), which has been approved by the Federal Drug Administration (FDA) for the treatment of hormonally related diseases in women and as a contraceptive.[20] MPA is also clinically appropriate to reduce abnormally strong sex drive or sexual fantasies. Cyproterone acetate (CPA) is the primary drug used to block uptake of testosterone by androgen receptors.

Both types of drugs may result in an asexual individual who loses both deviant and nondeviant sex drive and fantasies. A more ideal result would be the loss of only deviant fantasies and urges.[21] In any event, their use may provide relief from intrusive sexual fantasies and urges or help individuals

---

[15] *Id.* at 371 *citing* G.K. Stürup, *Treatment of Sexual Offenders in Herstedvester, Denmark, the Rapists*, 204 ACTA PSYCHIATRY SCANDANAVIA 14 (1968).

[16] Winslade et al., *supra* note 11, at 371, *citing* Reinhard Wille & Klaus M. Beier, *Castration in Germany*, 2 ANNALS SEX RES. 103 (1989).

[17] *Anti-Androgen Therapy and Surgical Castration*, *available at* http://www.atsa.com/ppantiandro.html (last visited Feb. 9, 2004).

[18] American Psychiatric Association, *supra* note 10, at 106.

[19] *Id.*

[20] *See* Miller, *supra* note 1, at 181.

[21] American Psychiatric Association, *supra* note 10, at 103. There is some evidence that cyproterone acetate (CPA), a form of chemical castration, may suppress a pedophile's arousal to children, while enhancing his arousal to adult consensual adult activity. *Id.* at 119.

resist acting on the prohibited urges. Taking testosterone or discontinuing the drugs may reverse this effect, although blood tests would reveal this.[22] Unlike surgical castration, chemical castration can be reversed.[23]

The side effects of these drugs are similar to those caused by surgical castration, although some scholars believe that chemical castration's side effects may be more serious.[24] These effects include weight gain, hyperinsulinemic response to glucose, diabetes mellitus, irregular gallbladder functioning, fatigue or lethargy, testicular atrophy (i.e., decrease in size of the testes), sweats, nightmares, dyspnea (i.e., difficulty breathing), hypogonadism (i.e., impaired capacity of the testes to produce male hormone), hot and cold flashes, leg cramps, hypertension, thrombosis (i.e., blood clot), and insomnia. Some dispute exists over whether feminization occurs.[25]

The American Psychiatric Association Task Force on Dangerous Sex Offenders is optimistic that chemical castration can be effective in reducing sexual reoffending and, in selected cases, it would support the use of these drugs for *treatment*. It concluded that pharmacological treatment of sex offenders with these drugs "is successful in reducing recidivism rates through the reduction of sexual fantasies, sexual drive, sexual arousal, and sexual behavior."[26] Although not stating its opposition explicitly, a fair reading of the Task Force Report clearly indicates that the American Psychiatric Association would not support *involuntary* surgical castration of sex offenders for *any* purpose.[27]

THE IMPACT OF CASTRATION ON SEXUAL RECIDIVISM

Surgical castration, because of its intrusiveness, has been used infrequently and primarily on the most serious sex offenders, such as rapists and those who victimize children. Studies conducted primarily in Europe report sexual offense recidivism after this procedure of less than 5% over 20 years in large numbers of sex offenders. These studies on surgical castration provide the theoretical basis for using drugs to reduce testosterone for the purpose of reducing deviant sexual urges and sexual reoffending.[28]

Despite its intrusiveness, some scholars are very confident this research establishes that surgical castration is effective in reducing sexual recidivism. Winslade and his colleagues state that a 30-year follow-up of 900 men who

---

[22] Bailey & Greenberg, *supra* note 11, at 1235–36.
[23] Miller, *supra* note 1, at 181–82.
[24] Bailey & Greenberg, *supra* note 11, at 1230.
[25] Miller, *supra* note 1, at 182.
[26] American Psychiatric Association, *supra* note 10, at 118.
[27] *Id.* at 103–04.
[28] *Id.* at 104.

underwent voluntary castration in Denmark found that only 20 of them had committed another sex crime during that time. This number is a reoffense rate of 2.2%.[29] Another study followed 738 sexual offenders castrated between 1929 and 1959; it found that only 10 of them committed another sex crime. This number is a relapse rate of 1.4% to 2.4% (depending on adjustments for shorter follow-up time for some of the men).[30] After reviewing the research literature, and noting that castration is no longer practiced in Denmark and is becoming less common in Germany, Winslade et al. concluded the following:

> In sum, there is clear and uncontroverted evidence that surgical castration as a therapeutic intervention for persons who have pedophilic disorders is effective, both with respect to libido and sexual activity and, importantly reduced sexual offending. While castration does have side effects, this is true for alternatives such as pharmacological regimes . . . For purposes of providing a clinically appropriate means for providing relief from what is a debilitating and life-long disorder, surgical castration cannot be discounted.[31]

Several studies involving small sample sizes support the conclusion that drugs, particularly CPA, can substantially reduce sexual recidivism in some sex offenders and that these positive effects continue even after the end of treatment. Thus, CPA can be used intermittently and still be effective in reducing sexual recidivism.[32] The American Psychiatric Association Task Force Report supports the use of drugs to treat sex offenders in appropriate cases. It has concluded, "The pharmacological treatment of the paraphilias (including sex offenders) with antiandrogens and hormonal agents is successful in reducing recidivism rates through the reduction of sexual fantasies, sexual arousal, and sexual behavior."[33]

Although the European research seems to show great promise that surgical castration reduces sexual reoffending, it is subject to serious methodological limitations. Most of these studies were uncontrolled or partially controlled and generally compared sex offenders who had *consented* to castration with similar sex offenders who either had not consented or were not offered castration.[34] Thus, the two groups are not similar in important re-

---

[29] Winslade et al., *supra* note 11, at 372–73, *citing* G.K. Stürup, *Treatment of Sexual Offenders in Herstedvester, Denmark, the Rapists*, 204 ACTA PSYCHIATRY SCANDANAVIA 14 (1968).
[30] Winslade et al., *supra* note 11, at 372–73, *citing* Jorgen Ortmann, *The Treatment of Sexual Offenders*, 3 INT'L J. L. & PSYCHIATRY 443 (1980).
[31] Winslade at al., *supra* note 11, at 376.
[32] American Psychiatric Association, *supra* note 10, at 110–11.
[33] *Id.* at 118.
[34] Grant T. Harris et al., *Appraisal and Management of Risk in Sexual Aggressors: Implications for Criminal Justice Policy*, 4 PSYCHOL. PUB. POL'Y & L. 73, 96 (1998).

spects. As a result, it is not clear that the reduction in sexual offending for the castrated group was caused solely by castration. It might be attributable, instead, to their desire to stop offending, as manifested by their consent to castration, rather than to the effect of the surgical procedure. Because of this significant flaw in the research design, it is impossible to attribute with certainty the reduction in sexual recidivism to castration.

Other factors also confound the studies' results. Some studies included individuals who would not now be considered sex offenders, such as adult homosexuals.[35] Most studies included heterogeneous sex offenders, including, for example, both pedophiles and adult rapists of women. Some have also included mentally ill or retarded sex offenders as well as exhibitionists.[36] Consequently, most studies do not differentiate recidivism rates for different types of offenders.[37] Simply put, these studies cannot establish which types of sex offenders might have lower recidivism rates if castrated and which might not. For example, experts cannot say that child molesters might have a lower recidivism rate if castrated, but rapists of adult women would not. And, of course, as noted in chapter 2, measuring recidivism rates accurately for sex offenders is difficult.[38]

Harris et al.[39] reviewed a number of studies, conducted primarily in Europe (especially Denmark), on the effect of surgical castration on sex offense recidivism.[40] They reviewed two major studies, one by Stürup in 1968[41] and 1972 and another by Freund in 1980,[42] that examined the impact of surgical castration on sexual recidivism. On the basis of results from a small sample, Stürup concluded that castration reduced sexual recidivism. Freund, who reviewed more studies involving more sex offenders, concluded that sexual recidivism was very low among castrated sex offenders, even though sex offenders considered for castration were at relatively high risk for sex offending.[43] After reviewing these studies, Harris and his coauthors concluded the following:

> [I]t seems beyond doubt that castration reduces sexual drive, and it may reduce the risk of sex offending among offenders whose offenses are

---

[35] Id. at 95–97.

[36] Bailey & Greenberg, supra note 11, at 1232.

[37] Id.

[38] See chapter 2, notes 39–45 and accompanying text.

[39] Harris et al., supra note 34, at 95–97.

[40] Surgical castration was conducted in Germany during the Nazi regime. It was also used with some frequency in Denmark and Germany until the early 1970s. Its use in Europe has diminished significantly. Winslade et al., supra note 11.

[41] Id. citing G.K. Stürup, Treatment of Sexual Offenders in Herstedvester, Denmark, the Rapists, 204 Acta Psychiatry Scandanavia 14 (1968).

[42] Harris et al., supra note 34, at 96–97, citing Kurt Freund, Therapeutic Sex Drive Reduction, 62 (Supp. 287) Acta Psychiatry Scandanavia 5 (1980).

[43] Harris et al., supra note 34, at 96.

limited to sexual ones and who regard themselves as having freely consented. However, it seems that it cannot provide a solution to the problem of reducing sexual recidivism until the issue of consent is resolved.[44]

NEW STATE CASTRATION LAWS

Legislation in various jurisdictions in the mid-1990s allowed castration as either a form of punishment or, in one case, as a form of treatment for sex offenders. I examine these new laws by state in this section.

Chemical Castration as Punishment

A number of state legislatures have recently enacted laws that require or permit sex offenders to be chemically castrated as part of sentencing them after conviction of a sex crime. Some *permit* judges to impose chemical castration as punishment on first-time sex offenders who commit sex crimes against underage victims. Others *require* judges to impose such punishment on sex offenders who commit a second offense of this kind.

California

In 1996, a California law that authorized this type of scheme went into effect.[45] Anyone convicted of a first-time, specified sex offense against a female victim under 13 years old may be subjected to chemical castration as a condition of parole. Anyone who commits a second such crime *must* be chemically castrated as a condition of parole;[46] however, a defendant may choose surgical castration instead.[47] If the defendant refuses to accept chemical castration, or surgical castration in its place, then he may not be paroled and will remain in prison until the end of his sentence.

The law is designed to reduce sexual recidivism. The statutory language clearly indicates a punitive intent. The law does not require any assessment of the offender by a medical professional to determine whether the offender suffers from a paraphilia, which is a recognized sexual mental disorder, or to determine whether these drugs are clinically indicated or medically

---

[44] *Id.*
[45] *See* Act of Sept. 17, 1996, ch. 596 §2, 1996 Cal. Legis. Serv. 2711 (West) (codified as amended at CAL. PENAL CODE § 645 (West 2004)).
[46] The defendant must be informed about the treatment and its side effects.
[47] CAL. PENAL CODE § 645(f) (West 2003).

appropriate for him or whether they are likely to cause adverse side effects if given to a particular individual. It only requires that the defendant be informed about what these drugs will do and their potential side effects.[48] The offender cannot refuse chemical castration if he wants to be released on parole.[49]

Florida

Florida passed a similar law, which went into effect on May 30, 1997.[50] A court may impose chemical castration as a punishment on first-time sex offenders who commit a sexual battery, and *must* impose it on repeat offenders. A court-appointed medical expert (undefined in the law) must first find that the offender is an "appropriate" candidate for the treatment, though it is not clear whether the expert must examine the offender or his records or simply make a determination on other grounds.[51] Failure to submit to chemical castration no later than 1 week prior to his release from prison is itself a felony in Florida, and the offender can be convicted and imprisoned if he refuses to take the drugs.[52] This law effectively coerces a prisoner to either submit to castration or have his prison sentence extended. The law does allow an offender to undergo surgical castration instead of chemical castration.[53]

Montana

In 1997, Montana passed a law similar to that of California.[54] Unlike the California law, however, it allows a judge to impose chemical castration only on certain sex offenders; it does not require him or her to impose it. Like the Florida law, the offender must start taking drugs 1 week before his release from prison and continue on them after his release. The law was subsequently amended to require that chemical castration be "medically safe" for the offender.[55] Presumably, it could not be imposed if there was a significant medical risk to the offender.[56]

---

[48] Winslade et al., *supra* note 11, at 377.
[49] CAL. PENAL CODE § 645(f).
[50] Act effective Oct. 1, 1997, ch. 97–184, 1997 Fla. Sess. Law Serv. (West) (codified at FLA. STAT. ANN. § 794.0235 (West 2003)).
[51] Winslade et al., *supra* note 11, at 382.
[52] FLA. STAT. ANN. §§ 794.0235(1), (5)(a)-(b) (2003).
[53] Id. § 794.0235(1)(b).
[54] See Act of Apr. 19, 1997, ch. 334, 52, 1997 Mont. Laws (codified at MONT. CODE ANN. §45-5-512 (2003).
[55] See Act of Apr. 19, 1997, ch. 341, sec. 2, § 2(2)A, 1997 Mont. Laws (codified as amended at MONT. CODE ANN. § 45-5-512(a)(A) (2003)).
[56] Winslade et al., *supra* note 11, at 380–81.

Oregon

Oregon's 1999 law mandates chemical castration for selected sex offenders who are about to be released and whose "suitability" has been established by the Department of Corrections.[57] The department evaluates eligible sex offenders and decides who would most likely benefit from this regime. A competent physician then medically examines and evaluates the group. If chemical castration is determined to be medically inappropriate for any individual after this evaluation, that person is excluded. The purpose of this law is to "reduce the risk of reoffending after release on parole or postprison supervision."[58]

Other States

Other states have enacted "chemical castration" laws that allow or require courts or parole boards to condition probation, parole, or suspended sentences on selected sex offenders taking these drugs.[59] Even more states will surely enact similar laws.

Summary

Clearly, all of these statutes are punitive in purpose and effect. Castration is imposed as a direct result of a conviction for a specified sex crime, and no other factual finding is generally required. In some cases, the sentencing judge or parole board has no choice: The judge or the board *must* order the offender to be chemically castrated. Although chemical castration may be an appropriate treatment for some sex offenders who give their informed consent to it, no serious argument can be made that these laws do not impose punishment on criminals. Failure to take the drugs results in continued confinement rather than release on probation or parole. In some cases, not taking the drugs is itself a felony carrying an additional prison term. The clear purpose of such laws is to protect society by preventing the offender from committing another sex crime after his release from prison. Drugs are not used because they are clinically indicated or medically appropriate to treat an offender's diagnosed mental disorder, nor is the offender's informed consent required, as it would be for bona fide medical care that is intended to benefit the individual.

---

[57] A "suitable" inmate must satisfy three criteria. First and second, the inmate must have a current or past conviction of a sex crime and must be within 6 months of release on parole or postprison supervision. Third, the inmate's present incarceration must be for a second conviction of a sex crime, and the inmate must lack intellectual capacity for impulse control or have demonstrated that he/she has excessive sex drive. OR. ADMIN. R. 291-202-0030(1) (2002).
[58] OR. REV. STAT. § 144.625(1) (2001).
[59] These include Georgia, GA. CODE ANN. § 42-9-44.2 (2002); Iowa, IOWA CODE § 903B.1 (2003); Louisiana, LA. REV. STAT. ANN. 15:538 (West 2004); and Wisconsin, WIS. STAT. § 304.06 (2003).

Surgical Castration as Treatment

A Texas law, effective May 20, 1997, allows physicians to perform surgical castration on inmates, but only those who have been convicted twice for indecency, sexual assault, or aggravated assault involving a child younger than 17 years old.[60] Unlike the California, Florida, Montana, and Oregon laws, castration in Texas is not imposed to punish the offender. Instead, it is offered as treatment to sex offenders who give their informed consent to taking these drugs.

Admirably, the Texas statute tries to guarantee that the inmate's decision to undergo this procedure is truly voluntary and that he does so only because it thinks it is in *his* best interest. The law makes it very clear that judges cannot require the offender to be castrated as a condition of being placed in community supervision and that parole boards cannot require the procedure as a condition of parole or release to mandatory supervision. Neither the prosecutor nor the defense counsel can introduce evidence that the offender will be castrated prior to sentencing. Thus, being castrated has no impact on an offender's sentence or release from prison. This removes any incentive for an offender to be castrated to shorten his period of confinement.

Procedural protections assure that a sex offender is castrated only for a therapeutic purpose. He must be over 21 and request castration in writing. The physician must also obtain his "informed, written consent" to the procedure. In addition, a psychiatrist and a psychologist experienced in treating sex offenders must evaluate the inmate and find that he is a "suitable candidate for the procedure." A monitor with experience in mental health, law, and ethics must consult with the inmate to ensure that he has been fully informed about the procedure and that his consent is voluntary.[61] If the monitor concludes that the inmate's decision is not free from coercion, the monitor has a legal duty to advise the inmate to withdraw his consent to the procedure.[62]

CONSTITUTIONAL ANALYSIS

In this section, I analyze point by point whether castration is constitutionally permissible. I use the usual factors for analyzing a punishment's constitutionality: Does it constitute cruel and unusual punishment? Does it violate substantive due process? Are other rights infringed upon?

---

[60] *See* Act of May 5, 1997, ch. 14 §§ 1-5, 1997 Tex. Sess. Law Serv. 287 (Vernon) (codified as amended at TEX. GOV'T CODE ANN. §§ 501.061-.062 and partially at TEX. CODE CRIM. PROC. ANN. art. 37.07, § 3(h)).
[61] Winslade et al., *supra* note 11, at 385.
[62] *Id.* at 385–86.

Cruel and Unusual Punishment

The Eighth Amendment to the U.S. Constitution forbids punishment that is "cruel and unusual."[63] The Supreme Court would undoubtedly conclude that any statute that authorizes or requires surgical or chemical castration on conviction of a criminal offense or as a condition of parole is *punitive* in purpose and effect and, consequently, subject to scrutiny under this constitutional clause.[64] The more difficult question would be whether the Court would hold that either type of castration is "cruel and unusual" punishment under Eighth Amendment jurisprudence and, thus, prohibited by the Constitution.[65]

Early Cases

Cases from the first half of the 20th century, although somewhat mixed, on balance seemed to conclude, without actually so holding, that surgically castrating sex offenders to punish them would be unconstitutional. For example, in a 1910 case, *Weems v. United States*,[66] the U.S. Supreme Court described surgical castration as "barbaric" and disproportionate for the offense of conviction.[67] In 1942, in *Skinner v. Oklahoma*, the Court prohibited a forced vasectomy on the grounds that the Oklahoma Habitual Criminal Sterilization Act ran "afoul" of equal protection and fundamental-rights considerations as applied to Skinner. The defendant had been sentenced to a forced vasectomy after his third conviction for crimes that involved "moral turpitude" (such as stealing chickens) under the Oklahoma statute.[68] These cases could be distinguished today because neither defendant was convicted of a sex crime and no serious argument was made then that castration was a reasonable means of preventing those convicted criminals from committing another nonsex crime.

Lower federal courts from the early part of the 20th century have concluded that compelled vasectomies, even when performed on convicted sex offenders, were "cruel and unusual punishment." In 1914, a federal court

---

[63] U.S. CONST. amend. VIII.

[64] In Kansas v. Hendricks, 521 U.S. 346, 361-63 (1997), the Court stated that a law will be considered punitive rather than civil in nature if it implicates either of the primary objectives of criminal punishment—retribution or deterrence—by, for example, requiring criminal conviction or criminal intent as a prerequisite to applying the law in question.

[65] *See infra* notes 66–96 and accompanying text.

[66] 217 U.S. 349 (1910).

[67] Weems, an employee of the Philippine government, was sentenced under Philippine law to 15 years in prison for falsifying a pay voucher for approximately 600 Philippine pesos. *Weems,* 217 U.S. at 357–58. The Court's reference to castration as "barbaric" was in the context of its discussion of the extent to which a 15-year sentence was excessive in view of the crime for which Weems had been convicted. *Id.* at 377.

[68] Oklahoma v. Skinner, 316 U.S. 535, 537, 541 (1942). *See also* Williams v. Smith, 131 N.E. 2 (Ind. 1921) (enjoining forced vasectomy on due process grounds).

struck down a law that authorized vasectomies to be performed on convicted sex offenders, concluding that castration constituted cruel and unusual punishment.[69] The court said,

> The physical suffering may not be so great, but that is not the only test of cruel punishment; the humiliation, the degradation, the mental suffering are always present and known by all the public, and will follow him wheresoever he may go. This belongs to the Dark Ages.[70]

In 1918, a federal court agreed, striking down a Nevada law that authorized a judge to compel a convicted sex offender to undergo a vasectomy:

> Reformation of the criminal is a wise and humane purpose of punishment, to be disregarded only when the death penalty is inflicted. It needs no argument to establish the proposition that degrading and humiliating punishment is not conducive to the resumption of upright and self-respecting life. When the penalty is paid, when the offender is free to resume his place in society, he should not be handicapped by the consciousness that he bears on his person, and will carry to his grave, a mutilation which, as punishment, is a brand of infamy. True, rape is an infamous crime; the punishment should be severe; but even for such an offender the way to an upright life, if life is spared, should not be unnecessarily obstructed. It will not do to argue that, inasmuch as the death penalty may be inflicted for this crime, vasectomy, or any other similar mutilation of the body, cannot be regarded as cruel, because the greater includes the less. The fact that the extreme penalty is not exacted is evidence that the criminal is considered worthy to live, and to attempt reformation.[71]

Although courts in these cases did not expressly consider surgical castration, they did condemn forced vasectomies as violating the Eighth Amendment's prohibition on "cruel and unusual punishment because they eliminated the offender's capacity to procreate. Because courts have struck down the lesser punishment of a coerced vasectomy as "cruel and unusual punishment," it is logical to assume they would also declare the harsher punishment of surgical castration unconstitutional.

Later Cases

No reported case since 1950 has been found in which a court approved surgical castration of a convicted sex offender over his objection. However,

---

[69] Davis v. Berry, 216 F. 413 (S.D. Iowa 1914), *rev'd*, 242 U.S. 468 (1917).
[70] *Davis*, 216 F. at 416. *But see* State v. Feilen, 126 Pac. 75 (Wash. 1912) (upholding trial court's order sentencing Feilen to life imprisonment and compelled vasectomy for crime of statutory rape).
[71] Mickle v. Henrichs, 262 F. 687, 691 (D. Nev. 1918). *See also* Coker v. Georgia, 433 U.S. 584, 592, 596 (1977), in which the Court ruled that imposition of the death penalty for the crime of rape constituted cruel and unusual punishment.

courts have taken contrary positions in cases in which the offenders consented to this procedure, even in cases in which the prosecutor or trial judge reduced the sentence because the offender agreed to, or did undergo, surgical castration.[72]

The Death Penalty Cases

During the 1970s, the Supreme Court handed down two important decisions reviewing Eighth Amendment challenges to the death penalty. In *Gregg v. Georgia*, the Supreme Court concluded that the meaning of this constitutional provision must be derived from the "evolving standards of decency that mark the progress of a maturing society."[73] In *Furman v. Georgia*,[74] the Court articulated a four-part test to be applied in determining whether a particular punishment violates that constitutional prohibition. In a concurring opinion, Justice Brennan concluded as follows:

> The test, then, will ordinarily be a cumulative one: If a punishment is unusually severe, if there is a strong probability that it is inflicted arbitrarily, if it is substantially rejected by contemporary society, and if there is no reason to believe that it serves any penal purpose more effectively than some *less severe punishment*, then the continued infliction of that punishment violates the command of the Clause that the State may not inflict inhuman and uncivilized punishments upon those convicted of crimes.[75]

Thus, the Court will consider whether a punishment is (a) too extreme or barbaric; (b) arbitrarily imposed; (c) excessive, disproportionate, or inconsistent with contemporary norms; or (d) unnecessary to achieve a penal purpose that could be served by a less severe punishment.[76]

More recently, in *Atkins v. Virginia*,[77] the Supreme Court held that the Eighth Amendment's prohibition on cruel and unusual punishment barred the imposition of the death penalty on a mentally retarded defendant. The Court reiterated the central principle of this constitutional protection: It prohibits "excessive sanctions."[78] Thus, punishment for a crime must be

---

[72] *See infra* note 130 and accompanying text.
[73] Gregg v. Georgia, 428 U.S. 153, 172 (1976) (quoting Trop v. Dulles, 356 U.S. 86, 101 (1958)).
[74] 408 U.S. 238 (1972).
[75] 408 U.S. at 283 (Brennan, J., concurring) (emphasis added).
[76] *See, e.g.*, Mark Spatz, Comment, *Shame's Revival: An Unconstitutional Regression*, 4 U. PA. J. CONST. L. 827 (2002) (discussing use of "shaming punishments" in light of *Furman's* Eighth Amendment analysis of the factors that constitute cruel and unusual punishment) and Kimberly Orem, *Evolution of Eighth Amendment Dichotomy: Substantive and Procedural Protections Within the Cruel and Unusual Punishment Clause*, 12 CAP. DEF. J. 345 (2000) (discussing post-*Furman* Eighth Amendment jurisprudence in capital cases).
[77] 536 U.S. 304 (2002).
[78] *Id.* at 310.

"graduated and proportional to the offense."[79] Note that constitutional review to ensure proportionality strongly suggests that the Eighth Amendment limits the magnitude of a punishment that is imposed on an offender for a retributive purpose (i.e., punishment intended to be a penalty imposed on a criminal as a necessary and appropriate response to his crime must be commensurate in degree to the harm he has caused).

In *Atkins*, the Court also reaffirmed earlier holdings that whether a punishment is excessive must be judged by "evolving standards of decency that mark the progress of a maturing society."[80] Thus, proportionality review must be informed by "objective standards" as much possible. The best evidence of these standards is "legislation enacted by the country's legislatures."[81] The Court observed that its own judgment would also inform its decisions when it resolves a challenge based on a claim of cruel and unusual punishment. It would have to consider whether "there is reason to disagree with the judgment reached by the citizenry and its legislators."[82]

The Eighth Amendment's ban on cruel and unusual punishment is an *absolute* limitation of governmental power. The government is not free to argue that it has extremely important interests that can only be achieved by such practices. Consequently, if courts conclude that castration is "cruel and unusual punishment," the inquiry stops there, and the practice must stop.

To date, the Supreme Court has not been called on to determine whether surgical or chemical castration imposed to punish a sex offender—with or without his consent—is cruel and unusual punishment. It seems fair to conclude that the Court will apply the general Eighth Amendment's "cruel and unusual punishment" jurisprudence that it has developed in the last half of the 20th century and is still vital today. Are these laws "cruel and unusual punishment?"

Retribution and Proportionality

No doubt exists that the Supreme Court would conclude that contemporary laws, which require that sex offenders convicted of specified sex crimes be castrated, are punitive and therefore subject to scrutiny under the Eighth Amendment. In *Kansas v. Hendricks*,[83] the Court explained the circumstances under which it might consider a law to be punitive:

---

[79] *Id.* (*citing* Weems v. United States, 217 U.S. 349 (1910), in which the Court held that incarceration for 15 years for the crime of falsifying records was excessive).

[80] *Atkins*, 536 U.S. at 312 (*quoting* Trop v. Dulles, 356 U.S. 86, 100-01 (1958)).

[81] *Atkins*, 536 U.S. at 312 (*citing* Harmelin v. Michigan, 501 U.S. 957 (1991)).

[82] *Atkins*, 536 U.S. at 310–13.

[83] Kansas v. Hendricks, 521 U.S. 346 (1997) (Kansas Sexually Violent Predator Act held to be non-punitive in nature and a constitutional exercise of state's police power to protect the public against mentally abnormal and dangerous sex offenders). See chapter 5 for a discussion of Sexually Violent Predator (SVP) Laws.

As a threshold matter, commitment under the [Kansas SVP] Act does not implicate either of the two primary objectives of criminal punishment: retribution or deterrence. The Act's purpose is not retributive because it does not affix culpability for prior criminal conduct. . . . In addition, the Kansas Act does not make a criminal conviction a prerequisite for commitment. . . . An absence of the necessary criminal responsibility suggests that the State is not seeking retribution for a past misdeed. . . .

Moreover, unlike a criminal statute, no finding of scienter is required to commit an individual who is found to be a sexually violent predator; instead, the commitment determination is made based on a 'mental abnormality' or 'personality disorder' rather than on one's criminal intent. The existence of a scienter requirement is customarily an important element in distinguishing criminal from civil statutes. . . .

Nor can it be said that the legislature intended the Act to function as a deterrent. Those persons committed under the Act are, by definition, suffering from a 'mental abnormality' or a 'personality disorder' that prevents them from exercising adequate control over their behavior. Such persons are therefore unlikely to be deterred by the threat of confinement. . . . Because none of the parties argues that people institutionalized under the Kansas general civil commitment statute are subject to punitive conditions, even though they may be involuntarily confined, it is difficult to conclude that persons confined under this Act are being "punished."[84]

Contemporary castration laws, which permit or require the use of drugs on convicted sex offenders, satisfy all of the criteria for a punitive statute set out by Justice Thomas in the *Hendricks* case. They provide that drugs can be used only on conviction of a specified crime; this conviction, in turn, requires the finding of scienter or *culpability* (to use the more precise criminal law term). No finding of mental disorder of any kind is required by these laws. A primary purpose is specific deterrence of the offender and, in all probability, general deterrence of other potential sex offenders. Castrated sex offenders are subject to parole supervision and monitoring, like all other convicted criminals. Finally, these laws are generally enacted and placed in the state's penal code and actually characterize chemical castration as punishment.[85] Surely, no serious argument can be made that these laws are not punitive.

---

[84] *Hendricks*, 521 U.S. at 361–63.

[85] California's Penal Code §645(b), for example, provides the following: "Person guilty of a second conviction of any offense specified in subdivision (c) where the victim has not attained 13 years of age shall, upon parole, undergo medroxyprogesterone acetate treatment or its chemical equivalent *in addition to any other punishment* [emphasis added] prescribed for that offense or any other provision of law."

The only real question for the Court would be whether the punishment inflicted by these laws is "cruel and unusual." Until recently, no state had enacted a sentencing law that required all offenders convicted of specified sex crimes to be surgically or chemically castrated as part of their sentence or as a condition of parole. The recency of these laws, and the vengeful rhetoric from public officials that often accompanied their enactment, clearly suggest that they are vindictive in nature and intended to inflict the same type of sexual brutality on the offender that he inflicted on his victim.[86]

Proponents might argue that "evolving standards" can become *more* punitive as well as less punitive—the direction in which the Supreme Court's sense of evolving standards has been moving. They would argue that the Eighth Amendment does not prevent society from inflicting more damaging punishments on criminals, especially if society's perception of the magnitude and scope of the harm caused by criminals escalates dramatically. Simply put, supporters might argue that we have only recently come to realize how much damage sex offenders inflict on their victims, and it should be no surprise that society wants to inflict more harm on the offenders.

Although this is a clever argument, it is not persuasive. In the first case, it is unlikely that the supporters of castration laws would candidly acknowledge in court that castration was intended as a proportional "pay back" to the offender for the harm he has caused. Such an argument, if successful, would open up a wide range of potentially brutal punishments that have no other legitimate penological purpose than to pay back criminals for the harm they have done. For example, these might include breaking limbs of drunken drivers who have seriously hurt other drivers in an accident. The human imagination for painful punishments is unbounded; the very purpose of the Eighth Amendment is to prevent this sort of unconstrained mob vengeance.

Even if supporters did argue that physical or chemical castration is a civilized manner of responding to a sex crime and that it complies with the principle of proportionality, this argument is unlikely to succeed. In the United States, we do not cut off a thief's hand to punish him for theft or rape an offender to punish him for rape. We should certainly not cut off (literally or equivalently) a sex offender's testicles to punish him for committing a sex crime. In short, it is extremely unlikely that the Court would uphold mandatory castration as a proportional response to harm done.

---

[86] *See, e.g.,* Steven Walters, *Chemical Castration Measure Advances,* Milwaukee J. Sentinel, Feb. 13, 1998, at 1, *available at* 1998 WL 6300730 (state representative who voted against proposed chemical castration bill thought it was "too kind," and that sex offenders should "have their genitals mutilated." *See also Panel Favors Chemical Castration,* Colo. Springs Gazette Telegraph, Jan. 31, 1997, at B1, *available at* 1997 WL 7449126 (proponent of bill requiring the use of chemical castration refers to those who would be thus treated as "scum of the earth" and states that first preference would be "locking them up and throwing away the key").

It would, and should, hold that either type of castration inflicted for a retributive purpose violates the Eighth Amendment's ban on "cruel and unusual punishment."

Crime Prevention

If this type of mandatory biological modification is to be justified and upheld against claims that it is "cruel and unusual punishment," proponents will probably have to persuade the Court that these laws have a legitimate penological purpose and that they are not an extreme manner of achieving those ends. In short, the government must argue that castration laws are a reasonable and effective means of *preventing* convicted sex offenders from committing more sex crimes. It could point to the body of research discussed earlier to support the legislative judgment that castration is an effective means of reducing sexual recidivism.[87]

Critiques of Castration to Prevent Crime

Although plausible and having some grounding in research, these arguments are likely to fail for a number of reasons.

First, these laws are overly broad because they assume that *all* sex offenders convicted of a specified crime (or crimes) are likely to commit another sex crime. This is simply not true.[88] Most sex offenders do not reoffend.[89] Any claim that castration is necessary to prevent future sex crimes would have to be made in each individual case, on the basis of a sound medical evaluation and state-of-the-art risk assessment techniques.[90] As they now stand, these laws will result in many sex offenders being castrated who are not in fact dangerous. Therefore, using this drastic solution is unnecessary and excessive. Second, castration does not necessarily eliminate sexual drive or function.[91] Some castrated men retain both.

Third, both types of castration are reversible. Virtually all castrated men can readily restore precastration drive and function by taking testosterone or other male steroids.[92] These preventive measures are not permanent and not always effective, and would not necessarily accomplish their intended preventive purpose. Even if they were effective initially in eliminating sex drive, a castrated sex offender would have to be monitored on an ongoing basis to ensure that he took the sex-drive-reducing drugs and did not take other drugs that would restore his drive and function. Given the inevitable

---

[87] See *supra* notes 45–59 and accompanying text.
[88] See chapter 2.
[89] See chapter 2
[90] See chapter 2.
[91] See *supra* notes 13–14 and accompanying text.
[92] See *supra* note 14 and accompanying text.

necessity of surveillance that must accompany castration, other less drastic measures, like risk management, would probably be just as effective.[93] Fourth, the state has other means for controlling sex offenders and preventing sexual recidivism that are less intrusive to the human body and mind and do not require artificially altering human biology. These measures include community containment and aggressive, long-term parole.[94]

Finally, it may also be true, as some observers argue, that not all sex crimes spring from sexual urges. As pointed out in chapter 1, many experts maintain that sex crimes are caused by social and cultural forces, such as a desire to ensure domination and subordination of women.[95] If they are correct, then castrating a man to reduce his sex drive would not necessarily extinguish nonsexual motivations to commit sex crimes. Quite the contrary, castration might increase the offender's anger, intensifying his desire to retaliate.

The State's Response

Obviously, the state will contest these critiques on the merits. In all probability, it will also argue that these laws do not *require* convicted sex offenders to undergo chemical castration. Instead, they only impose a condition of parole on sex offenders; if these offenders do not wish to be castrated, they can avoid the procedure by staying in prison. Consequently, the government would argue, castration should be considered voluntary.

This argument should fail. If the Eighth Amendment precludes the state from imposing a particular criminal punishment as part of a criminal sentence, then it should not be allowed to use that same punishment as a condition of parole. This use of an unconstitutional condition is well established. This doctrine holds that the government cannot confer a benefit, even one that it may withhold entirely, on the condition that the recipient surrender a constitutional right.[96] In effect, the government is using an incentive—freedom from prison subject to parole or conviction of a new felony and another prison term—to coerce a defendant to undergo an unconstitutional punishment.

Substantive Due Process

Even a convicted felon confined in prison has a liberty interest in the integrity of his body that is protected by the due process clause of the

---

[93] *See* chapter 7 for a description of risk management strategies.
[94] *See* chapter 7.
[95] *See* chapter 1.
[96] Legal Services Corp. v. Velazquez, 531 U.S. 533 (2001). *See generally* Kathleen M. Sullivan, *Unconstitutional Conditions*, 102 HARV. L. REV. 1415 (1989).

Fourteenth Amendment.[97] In castration cases, the individual's interest is even stronger because this procedure adversely affects his right to procreate, which is also protected by the Constitution.[98] It is very likely that the Supreme Court will consider the individual interest here to be extremely important and entitled to robust constitutional protection.

This protected liberty interest in bodily integrity and procreational capacity is not absolute, however. The State may infringe on that interest under certain circumstances. In the case of an incarcerated prisoner, the Court has not required the state to prove that it has a "compelling state interest," as it often does when an individual's right to thinking as he chooses is involved. Because prisons are very difficult and dangerous institutions to manage, the Court has shown a great deal of deference to prison administrators' professional judgment as to how to run the prison and to deal with disordered and dangerous inmates.[99]

In *Washington v. Harper*,[100] the Court upheld the constitutionality of a prison policy pursuant to which prison psychiatrists had been administering antipsychotic drugs to an unconsenting inmate, Walter Harper, who suffered from schizophrenia. The Court acknowledged that Harper had a liberty interest, protected by the due process clause of the Fourteenth Amendment, in avoiding unwanted medication, but found that the State had a legitimate interest, as well, in protecting other inmates, prison staff, and Harper himself.[101] The Court also noted that the State's interest was reasonably related to ensuring the safety of Harper, staff, and other prisoners, and that the State had taken adequate steps to ensure that those measures were in Harper's medical interest.[102] Thus, *Harper* allows prison officials to give drugs to unconsenting inmates *confined in a prison facility* who suffer from a serious mental disorder that makes them dangerous if the drugs will protect the prisoner and others *and* if the medication is medically appropriate.

In another case, *Riggins v. Nevada*,[103] the Court reversed the conviction of a criminal defendant who had been treated against his will throughout his trial with antipsychotic drugs. Distinguishing the case from *Harper*, the Court noted that Riggins had been denied adequate due process safeguards because Nevada had failed to demonstrate either that the treatment was

---

[97] *See, e.g.*, Harper v. Washington, 494 U.S. 210 (1990); *see also* William Green, *DeproProvera, Castration, and the Probation of Rape Offenders: Statutory and Constitutional Issues*, 12 U. DAYTON L. REV. 1 (1986); Kari A. Vanderzyl, *Castration as an Alternative to Incarceration: An Impotent Approach to the Punishment of Sex Offenders*, 15 N. ILL. U. L. REV. 107 (1994).
[98] *See e.g.*, Skinner v. Oklahoma, 316 U.S. 535, 541 (1942); Griswold v. Connecticut, 381 U.S. 479 (1965); Eisenstadt v. Baird, 405 U.S. 438, 453 (1972); Roe v. Wade, 410 U.S. 113, 152-53 (1973).
[99] *See, e.g.*, Harper v. Washington, 494 U.S. 210, 223-24 (1990).
[100] *Id.*
[101] *Id.* at 222–23, 225–27.
[102] *Id.* at 225–27.
[103] Riggins v. Nevada, 504 U.S. 127 (1992).

medically appropriate or that it was essential for the safety of Riggins or others.[104]

Both the *Harper* case and the *Riggins* case involved individuals with serious mental disorders, with manifest and severe symptoms, who were confined in a state prison or a state criminal mental hospital. Harper was a serious threat to himself and other prisoners. Riggins was charged with capital murder. The government had very strong interests in ensuring that both individuals did not hurt themselves or others, and it also had a duty to provide both of them with appropriate medical treatment for their mental disorders.

Substantive Due Process and Chemical Castration

In chemical castration cases, the government could argue that requiring a dangerous sex offender to be castrated as a condition for releasing him into the community serves an important interest in preventing that individual from committing another sex crime. However, there is no serious claim that all offenders convicted of specified sex crimes suffer from a "serious mental illness" that causes them to be dangerous. Nor is it likely that a court would be persuaded that this procedure is in the offender's "medical interest." After all, these laws require chemical castration based on the offense for which the individual was convicted; they do not require a medical evaluation or diagnosis or a finding that the procedure is in the individual's medical interest. This is not surprising. There is no pretense that these individuals suffer from a recognized mental disorder that causes them to be dangerous or that chemical castration is in their medical interest and for their benefit. Surely, a court would see through the hypocrisy of such an argument.

The fact that some state laws give judges discretion to order chemical castration should not change the analysis or the result. In exercising that discretion, judges are not allowed to ascertain whether the offender suffers from a serious mental disorder that causes him to be sexually dangerous or to consider whether chemical castration is in the offender's medical interest. On the contrary, judges are instructed to make their decision exclusively on the basis of public safety considerations.[105]

The Constitutional Right to Sexual Intimacy

Sex offenders released on parole or probation presumptively regain their constitutional right to engage in sexual intimacy with legally competent

---

[104] *Id.* at 135.

[105] *See supra* notes 45–59 and accompanying text discussing various state punitive chemical castration laws in this chapter.

and consenting partners. (Aside from constitutional considerations, finding appropriate partners to share in normal sexual activity after release from prison is often crucial to the successful reintegration of a sex offender into the community.) The state would have to make an extremely persuasive showing that eliminating an individual's physiological capacity to exercise this fundamental right is essential to accomplish an important state interest of preventing future sex crimes.

The government is unlikely to succeed in making such a showing. There are less drastic means available to the state to protect the public from the risk of sexual recidivism posed by a few of these men. These strategies include community containment and aggressive, long-term parole.[106] It is not clear that the Supreme Court would necessarily require the use of such "less restrictive means," because these individuals are still subject to state control as a result of their conviction and, consequently, have a diminished liberty interest. But the Court would certainly give serious consideration to the importance of sex offenders' interest in bodily integrity, their right to share sexual intimacy with appropriate partners, and the availability of other effective control systems that do not require changing human biology and personality.

Other Constitutional Rights

Other constitutional claims could be made against punitive castration laws. Opponents will surely include these arguments in their constitutional attacks. Because the Court will most likely decide these cases on Eighth Amendment and substantive due process grounds discussed previously, I describe other constitutional challenges to castration laws very briefly.

Procedural Due Process

Both the Fifth[107] and Fourteenth[108] Amendments to the United States Constitution require the government to provide adequate procedural due process to people whose constitutional rights will be adversely affected by state action.[109] The Supreme Court has recognized that due process is flexible and that constitutional sufficiency may vary, depending on the private and state interests involved, the value of a specific procedural protection, and the potential impact of an erroneous decision.[110] Nevertheless, the state generally must provide notice—an opportunity to be heard by a neutral

---

[106] *See* chapter 7 for a thorough discussion of these strategies.
[107] U.S. CONST. amend. V.
[108] U.S. CONST. amend. XIV.
[109] Mathews v. Eldridge, 424 U.S. 319, 332 (1976).
[110] *Id.* at 334.

decision maker—to confront the evidence against him, and the assistance of counsel. These laws do not provide any opportunity for the offender to argue that he should not be castrated.

The Right to Think

The First Amendment protects an individual's right to generate his own thoughts and ideas.[111] It prevents the government from engaging in "mind control." A powerful case can be made that the Constitution protects a person's sexual thoughts[112] so long as he does not act inappropriately on them by committing a crime. Because chemical castration is intended to eliminate an offender's having sexual content in his psychological life, and because the government's interference with the offender's mentation must occur over a long time to be effective, it is even more objectionable.[113] Because these laws require all offenders convicted of specified crimes, including many who will not commit another sex crime, they are overly broad in identifying the class of individuals who will be subjected to chemical interference with their normal thought processes.

Recommendation

Laws that authorize or require judges to sentence convicted sex offenders to undergo surgical castration or chemical castration are clearly punitive in purpose and effect. For the reasons discussed earlier in this chapter, courts should hold that they violate the Eighth Amendment's prohibition against "cruel and unusual punishment" and other important constitutional rights and enjoin their implementation.

These laws alter basic body chemistry to change essential human biology. Their only possible justification is to prevent sexual recidivism. These laws are overly broad, sweeping within their scope all sex offenders convicted of a specified crime. Most do not require or even allow a medical evaluation to ascertain whether this procedure is clinically indicated or in the medical best interest of the offender. Instead, they simply seek to eliminate sexual thoughts and desires in a large and diverse class of sex offenders. They may not even be effective in achieving their intended goal.

The state has less intrusive and more effective means in its crime-fighting arsenal to protect society from dangerous sex offenders. There is no good reason why courts should not require the government to rely on accepted and proven crime-control measures to prevent sexual recidivism, and there is no good reason why the Eighth Amendment's historic ban on

---

[111] U.S. CONST. amend. I.
[112] Stanley v. Georgia, 394 U.S. 557 (1969).
[113] Green, *supra* note 96.

physical mutilation for behavioral control[114] should be lifted. Once society starts using drugs to change thinking and behavior in people who are not mentally ill, there is a very serious risk that it will engage in more drastic biological engineering in the name of crime prevention.

Castration as Treatment

Because all of the castration statutes enacted to date (except the Texas law) are punitive in purpose and impact, it is hard to imagine that states would seriously argue that these statutes in fact are therapeutic and intended to benefit those subject to them. Castration as authorized or required by these laws is not intended to be in the medical interest of the offender. Quite the contrary, they are intended to protect society from sexual recidivism.[115]

Does the constitutional analysis change if the government argues that castration should be considered "treatment" that is authorized or required as a component of punishment? Put differently, what if the government claims that castration is simply an appropriate *therapeutic* means to change the offender's behavior that is a constitutionally permissible part of his punishment? It is analogous, so the government might argue, to allowing a criminal acquitted of a serious crime by reason of insanity to be released into the community if, and only if, he continues to take the psychotropic drugs that staff have prescribed for him to control his mental disorder and the resulting dangerousness.

Such a claim should not be taken seriously. Unlike psychotropic drugs that are medically recognized as an appropriate treatment for the symptoms of mental disorder,[116] chemical castration is a medically recognized treatment for only a small group of sex offenders, namely, those who have a hypersexual drive and who constantly experience intrusive sexual fantasies and urges. As discussed earlier, the legislature is prescribing drugs on the basis of past criminal behavior, not on a current diagnosis of medical illness and a professional determination that it is in the medical interest of the offender.[117]

Only the Texas law would probably withstand a constitutional challenge. It is a bona fide treatment law that lets the *offender* decide whether he wants to undergo surgical castration. Appropriate procedures are in place

---

[114] See *supra* notes 63–71 and accompanying text. See generally Kaimowitz v. Dept. of Mental Health, No. 73-19434 (Cir. Ct. Wayne County, Mich. July 10, 1973).

[115] For a more thorough analysis of these laws individually, *see supra* notes 45–58 and accompanying text.

[116] See, e.g., Michelle Tansella, *Making Mental Health Services Work at the Primary Level,* 78 BULL. OF THE WORLD HEALTH ORG. 501 (2000), *available at* 2000 WL 17372482 (psychotropic drugs effective treatment for people with mental disorders). *See also* Washington v. Harper, 494 U.S. 210, 226 n.9 (1990) (psychotropic medication widely accepted within psychiatric community as "extraordinarily effective" treatment).

[117] Miller, *supra* note 1.

to ensure that he gives his informed consent to the operation. He is given sufficient information to make a knowledgeable choice and ensure that he is not being coerced into agreeing to it. Physicians must examine him and conclude that he is a suitable candidate for the procedure. This should also ensure that the operation is in his "medical interest" as required by constitutional precedent. Finally, having the operation has no impact on the sentence he will receive. Thus, neither the prosecutor nor the judge can use sentencing as an improper incentive to influence his decision. States that are serious about providing castration to sex offenders as *treatment* should consider adopting the Texas approach.

CONSENT TO SURGICAL CASTRATION AS PUNISHMENT

Even if the state cannot force convicted sex offenders to be chemically castrated, can offenders on their own initiative consent to surgical castration as part of their punishment to get out of prison sooner, or to avoid imprisonment entirely? This is an extremely difficult question. At the very least, consent must be competent, knowing, and voluntary to be legally effective.[118]

Competence

In most cases, a convicted sex offender will be competent to make this decision. Unless he is mentally retarded or suffers from a serious mental disorder that adversely affects his thinking, he should have the requisite intelligence and rational decision-making capacity to understand the nature of the operation, with its physical and emotional consequences, and to make a decision that would be in his self-interest.

Knowledge

Most sex offenders should also satisfy this requirement. Experts can provide them with all the information currently available about the procedure and its effects, including side effects. They can also explain what we do not know about the procedure and its consequences.

Voluntary

The most difficult query to address is whether the convicted offender is voluntarily consenting to this procedure. If so, should this be considered punishment or treatment? Does it matter?

---

[118]Cruzan v. Director, Mo. Dept. of Health, 497 U.S. 261 (1990). *See also* Kaimowitz v. Dept. of Mental Health, No. 73-19434 (Cir. Ct. Wayne County, Mich. July 10, 1973).

Certainly, the offender must choose between two difficult alternatives. The government is offering the offender something of considerable value in exchange for undergoing surgical castration, namely, a shorter term of incarceration or no incarceration at all. This inducement is very powerful and arguably might leave the offender with no "real choice." One could even argue that this decision is made under duress. If one alternative has significantly harsher or permanent results, can it still be considered a voluntary decision to "choose" the less onerous option? Others might argue that the offender still has a choice, although it is surely a *difficult* choice; he may undergo surgical castration or go to prison. It is still up to the offender to decide.

Punishment or Treatment?

The government is surely not offering this bargain for the offender's benefit. Quite the contrary. Only because the government believes that surgical castration will incapacitate the offender and prevent him from committing another sex crime is it even making the procedure available to the offender. Protecting society from future crimes is a classic purpose of punishment. Thus, any "bargain" in which the government offers an offender a substantial "discount" in his prison sentence in exchange for being castrated should be considered punishment rather than treatment. As noted earlier,[119] the government cannot impose an unconstitutional condition, even one mischaracterized as "treatment," on an offender to induce him to surrender his constitutional rights.

The Views of Scholars

Not unexpectedly, scholars have differing views on whether the state should be allowed to castrate sex offenders in exchange for a reduction in their criminal sentence.

Some argue that the government should be allowed to offer that bargain to sex offenders and that sex offenders should be allowed to accept it. Bailey and Greenberg take the view that all actions taken in response to even the strongest incentives are conscious and intentional, thus making them voluntary.[120] So long as one of the choices is a "fair" punishment for his offense (e.g., a 30-year prison term), they would let the offender choose an

---

[119] *See supra* note 95.
[120] Bailey & Greenberg, *supra* note 11, at 1242.

"unfair punishment" (e.g., surgical castration). The offender's position with the castration alternative will be better than or the same as, but never worse than, his position without the alternative.[121]

But that is the wrong focus. The real question that must be asked is whether it is morally acceptable for the *government* to put the offender in the position of being subjected to *any* of the alternatives.[122] If the government could not constitutionally impose castration on a sex offender (whether characterized as punishment or treatment), then it should not be allowed to finesse this fundamental limitation on its power by offering a reduced sentence to the offender in exchange for his undergoing an unconstitutional procedure.[123] Such a *quid pro quo* exchange is not constitutionally acceptable.[124]

The Position of the American Psychiatric Association

The American Psychiatric Association has strongly criticized laws that identify sex offenders for treatment by chemical castration solely on the basis of the crime for which they were convicted. In its view, this approach "equates psychiatric diagnosis with criminal behavior."[125] This definitional equivalence, in turn, stigmatizes people who really do suffer from a mental disorder and may discourage them from seeking treatment. Many convicted sex offenders cannot legitimately be diagnosed with a psychiatric disorder, or if they can be so diagnosed, the disorder may not be one that would warrant this particular treatment.[126]

Simply put, treatment must be provided on the basis of clinical criteria, not legal criteria. In the association's view, the criminal justice system has no business using pharmacological treatment as a means of social control. Using medicine for this purpose undercuts the integrity of psychiatry. The association believes that treatment should be offered to those for whom it is medically appropriate and who are motivated to change and voluntarily consent to it.[127]

---

[121] *Id.* at 1244.

[122] *Id.* at 1243 (1998).

[123] *See supra* note 96 and accompanying text.

[124] O'Connor v. Donaldson, 422 U.S. 563, 585–87 (1975) (Burger, J., concurring) Justice Burger rejected the argument that the State could indefinitely confine in a mental hospital an individual who was not dangerous to others in exchange for the individual giving up the protections of the criminal justice system, confinement for a fixed period for a past crime and protective procedures, on the theory that the State offered treatment as a *quid pro quo*.

[125] American Psychiatric Association, *supra* note 10, at 179.

[126] *Id.*

[127] *Id.*

Actual Cases

As it turns out, this is not a "hypothetical case" imagined by creative law professors. Some sex offenders have actually undergone surgical castration in hopes of obtaining a lighter prison sentence.

Illinois

William Mingus pled guilty to sexual assault of a child and, before sentencing, voluntarily underwent physical castration. Mingus claimed that he did this only to help himself, not to reduce the maximum 15-year penalty in Illinois. However, he did ask the judge to grant him probation as opposed to jail time. No Illinois law explicitly authorized a sentencing judge to issue a lighter sentence to a sex offender who had voluntarily undergone surgical castration, and judges are generally wary of striking such a bargain lest it set a precedent. The judge ruled that, even though Mingus had been castrated, he was a second-time sex offender and there was still no guarantee he would not offend again. Despite the judge's disclaimer that he was not giving him a lighter sentence in exchange for being castrated, Mingus was sentenced to 6 years in prison, which was significantly less than the maximum penalty authorized by law.[128]

Kansas

In Johnson County, Kansas, Herbert Fox, a 66-year-old pedophile, was scheduled to go to trial in August 2002, when a jury was to decide whether he should be committed indefinitely as a sexual predator. In an effort to avoid possible lifetime commitment, Fox agreed to be surgically castrated in March 2002. As of this writing, his SVP trial has been delayed so that he can be reevaluated to determine whether he should still be tried as a predator.[129]

South Carolina

In 1985, the South Carolina Supreme Court held that castration of three convicted sex offenders, who had pled guilty to sex crime charges and had agreed to be castrated in exchange for reduced sentences, violated South Carolina's constitutional prohibition against cruel and unusual punish-

---

[128] Art Barnum, *Child-Sex Offender Fails to Avoid Prison; Man Gets 6 Years Despite Voluntary Castration*, CHI. TRIB., Oct. 17, 2000, at 3.
[129] T. Rizzo, *Man Who Chose Castration Over Predator Unit May Get Both*, THE KAN. CITY STAR, June 29, 2002, at B2.

ment.[130] The court ruled that the trial court's conditional suspension of the prison term was improper because it violated public policy—even though all three sex offenders *wanted* to undergo castration and serve the suspended sentence. Simply put, the court said, "Article I, §15, of our Constitution prohibits the infliction of cruel and unusual punishment."[131] In this court's view, the state constitution's ban on cruel and unusual punishment automatically limited the types of punishment that the government could inflict on its citizens even with their consent.

Arkansas

In 1998, a judge gave James Ray Stanley, who had pled guilty to rape and sexual solicitation of a child, a 30-year sentence in prison, 10 years of which were suspended on condition that Stanley undergo physical castration and complete the sexual offender program.[132]

In 1999, the Supreme Court of Arkansas implicitly upheld the judge's sentence in the *Stanley* case.[133] The American Civil Liberties Union tried to intervene in this case, seeking to have the castration condition set aside as unconstitutional and illegal.[134] Stanley opposed the ACLU, arguing that "surgical castration falls within the category of 'available medical or psychiatric treatment,'" which the legislature authorizes the trial court to require as a condition of a suspended sentence.[135] The court dismissed the ACLU's appeal, holding that it did not have the legal right to intervene in the case.[136] Without legally authorized third-party intervention, the court concluded that it did not have authority to reach the merits of the case.[137] As a practical matter, this meant the Arkansas Supreme Court, in the absence of any party who objected, would not stop the operation. It refused to decide whether either the state or federal constitution prevented the government from castrating a sex offender willing to undergo the procedure in exchange for a reduced sentence.

Justice Brown strongly disagreed in dissent, concluding "[s]urgical castration is also unique and irreversible. In addition, unlike the death sentence, it is not a penalty authorized by the laws of this state."[138] He argued that the

---

[130] State v. Brown, 326 S.E.2d 410 (S.C. 1985). There is some indication that the trial judge deliberately sought to coerce the defendants into agreeing to be surgically castrated. He sentenced them to a 30-year prison term, which was the maximum he could impose under the law. However, he agreed to suspend the sentence and place the defendants on probation for 5 years if they successfully underwent the procedure. *Id.* at 409, 411.

[131] *Id.* at 412.

[132] ACLU of Ark. v. State, 5 S.W.3d 418, 419 (1999).

[133] *Id.*

[134] *Id.* at 419.

[135] *Id.* at 422 (Brown, J., dissenting).

[136] *Id.* at 420.

[137] *ACLU of Ark.* at 421.

[138] *Id.* at 422.

state supreme court should recognize the "severe public policy implications of allowing surgical castration to proceed when there is no authority for doing so."[139] Before wading into such "treacherous waters," Justice Brown believed the court should be assured that due care and consideration had been extended to issues such as the following:

- Should the General Assembly consider chemical hormonal medications as an alternative to surgical castration?
- Should the defendant be given a psychological examination before agreeing to castration, as is done in Texas?
- What steps have been taken to assure that the defendant's consent to castration is an informed consent?
- What is the potential liability of the surgeon who performs the castration?
- If castration is deemed "treatment," must it be made available to other sex offenders who are currently incarcerated?
- Castration may be a cheaper alternative to long-term incarceration, but which is the more effective deterrent? (Apparently, surgical castration may not completely eliminate the sex drive in all cases.) What safeguards are in place to protect against abuse?[140]

RECOMMENDATIONS

In light of these laws, what we know about surgical and chemical castration, and this constitutional analysis, I make the following recommendations regarding castration. Because surgical and chemical castration involve different issues, I discuss these practices separately.

Surgical Castration

It is simply unacceptable to impose surgical castration on a convicted sex offender to punish him. Inflicting this physical and psychological loss and scarring simply to pay back the offender is uncivilized and not worthy of America. Nor can threatening such a harsh and irrevocable punishment to deter other potential sex offenders justify maiming human beings. Preventing future sex crimes is the only legitimate purpose of punishment that could possible justify such a brutal practice.

Whether the state should be in the business of physically castrating sex offenders in exchange for reducing their prison sentences is a more

---

[139] Id. at 422.
[140] Id. at 422–23.

complex question. One could argue that a convicted sex offender should be able to choose the lesser of two punishments as he calculates his personal preference, so long as one of those choices, imprisonment, is a fair and proportional punishment for his offense. The matter of punishment is simply a bargain, analogous to a private contract between the state and the criminal. In this view, it is necessary only that adequate procedures be in place to ensure that the defendant is competent to consent, has all relevant knowledge, and receives accurate advice from the court about his choices. Legal controls in the form of procedural due process are all that is necessary; the offender has legal authority to make the substantive decision that he considers to be in his own best interests.

But this view is incomplete and incorrect. The state operates a criminal justice system and inflicts punishment on convicted offenders in the name of the community and as a symbolic reflection of its basic value system. In part, this system channels the urge for private vengeance into public institutions subject to broader considerations than simply that of the victim. The criminal justice system also teaches values and shapes the culture in light of those values. Physical mutilation is not part of our fundamental value system.

Even if one were to believe that sex offenders should be allowed to make this Faustian bargain so long as the bargaining process is carefully regulated, operational and practical problems are insurmountable. Allowing offenders to consent to castration in exchange for a lighter sentence would be difficult to regulate because the plea-bargaining process is easily abused. Legislatures could up the ante drastically by imposing lifetime sentences, and then allow sex offenders to "buy down" their sentence by agreeing to castration. Judges can also abuse the system, imposing improper pressure on defendants. Several trial courts have imposed the maximum sentence and then offered the defendant a deal: Be surgically castrated and this court will give you your freedom. It is virtually impossible to know what the judge's sentence would have been if castration had not been available. Moreover, what should victims think when they see the perpetrator go free simply by agreeing to the surgery?

In this day and age, the government should simply not consider permanent maiming of its citizenry as a legitimate and constitutional means of punishment. Less drastic and more effective means are readily available to prevent the offender from committing future sex crimes. Once we start down this road, there is no way of knowing where it will lead.

Chemical Castration

Should we use chemical castration to punish sex offenders? With or without their consent? Is it sufficiently different from surgical castration to justify its use? Unlike surgical castration, chemical castration does not involve an irreversible physical change. The side effects of chemical castration, however, are different and arguably more severe than those of surgical castration.

Chemical castration laws enacted recently by several states make it abundantly clear that their purpose is punishment. These laws apply to all sex offenders convicted of specified sex crimes. Their language[141] and placement in the state's legal code[142] make it clear that the legislature intended to sentence a convicted sex offender to chemical castration. There is no discussion of this regime as a treatment for mental disorder, such as a paraphilia, nor do these laws generally require a clinical evaluation by a qualified psychiatrist to determine whether these drugs are medically appropriate treatment for the offenders.[143] Nor do these laws require that the offender give informed consent. This requirement is essential in a bona fide treatment regime. Clearly, the only plausible rationale for chemical castration laws is to prevent future crimes.

There is no need to use chemical castration as punishment. The state has other less intrusive measures available to prevent sexual reoffending, including incarceration, community containment, and lifetime parole. If recently enacted chemical castration laws are upheld, it is almost certain that the legislatures will expand their reach, imposing chemical castration on virtually all sex offenders as a condition of parole and enacting sentencing schemes that authorize extended or lifetime parole for them. In short, it is not unrealistic to expect legislatures to effectively require almost all sex offenders who want to be released from prison to undergo chemical castration for the rest of their lives. There is surely no need to use a nuclear bomb on all sex offenders to control the relatively few sex offenders who are truly dangerous.

In summary, then, the state has no business imposing chemical castration on a sex offender or inducing offenders to undergo this procedure by offering them a lighter sentence. Nor should the state be allowed to impose castration as a condition of parole or release from prison. Simply put, chemical castration is not a constitutionally or morally acceptable punishment.

Chemical Castration of SVPs

California is imposing chemical castration on SVPs who seek to be released from institutions and released as outpatients in the community.[144]

---

[141] Both the California and Florida codes state that, on the second conviction, a sex offender "shall" undergo chemical castration, indicating a sentence of punishment.
[142] The California castration law is under their Penal Code at Part 1, Crimes & Punishments.
[143] Miller, *supra* note 1.
[144] People v. Ghilotti, 44 P.3d 949 (Cal. 2002).

In these cases, the state can make a more persuasive case that chemical castration is not being imposed to punish sex offenders, but to treat them. True, the state's primary purpose is to prevent SVPs from committing new sex crimes in the community, but chemical castration, even over the offender's objection, should be allowed as bona fide treatment, provided certain stringent conditions are met.

The Task Force identified when chemical castration is acceptable as treatment and supports its use for sex offenders in very limited situations. The Task Force recommended that cognitive–behavioral treatment should be used initially.[145] If that fails, or if there is evidence of hypersexuality,[146] then drugs should be used in patients who have been selected for treatment by psychiatrists "based on clinical criteria, including diagnosis of a disorder indicating treatment, the absence of disorders contraindicating use of these agents, and motivation for treatment." These patients may benefit from this treatment.[147] There are some patients, then, who suffer from a recognized sexual disorder and for whom chemical castration is a recognized and clinically appropriate treatment if other, less intrusive treatments prove ineffective.

Courts, however, must be vigilant to ensure that state officials do not simply impose chemical castration on *all* SVPs who are being placed on outpatient commitment. Most SVPs are not diagnosed as suffering from a paraphilia, and even when they are, cognitive–behavioral treatment should be effective in most of those cases. There is every reason to believe that state officials will significantly overuse chemical castration in placing SVPs on outpatient commitment to maximize their chances of preventing sexual recidivism. In the *Ghilloti* case, state officials insisted that an SVP be chemically castrated as a condition of being placed on outpatient commitment even though *three independent mental health professionals* concluded that he no longer fit the state's criteria for an SVP and should be given his freedom.[148] Of course, one can understand the political backlash that will occur *when*— not if—an SVP on community release commits another sex crime. But that does not justify using chemical castration for all SVPs when it is not medically indicated as the appropriate treatment.

CONCLUSION

Surgical castration should never be imposed on sex offenders as punishment, and sex offenders should not be allowed to bargain away body parts

---

[145] American Psychiatric Association, *supra* note 10, at 119.
[146] *Id.*
[147] *Id.* at 179.
[148] *Ghilotti*, 44 P.3d 949.

for a lighter sentence. The state has no legitimate business maiming its citizens, even with their supposed consent, in the name of crime control.

Chemical castration presents a more complex case. It does not involve physical maiming and is reversible. An argument can be made that it is simply a new and effective technology that has become available and that should be used to protect society from the ravages of sex offenders.

Although initially persuasive, this argument should be rejected. Chemical castration is an acknowledged treatment for a very small number of sex offenders who suffer from a recognized serious sexual disorder and for whom other less intrusive treatments have proved ineffective. Whether characterized as punishment or treatment, it should not be used on a group of sex offenders identified by a legal category, like those convicted of specified sex crimes or those committed as SVPs. Society has effective crime control measures at its disposal to prevent sexual recidivism. There is no need to misuse medicine for social control. Once that boundary is violated, who knows what the future will hold? Instead, chemical castration may be used when it is clinically appropriate, is offered for the medical benefit of the patient, and the patient gives informed consent.

Society should not be seduced by the promise of a quick technological fix that requires reengineering human biology to prevent sexual recidivism. Human beings should be held accountable and punished for their crimes, and crime control measures should presume that all offenders, including sex offenders, are moral agents. There is no need to maim or drug them. We should respect and use our traditional methods of punishing criminals, including sex offenders.

7

DOES RISK MANAGEMENT MAKE MORE SENSE?

The number of adults convicted each year of rape, child molestation, and other types of sexual assaults and sentenced to state prison more than doubled between 1980 (8,000) and 1992 (19,100, almost 5% of all state prison admissions that year). Most of them *will* return to the community after serving their sentences. In 1992, states paroled 7,382 prisoners convicted of sex offenses. Many sex offenders will not be sentenced to jail or prison at all. Instead, they will be convicted and given a sentence of probation.[1] It makes sense, then, to implement cost-effective strategies to prevent these offenders from committing more sex crimes when they return to our neighborhoods.

Despite the current climate of fear, convicted sex offenders, as a group, are not particularly dangerous. Research shows that they are less likely to commit another crime than most other violent criminals. However, if they do reoffend, sex offenders are more likely to commit another sex crime than other convicted criminals who reoffend. The available evidence

---

[1] Kim English, Suzanne Pullen, & Linda Jones, *Managing Adult Sex Offenders in the Community—Containment Approach*, National Institute of Justice Research in Brief, Jan. 1997, *available at* http://www.ncjrs.org/pdffiles/sexoff.pdf (last visited Feb. 11, 2004). "State prisons held 20,500 sex offenders in 1980, 75,900 in 1992, 81,100 in 1993, and 88,100 in 1994." (citation omitted).

demonstrates that many of them can be safely released after they have served their criminal sentences without any realistic fear that they will reoffend.[2]

There is, however, a small number of sex offenders who are very dangerous and likely to commit another sex crime if released into the community without supervision. And there are other sex offenders who fall somewhere in between the nondangerous and the truly dangerous. Given these facts, do the legal strategies enacted since 1990 to protect the community from dangerous sex offenders make sense? Are they based on sound empirical evidence? Do some strategies make more sense than others?

In this chapter, I demonstrate that risk management must be an essential strategy for releasing many convicted sex offenders into the community if we are to prevent them from committing more sex crimes. In so doing, I also show that many of the key strategies put in place recently, in which we place so much confidence, simply will not work and should be abandoned or modified.

STARK CHOICES: INCAPACITATION OR RELEASE?

Legal strategies enacted in the United States since about 1990 to protect society from dangerous sex offenders assume that sex offenders are especially dangerous and that many of them pose a high risk of committing more sex crimes for their entire lives. To respond to this never-ending threat, legislatures have generally relied on two very different approaches to prevent them from committing more sex crimes: long-term and indefinite incapacitation[3] or release into the community subject to a registration requirement and possible community notification.[4] These strategies require public agencies to *choose* between confining convicted sex offenders for a very long time or releasing them subject to minimal supervision achieved by information compilation and dissemination.[5] This choice also requires public officials to predict at a single moment in time whether a sex offender is at high risk of committing a new sex crime if he is placed in the community.

Long-Term or Indeterminate Incapacitation

Longer Criminal Sentences

Many states have used the criminal justice system to protect the community. As noted in chapter 1, legislatures increased sentences for sex

---

[2] *See* chapter 1 for a discussion of whether sex offenders are dangerous.
[3] *See* chapter 1 and chapter 5.
[4] *See* chapter 4.
[5] John Q. La Fond & Bruce J. Winick, *Sex Offender Reentry Courts: A Cost Effective Proposal for Managing Sex Offender Risk in the Community*, 989 ANNALS N.Y. ACAD. SCI. 300 (2003); John Q.

offenses, passed tough mandatory minimum sentences for repeat offenders, including sex offenders, and enacted lifetime sentencing laws called "three-strike" laws. Between 1993 and 1995, 24 states and the federal government passed "three-strike" laws that extended criminal sentences for serious repeat offenders, including sex offenders. Some required lifetime sentences for certain repeat offenders.[6] Many sex offenders were sentenced to longer prison terms and served more of their sentences.

Critiques of Criminal Sentencing

Criminal punishment serves many purposes, including specific and general deterrence, retribution, rehabilitation, and social defense through incapacitation.[7] To the extent that sex offenders are sentenced to jail or prison to protect the community from dangerous offenders by incapacitating them, confinement in secure institutions will prevent them from committing more sex crimes in society.

Mandatory minimum and lifetime sentencing laws, however, are *overin-clusive* in identifying dangerous sex offenders because they use only the offender's history of criminal convictions to determine his risk of sexual recidivism. This is a flawed way to assess the offender's risk of committing another sex crime. Actuarial tools (discussed in chapter 2) do a much better job of identifying high-risk sex offenders than these sentencing laws. Consequently, most of these sentencing laws are likely to incarcerate many sex offenders who do not pose a significant risk of committing another sex crime. Many will be confined for longer periods even though they are not likely to commit another sex crime.[8] These laws often inflict excessive punishment in individual cases[9] and will continue to fill our already crowded

---

La Fond & Bruce J. Winick, *Sex Offender Reentry Courts: A Proposal for Managing the Risk of Returning Sex Offenders to the Community*, 34 SETON HALL L. REV. 1173 (2004).

[6] John Clark et al., *"Three Strikes and You're Out": A Review of State Legislation*, NAT'L INST. OF JUST. RES. IN BRIEF (Sept. 1997), *available at* http://www.ncjrs.org/pdffiles/165369.pdf (last visited Feb. 11, 2004).

[7] *See, e.g.*, Kansas v. Hendricks, 521 U.S. 346, 361–62 (1997) (the two primary objectives of criminal punishment are retribution and deterrence); *see also* Michelle Cotton, *Back With a Vengeance: The Resilience of Retribution as an Articulated Purpose of Criminal Punishment*, 37 AM. CRIM. L. REV. 1313 (2000) (commonly cited goals of criminal punishment are retribution, deterrence, rehabilitation, and incapacitation); and WAYNE R. LAFAVE, CRIMINAL LAW § 1.5 (4th ed.) (2003) (theories of punishment include prevention, restraint, rehabilitation, deterrence, education, and retribution).

[8] Of course, the long sentences provided by these laws may be appropriate in individual cases to serve other purposes, including retribution for harm done by the offender and specific deterrence of the offender. Our focus here is on protecting the community against sexual violence.

[9] *See, e.g.*, Andrade v. Att'y Gen., 270 F.3d 743 (9th Cir. 2001), *rev'd sub nom.* Lockyer v. Andrade, 538 U.S. 63 (2003). Andrade was convicted of two counts of petty theft for shoplifting from two K-Mart stores, ordinarily misdemeanor offenses under California law. Unfortunately, Andrade had been previously convicted of several offenses, all nonviolent. As a result, Andrade's petty thefts, which normally would have carried a sentence of up to 6 months and a $1,000 fine each, were enhanced to felonies, and then enhanced again to third and fourth strikes, under California's "three-strike" law. In the end, for the theft of approximately $150 worth of videotapes, Andrade was

jails and prisons. No wonder sex offenders are the second largest "growth industry" in our penal system[10] and contribute so much to its burgeoning costs.

These sentencing laws will also be *underinclusive* in identifying dangerous sex offenders, failing to confine many who would be found to pose a higher risk of sexual recidivism if state-of-the-art risk assessment techniques were used. Many sex offenders will either be placed on probation or released back into the community after they serve their sentences, despite their ongoing high risk of committing more sex crimes.

Sexually Violent Predator (SVP) Laws

SVP laws will protect the community from those sex offenders placed in secure mental health institutions and, to a lesser extent, from sex offenders placed in a community release program.[11] The Supreme Court has upheld these laws against various constitutional challenges. Consequently, states are free to use them to confine mentally abnormal sex offenders who have serious difficulty in controlling their sexual behavior.

Critiques of SVP Commitment

SVP laws are unbelievably expensive to implement[12] and, because of statutory definitions, constitutional limitations, and high costs,[13] they will incapacitate only a relatively small number of dangerous sex offenders. As of summer 2002, 2,478 men (and a few women) were committed as SVPs under these laws.[14] SVP commitment can be used in only a relatively small number of cases. In that sense, SVP laws are *underinclusive*, because many sexually dangerous offenders will be released at the end of their prison sentence rather than be committed as an SVP.

Because conviction of a qualifying sex crime is necessary before prosecutors can seek commitment under an SVP law, these laws create disincentives

---

sentenced to life with no possibility of parole for 50 years. Ultimately, the Ninth Circuit granted Andrade a certificate of appealability and ruled that, as applied to Andrade only, California's "three-strike" law violated the Eighth Amendment's prohibition against cruel and unusual punishment in that it imposed a sentence grossly disproportionate to the crimes of conviction. *Id.* at 767.

[10] *See* chapter 1.

[11] For a thorough discussion of a community release program, *see* John Q. La Fond, *Outpatient Commitment's New Frontier: Sexually Violent Predators*, 9 PSYCHOL. PUB. POL'Y & L. 159 (2003).

[12] *See* John Q. La Fond, *The Costs of Enacting a Sexual Predator Law and Recommendations to Keep Them From Sky-Rocketing, in* PROTECTING SOCIETY FROM SEXUALLY VIOLENT OFFENDERS: LAW, JUSTICE, AND THERAPY 283 (Bruce J. Winick & John Q. La Fond eds., 2003) [hereinafter PROTECTING SOCIETY]; *see also* La Fond, *infra* note 30.

[13] In *Kansas v. Crane*, 534 U.S. 407 (2002), the Supreme Court held that the state must prove that, as a result of mental abnormality or personality disorder, an individual has "serious difficulty" in controlling his sexual behavior. Most mental health experts agree that proving volitional impairment is difficult.

[14] W. Lawrence Fitch, *Sexual Offender Commitment in the United States: Legislative and Policy Concerns*, 989 N.Y. ACAD. SCI. 489, 492 (2003).

for sex offenders to accept criminal responsibility for their behavior by pleading guilty. Instead, many sex offenders will offer to plead guilty only to a nonsexual crime or will go to trial. SVP laws also create barriers to convicted sex offenders participating in treatment while in prison or, if they do participate, to doing so in earnest.[15] In most states, anything a sex offender says to his therapist during the course of prison treatment can be used later on to commit him as an SVP. As a result, SVP laws may actually undermine prison treatment programs, which have much greater potential for success than SVP treatment programs, because prison treatment is offered much closer in time to the sex offense, thereby discouraging the offender from denying and minimizing his crime while he serves his sentence.[16]

Collecting and Publicizing Information About Sex Offenders

This second option relies primarily on sex offender registration and community notification laws. These laws require the compilation of information about sex offenders and, in many cases, its dissemination to the community.[17]

Registration Laws

Under Congressional pressure and without Congressional funding, all 50 states have enacted a sex offender registration law that requires most sex offenders to register with a law enforcement agency where they live and to provide information about their residence, employment, and criminal history. They may also have to provide additional information about themselves, including a photograph, fingerprints, and a DNA sample. Policymakers hope that registration laws will deter sex offenders from committing another sex crime and aid the police in investigating sex crimes.

Notification Laws

Also under Congressional pressure, all 50 states have enacted a notification law. They authorize or require the police to provide information about registered sex offenders to communities where these offenders live. Legislators passed these laws because they believed that registration laws would not adequately protect the community.

---

[15] Bruce J. Winick, A *Therapeutic Jurisprudence Assessment of Sexually Violent Predator Laws, in* PROTECTING SOCIETY, *supra* note 12, at 317.
[16] Robert M. Wettstein, A *Psychiatric Perspective on Washington's Sexually Violent Predator Law,* 15 U. PUGET SOUND L. REV. 597 (1992).
[17] *See* chapter 4 for a thorough analysis of registration and notification laws.

Critiques of Registration and Notification Laws

These laws are rigid and too broad, requiring most sex offenders, including many who have lived safely in the community for years, to register for at least 10 years and often for much longer. The laws can disrupt families and hinder successful reintegration of offenders into society and the development of offender support groups that could monitor the offender and help prevent his reoffending. Most provide no inducement for sex offenders to engage in treatment or to prove by their law-abiding behavior that they are not dangerous and should no longer have to register. No sound research has established that they prevent sexual recidivism.[18] This result is not surprising, because these laws are really passive; they only collect information and distribute it haphazardly and infrequently.

Neither type of law requires the state to impose direct control over how sex offenders live in the community or subject them to ongoing supervision. Indeed, one could argue that notification laws are an attempt by the state to absolve itself of any duty to prevent sexual recidivism.[19]

Summary

Severe sentencing laws and SVP commitment laws on the one hand, and registration and notification laws on the other hand, leave the state only two extreme options to prevent sexual recidivism: confine convicted sex offenders for a long time or release them into the community subject to information control. However, these laws overconfine, locking up large numbers of offenders who could live safely in the community if released or, if necessary, subject to appropriate supervision in the community.

Most sex offenders will come back to the community eventually. Once they are released from prison and parole, there is not much the state can do under these laws to protect the community from those sex offenders who are at risk of committing another sex crime. The state can indefinitely commit a relatively small number of them as SVPs or release most of them with no control other than compiling some information about them and sometimes providing it to the community. These are rather stark choices: indeterminate confinement or release with no supervision.

---

[18] Peter Finn, *Sex Offender Community Notification*, National Institution of Justice Research in Action, Feb. 1997 *available at* http://www.ncjrs.org/pdffiles/162364.pdf (last visited Feb. 11, 2004).
[19] La Fond, *supra* note 11.

THE PREDICTION MODEL OF DANGEROUSNESS
AND ITS LIMITATIONS

Both strategies depend on a prediction model of dangerousness. This model requires the state to make a determination—at a single point in time—of whether the offender will commit another sex crime if he is released to the community. Authorities must make this determination based on information known at that moment about the offender. They cannot take into account new information learned about him *after* the prediction is made and, unless he is on probation or parole, it is almost impossible for them to *adjust* the degree of control they exercise over the offender in light of that new information.

Mandatory minimum sentencing laws rely on a categorical approach, basing the prediction solely on the offender's criminal offense history. SVP laws give specified officials discretionary authority to initiate commitment based on their one-time prediction of risk. Registration laws are expansive and effectively predict that most sex offenders may reoffend over a 10-year period; consequently, most sex offenders must register for at least 10 years and often much longer. Notification laws either specify which offenders will be subjects of notification, and the extent of notification, or give specified agencies limited discretion in making these decisions.

Duration

Predictions of sexual dangerousness generally apply to an extended time period. It is essentially a forecast made at one point in time that during a specified future period the offender probably will—or will not—commit another sex crime.

Criminal sentences protect the community against sexual reoffending as long as the individual is incarcerated and, to a lesser degree, on parole or probation. SVP laws protect the community while the offender is committed to an institution or, to a lesser extent, placed on community release.[20] Registration law protection, modest at best, lasts during the required registration period. How long notification law protection lasts is not clear, because notification may be a one-time event or require someone in the community to seek this information.[21] Thus, its protective effect probably dissipates quickly with the passage of time and as new neighbors move in after notification. None of these approaches provides substantial protection to the community after a sex offender has been released from the duty to register.

---

[20] *Id.*
[21] *See* chapter 4.

The Categorical Approach

As I noted earlier, mandatory minimum sentencing laws use a categorical approach to predicting sexual dangerousness; it is based exclusively on the offender's criminal history. Although some types of offenses are relevant to predicting sexual dangerousness, many are not. Moreover, many factors now known to predict sexual recidivism, such as male victims, age of first offense, deviant sexual preference, will not be considered in this scheme.[22] No one seriously argues that this approach is accurate in predicting sexual reoffending.

The Discretionary Approach

SVP laws confer discretion on public officials, and they can usually consider more information than just an offender's official conviction record in deciding whether a convicted sex offender poses a serious risk of reoffending sufficient to justify seeking his commitment under an SVP law. Nonetheless, most of the information these officials actually use is "stale": The events usually occurred many years ago. By definition, it is also fixed and will not change. In addition, it is difficult (though not impossible) for officials to gather and use more recent information about the offender in predicting his risk. Sheer numbers, however, make it unlikely. For example, as of October 1, 2002, the California Department of Mental Health screened the records of 4,472 convicted sex offenders to determine their eligibility for commitment under its SVP law.[23] Thus, even in a discretionary model, officials are most likely to rely exclusively on an offender's conviction history in exercising their discretion.

The Actuarial Approach

Actuarial prediction methods are now the preferred approach to predicting sexual dangerousness. Actuarial tools, constructed by studying large numbers of repeat sex offenders and determining their common characteristics, have a robust power of predicting sexual reoffending.[24] Karl Hanson, a noted Canadian researcher, believes that actuarial risk assessment can identify a group of sex offenders who will reoffend at a rate that can "conser-

---

[22] See chapter 2.
[23] Cal. Dept. of Mental Health, Sex Offender Commitment Program (SOCP) Home Page, *available at* http://www.dmh.ca.gov/socp/default.asp (last visited Feb. 11, 2004).
[24] See chapter 2 for a thorough discussion of this approach.

vatively be estimated at 50% and could reasonably be estimated at 70% to 80%."[25]

Criticisms of Actuarial Predictions of Sexual Dangerousness

Actuarial predictions can only identify a range of risk for a group of sex offenders. They cannot identify the specific risk for any individual within the group. Nor can actuarial prediction specify where within the group range the individual lies. He may have a higher or a lower risk than the group's risk. If he does, then his *individual* risk of sexual recidivism is either higher or lower than the *group* risk.

Actuarial predictions make judgments about a person on the basis of his membership in a group and the characteristics of that group. Critics have faulted this approach because it does not make judgments exclusively on the basis of the individual and his characteristics; instead, it relies on his similarity to others. Even so, it should be noted that most public health information about risk is derived from this same approach.

Even if Hanson is correct that we can identify a group of sex offenders who will reoffend at a rate between 50% and 80%, those predictions will be *wrong* in 20% to 50% of the cases. Those predictions also suppose that *no control* will be exercised over these individuals while they live in the community. Moreover, these predictions project that the offender will reoffend at *one moment* in time sometime during a defined follow-up period, often about 4 or 5 years. To ensure that this prediction of dangerousness does not materialize at one moment during this period, we would have to confine the individual for the entire period. As we shall soon discuss, actual risk of even these high-risk offenders can be lowered considerably if they are aggressively supervised in the community.

Predictions about less dangerous sex offenders are likely to be less accurate because they have a lower base rate of offending. That is, as a group they do not commit as many sex crimes as the high-risk group does. Thus, sexual offending by any member of this group is less likely. Predictions about this group will be less accurate, resulting in more errors, including predictions of danger (i.e., an offender predicted to reoffend would not) and of safety (i.e., an offender predicted not to reoffend would). Errors of the first type, incorrect predictions of danger, are more likely than the other type for this group. Consequently, it is much less certain whether these offenders should be confined for a long period or released subject to registration and notification laws.

---

[25] *See* R. Karl Hanson, *Who Is Dangerous and When Are They Safe? Risk Assessment With Sexual Offenders*, in Protecting Society, *supra* note 12, at 63, *and* Hanson, *infra* note 44 at 67–68. *See* chapter 2 for a discussion of the use of actuarial instruments to assess risk for sex offenders.

Actuarial predictions shed absolutely no light on the psychology of the individual or why he has committed or is predicted to commit a sex crime. Consequently, we know nothing about what his precursors to offending are, what might trigger it, or how it might be prevented. In short, they shed light only on statistical group dangerousness and nothing else.

Summary

Actuarial predictions of sexual recidivism are the most accurate so far, but even at the highest level of confidence, they will have a significant error rate. They state only a group risk of reoffending, not an individual rate. The individual rate is likely to be different from the group rate. These predictions forecast a one-time event during a lengthy period. Actuarial risk predictions cannot take into account subsequent information about the offender that might significantly change the risk calculation. These predictions also assume that the offender will not be under intensive supervision.

THE PROBLEM OF ACCURATELY DETERMINING
SEXUAL RECIDIVISM

As noted in chapter 1, sexual recidivism (the commission of another sex crime) is generally determined by studying official records to see whether convicted sex offenders are subsequently arrested, charged, or convicted with another sex crime. As we saw in chapter 2, this records-based approach, which is generally used in measuring all criminal recidivism, shows that sex offenders, as a group, have a relatively low risk of sexual recidivism when compared with many other kinds of violent criminals.

On the other hand, as we also pointed out in chapter 2, victim surveys and sex offender self-reports indicate that many sex crimes are never reported to the police; consequently, they would not be counted in studies of sexual recidivism. Even if reported, the offender is not always arrested. If arrested, the case may not go to trial. If it goes to trial, the defendant may plead guilty to a nonsex crime or be acquitted. Consequently, recidivism studies undoubtedly underreport sex crimes and, necessarily, underreport sexual recidivism.

Given the apparent disagreement between research on sex offender recidivism, on the one hand, and victim surveys and offender self-reports, on the other hand, sex offenders as a group *may* be more dangerous than official records and recidivism research indicate. If they *are* more dangerous, then current methods of predicting sexual recidivism may grossly underpredict sexual dangerousness. There may also be a significant number of sex offenders who have committed more sex crimes than disclosed by official records. If so, then these offenders may be much more dangerous than actuarial instruments would indicate, because their history is incomplete and therefore inaccurate. Because the true rate of sexual recidivism is problematic, the use of risk-management strategies for preventing sex offenders living in the community from committing more sex crimes is imperative.

TREATMENT EFFICACY

As we saw in chapter 3, many mental health professionals believe that new treatment techniques can successfully reduce the risk of sexual recidivism for those who participate sincerely in these programs. Although recent research suggests some factual basis for optimism, the jury is still out on the question of whether treatment does reduce sexual dangerousness. It may or it may not. Consequently, we simply do not know with certainty whether sex offenders who have participated in treatment programs, whether in the community, in jail or prison, or in SVP facilities, are less likely to commit another sex crime once they are released. Until we know the answer to this question, it is not clear that treatment should change an earlier prediction of sexual dangerousness. In light of this uncertainty, it makes a great deal of sense to apply risk management techniques to many sex offenders living in society.

Even though treatment efficacy remains an open question, we should encourage sex offenders to participate in treatment whenever and wherever possible, while also monitoring them for a reasonable period of time to ensure that they implement what they have learned in treatment and do not reoffend. Risk management allows professionals to assess individual risk periodically and to increase or decrease the level of community supervision in light of this ongoing process and the new information. If in the future we gain more confidence in the efficacy of treatment for sex offenders, risk management may not be needed as much. Until then, however, it is only prudent to use it. Later in this chapter, I describe four different approaches to risk management that appear very promising.

PREDICTING SAFETY

Experts have made significant progress in predicting sexual dangerousness.[26] Unfortunately, they have not made nearly as much progress in predicting sexual safety. Simply put, experts do not know when sex offenders

---

[26] See chapter 2.

can be released to the community with little risk of committing another sex crime.[27]

There is a reason for this. Predictions of sex offending risk are based primarily on past facts that are static or fixed and do not change. These include age of first offense, number of convictions for sex crimes, male victims, and similar variables.[28] Predictions of safety, on the other hand, are based primarily on dynamic factors that can change over time. These might include, for example, developing empathy for victims, changing one's attitudes toward women, and successfully mastering techniques to prevent relapse. As of now, experts have been unable to identify which factors indicate reduced risk with sufficient accuracy to determine when high-risk sex offenders can be safely released into the community.[29] (Their present inability to determine with certainty whether treatment reduces sexual recidivism compounds this problem.)

As a result, researchers have been unable to develop actuarial instruments (or any instruments, for that matter) that identify a group of sex offenders or individual offenders whose recidivism risk has been reduced sufficiently to justify their conditional release from prison or commitment. Identifying SVPs who can be conditionally released from institutions and placed in a supervised community has been very troublesome for states with SVP laws. Many more sex offenders are being committed than are being released, and few SVPs have been given a final discharge from commitment.[30]

Assessing whether sex offenders confined in prisons or secure mental health facilities can be "safely" released into the community is extremely difficult because of the context in which that assessment is made. Most experts agree that accurate risk assessment is very difficult to conduct in a secure institution. The reason is quite simple: Men in secure confinement do not have the opportunities to reoffend that they will have in the community. In addition, an institutional environment does not afford a realistic environment in which sex offenders can apply what they have learned in treatment. Instead, it requires ongoing monitoring and assessment of how the offender behaves in the real world to see how he responds to the stimulation and opportunities there.[31] Even then, ongoing monitoring and

---

[27] See Hanson, supra note 25 in PROTECTING SOCIETY; and Hanson, infra note 44.

[28] See chapter 2 for a thorough discussion.

[29] Failure to complete treatment, however, does correlate with increased risk of sexual recidivism. R. Karl Hanson et al., First Report of the Collaborative Outcome Data on the Effectiveness of Psychological Treatment of Sex Offenders, 14 SEXUAL ABUSE: A J. OF RES. AND TREATMENT 169 (2002).

[30] See La Fond, supra note 12 in PROTECTING SOCIETY; and John Q. La Fond, The Costs of Enacting a Sexual Predator Law, 4 PSYCHOL. PUB. POL'Y & L. 468 (1998).

[31] See John Q. La Fond, Washington's Sexually Violent Predator Law: A Deliberate Misuse of the Therapeutic State for Social Control, 15 U. PUGET SOUND L. REV. 655 (1992) (Appendix I)

assessment is essential to confirm that the offender can live safely in the community and to make the necessary adjustments in control, including reinstitutionalization, if necessary, in light of this information to protect the community. Simply put, risk management can provide a reasonable backstop for what we do not know about predicting safety.

A BETTER ALTERNATIVE: RISK MANAGEMENT

Experts can predict dangerousness much more accurately than they can predict safety, and we do not know whether treatment reduces sexual recidivism. Predictions of risk made at one moment in time often become stale and inaccurate with the passage of time. New information about the offender may develop that indicates greater or lesser danger, requiring adjustments in the control exercised over the individual. Therefore, risk management is a much better system for protecting the community, because it allows controls on sex offenders to be adjusted in light of periodic risk assessments and updated information learned from them.[32]

Under a risk management model, an initial risk assessment for each sex offender, using state-of-the-art actuarial instruments and other techniques, would be conducted at the time of sentencing. Sentencing would be imposed and the release of the offender into the community would be managed using this model. Control both within the institution and in the community could be increased and decreased over time in light of ongoing assessments.

The criminal justice system already provides for risk management of offenders, usually through probation (i.e., an offender is released into the community subject to supervision by government agencies without serving any jail or prison time) or through parole (i.e., an offender is released into the community subject to supervision by government agencies after serving jail or prison time). Thus, one could reasonably wonder, what, if anything, is new in the concept of risk management?

The answer is that experts have developed new risk management regimes specifically for sex offenders. They are not foolproof, of course, but they appear to be effective in reducing sexual recidivism. We now know enough about sex offending and sex offenders to justify risk management

---

(reprinting in part Vernon L. Quinsey, Review of the Washington State Special Commitment Center Program for Sexually Violent Predators (Feb. 1992)) (unpublished manuscript on file with author); *see also* Anita Schlank, *Guidelines for the Development of New Programs, in* THE SEXUAL PREDATOR: LAW, POLICY, EVALUATION, AND TREATMENT 12-5 & 12-6 (Anita Schlank & Fred Cohen eds., 1999).

[32] *See, e.g.*, Kurt Heilbrun, Christine Maguth Nezu, Michelle Keeney, Susis Chung, & Adam L. Wasserman, *Sexual Offending: Linking Assessment, Intervention, and Decision Making*, 4 PSYCHOL. PUB. POL'Y & L. 138 (1998); Bruce J. Winick, *Applying the Law Therapeutically in Domestic Violence Cases*, 69 UMKC L. REV. 33 (2000).

approaches that differ significantly from general probation and parole strategies. If we are serious about protecting future victims, society must use containment strategies that are very aggressive and are tailored to each sex offender. Sex crimes thrive in secrecy because sex offenders are secretive and manipulative, and many of them have highly developed social skills that they use to further their offending. Many sex offenders have developed belief systems that allow them to deny or minimize the harm they do to others. Finally, many of them have an enduring propensity to reoffend.[33] Thus, new supervision strategies must deny them any opportunity to commit another sex offense, while simultaneously changing their attitudes and behavior.

Locator Technology

New technology makes surveillance of offenders more precise and economical. Home monitoring through electronic bracelets has been used for offenders, including sex offenders, released on bail or placed back into the community on parole or conditional release from SVP programs. These devices have advantages and disadvantages. They can only confirm whether a person is at a designated place at a designated time. They cannot tell authorities where he is if he is not where he is supposed to be.[34]

Bracelets or other devices using global positioning satellites (GPS), however, can provide continuous "real time" information on an offender's physical location,[35] thus ensuring that law enforcement knows almost instantly whether a sex offender is violating the conditions of his release by visiting people or places that he has been told to avoid.[36] The GPS system has another advantage over traditional electronic monitoring: Certain places, like schools, playgrounds, or victims' houses, can be designated as "hot zones" and placed off limits to sex offenders. If an offender tries to enter a hot zone or fails to return home when required, the GPS system can send an immediate alert. One senior probation supervisor in Florida described the GPS system this way: "It's like having a camera in the sky. We can follow them around."[37] Of course, this system cannot stop a sex offender determined to commit another sex crime from doing so. But, by subjecting sex offenders to intensive, ongoing, real-time surveillance, it can

---

[33] English et al., *supra* note 1.
[34] Jennifer Lee, *Putting Parolees on a Tighter Leash*, N.Y. TIMES, Jan. 31, 2002, at D1.
[35] Bill Douthat, *Tracking System Keeps Never-Blinking Eyes on Offenders: Satellites Monitor Whereabouts, Even Speed*, THE PALM BEACH POST, July 16, 2001, at A1.
[36] Stuart Pfeifer, *O.C. to Track Sex Criminals With GPS*, L.A. TIMES, Dec. 23, 2001, Part II at 1; Matthew P. Blanchard, *Satellite Monitoring Network Creates Virtual Jail for Suspects*, PITTSBURGH POST-GAZETTE, Sept. 8, 2001, at C8.
[37] Lee, *supra* note 34, at D6.

help prevent sex crimes. By proving where they have been, these devices can also clear sex offenders of suspicion if children are reported missing or if a sex crime has been committed. This information should help police eliminate suspects and conduct better investigations.

There are still some problems with these devices. They are somewhat bulky and may not always work when the offender is in a building, an area surrounded by tall buildings, or certain rural areas.[38] Advances in technology should remedy these limitations in due course.

Florida estimates the cost of monitoring a sex offender in the community with a GPS system at about $10 a day, compared with about $45 a day to keep him in a state prison.[39] Currently, 27 states are using some type of satellite surveillance to keep close watch on approximately 1,200 offenders.[40] Another 150,000 criminals or so are monitored by electronic supervision, such as home monitoring using an electronic bracelet or mandatory telephone checks. It costs at least $20,000 or more to confine a sex offender in most state prisons, not including new capital costs. It costs, on average, $100,000 a year to commit an SVP to an institution.[41]

Criminal Sentencing

Risk assessment should be used in sentencing convicted sex offenders. Offenders determined by actuarial instruments to be at high risk of reoffending should be given an additional sentence above and beyond their normal prison sentence. After the offender has served the normal sentence for his crime or crimes, another risk assessment would be conducted. Depending on its result, this additional increment would be served either in prison or on intensive parole, which uses a community containment approach to monitor the offender's behavior in the community. This approach should also create a strong incentive for sex offenders sentenced to this additional time to participate actively in prison treatment programs in order to reduce their propensity to reoffend and to earn the opportunity to live in the community subject to intensive supervision.

Washington State uses a somewhat similar approach, sometimes called *determinate plus* sentencing. It is based on the crime of conviction and the offender history. It *requires* a judge to give *nonpersistent* offenders who have committed a specified sex crime or sexually motivated crime the maximum sentence. The court may also sentence the offender to serve a period of the sentence after he is released from prison into community custody under the

---

[38] *Id.*
[39] *Id.* at D1.
[40] *Id.*
[41] *See* chapter 5.

supervision of the Department of Corrections.[42] This practice ensures that the offender is subject to aggressive community supervision for the maximum period.

Conversely, if an initial risk assessment indicates that the offender poses a very low risk of reoffending, and the crime is not a violent felony, then he may be a candidate for probation in the community, subject to aggressive community monitoring and intensive treatment as an outpatient. Of course, other important factors must be considered in making this decision, including the interests of the victim and the community. Sex offenders who are not dangerous do not have to be sent to jail or prison if a sound risk management program is in place.

Certain conditions must be met before an offender can be placed on community probation. First, sex offenders must plead guilty to the charged sex crime or crimes. They should not be allowed to enter an *Alford* plea, by which an offender maintains his innocence but acknowledges that the government could prove the charges. Nor should they be allowed to enter a *nolo contendere* plea, by which an offender does not admit guilt, but rather waives his right to make the government prove his guilt. Sex offenders should not be permitted to plead guilty to a nonsex crime, have a deferred judgment or sentence entered, or be diverted out of the criminal justice system. These strategems allow sex offenders to deny or minimize the harm they have done to their victim or victims and to maintain faulty thinking that facilitates the commission of sex crimes. Moreover, these dispositions suggest that their crime was a "one-time mistake," denigrate the harm done to the victim, and can leave an incomplete or inaccurate public record, thereby jeopardizing public safety. Instead, the offender must accept full responsibility for what he has done. A forthright guilty plea can begin the process of cognitive restructuring that brings home to the defendant the magnitude of his actions.[43] In addition, the offender should be sentenced to a jail or prison term that is suspended on condition of his compliance with the terms of his probation. This measure provides meaningful external control on the offender and gives him powerful incentives to succeed in treatment and on probation.

Postrelease Risk Management in the Community

Risk management also allows authorities to follow a sex offender into the community after he is released from jail or prison and to increase or decrease control over him in light of new information about his behavior

---

[42] WASH. REV. CODE §§ 9.94A.712, 713 (2004).
[43] English et al., *supra* note 1.

in his new environment. For example, a convicted child molester may start to visit playgrounds and talk to young children. If he does, then authorities should impose more stringent conditions on him or, if necessary, return him to prison. Or the offender may have successfully completed a community treatment program, established a support group to help him avoid opportunities to reoffend, and successfully avoided being around or talking to young children. In this case, authorities might allow him greater freedom in the community and lessen the surveillance and reporting requirements. In short, these sorts of dynamic risk factors are very important in determining with greater accuracy whether the offender is at greater or lesser risk of reoffending.[44] If so, then there is little justification for making a one-time assessment of risk that will apply to the individual for a long time, perhaps the rest of his life.

Sexual Predators

A risk management approach should also be used to commit SVPs *initially* to a least restrictive alternative (LRA; e.g., community placement) in appropriate cases or to release them from institutional commitment. This approach would be especially useful in determining and managing the release to the community of sex offenders committed under SVP laws. It would also reduce burgeoning SVP populations in institutions and significantly reduce costs incurred in confining them.[45]

Additional Advantages of Risk Management

Risk management can be used to supervise many more sex offenders as they are released from criminal confinement. Thus, more sex offenders can be monitored and controlled in the community. The level of control can be increased or decreased, depending on periodic risk assessments. This approach can create powerful incentives for offenders to change their attitudes and behaviors in prison and in the community in order to earn more freedom. It also assures the community that increased restraint, including reincarceration, will be imposed on the offender if necessary to protect the community.

Risk management should also be less expensive than confinement under a state SVP law or a criminal sentencing law.[46] It will be more effective than compiling relatively useless information in sex offender registries

---

[44] *See* R. Karl Hanson, *What Do We Know About Sex Offender Risk Assessment?* 4 PSYCHOL. PUB. POL'Y & L. 50 (1998).

[45] La Fond, *supra* note 12 *in* PROTECTING SOCIETY; La Fond, *supra* note 30.

[46] *Id.*

or warning the community to watch out for itself. Simply put, a risk management approach provides the best of both worlds: stronger community protection measures combined with strong incentives for sex offender rehabilitation.[47]

An example of how risk management might be applied to sex offender registration laws is instructive. Some sex offenders may have to be added to a registration list if they do not comply with the conditions of their parole or for other reasons should be considered at high risk of reoffending in light of information about their behavior in the community. Conversely, some offenders considered dangerous at release may be considered much less dangerous if they have lived safely in the community for a number of years. It makes sense to modify legal control in light of this new information.

SUCCESSFUL RISK MANAGEMENT PROGRAMS

Several risk management programs appear to successfully place sex offenders in the community while also monitoring them very intensively and adjusting supervision in light of new information about risk. It is well worth looking at them.

The Community Containment Approach

Colorado has pioneered an innovative, aggressive, and effective risk management program called *community containment*.[48] Its basic goal is public safety and preventing new sexual victimization. Its strategy is to deny offenders any access to victims and to prevent the offender from engaging in the type of conduct that he has used in the past to commit a sex crime.[49] Variations of this approach are used by other jurisdictions.[50]

A Team Approach

A multidisciplinary case management team composed of a probation or parole officer, a treatment provider who is treating the offender, and an experienced polygraph examiner is the core component of this approach. The team reviews an offender's criminal records to learn everything it can about his past pattern of sexual victimization, including how many crimes

---

[47] La Fond & Winick, *supra* note 5.
[48] Kim English et al., *Community Containment of Sex Offender Risk: A Promising Approach, in* PROTECTING SOCIETY, *supra* note 12, at 265.
[49] Kim English, *The Containment Approach: An Aggressive Strategy for the Community Management of Adult Sex Offenders*, 4 PSYCHOL. PUB. POL'Y & L. 218, 221 (1998).
[50] English et al., *supra* note 1.

he committed, who his victims were, how he committed his crimes, and where he committed them. If necessary, the team may interview neighbors, family members, and coworkers to supplement this information. The team also learns from the offender himself about his *modus operandi* and high-risk behavior patterns that only he knows. This information includes his preferred victim types, the frequency and intensity of his deviant sexual arousal patterns and behavior, and the events and emotional states that are precursors to his sexual offending. The offender must waive confidentiality protection for this information because it may be shared with others, including law enforcement agencies, family members, and others.

Polygraph Exams

The team's polygraph examiner uses the polygraph to verify all of this information and to update it periodically. The use of a polygraph significantly increases the amount and accuracy of information obtained from the offender. It also helps to break down the denial and minimization shown by many sex offenders that enables them to offend, and it enhances the process of cognitive restructuring that is essential for effective treatment.[51] Polygraph examinations have proved extremely effective in eliciting more admissions from sex offenders about the number of people they have victimized. In one study, offenders admitted to having six times more victims than offenders who were not given a polygraph test.[52] Although there may be many other possible explanations for these increased confessions, it is very likely that the polygraph testing strongly encouraged sex offenders to be candid about their offense history. Of course, polygraph exams are not 100% accurate, but as others have noted, they are far more accurate than sex offender self-reports of their sex crimes.[53]

Self-Incrimination

Self-incriminating answers by the offender during a polygraph exam raise serious Fifth Amendment issues. Can the government use these admissions to convict the offender of past crimes that were unknown to the prosecutor? This is a complicated issue that is beyond the scope of this book.[54] Many jurisdictions choose not to try to use these confessions to convict the offender; rather, they prefer to get accurate and honest information from him about his past sex crimes to make sure that he does not commit new ones.

---

[51] *See* chapter 3 for a discussion of cognitive restructuring.

[52] Jan Hindman & James M. Peters, *Polygraph Testing Leads to Better Understanding of Adult and Juvenile Sex Offenders*, 65 DEC. FED. PROB. 8, 9 (2001).

[53] English et al., *supra* note 1.

[54] For a general analysis of these issues, *see* La Fond & Winick, *supra* note 5.

A Containment Plan

Using information about his sexual history obtained from the offender, the team prepares a supervision and surveillance plan, which is tailored to the offender and his offense pattern. The plan establishes tight boundaries on his daily routine, his access to erotic material, and other activities that are part of his offense pattern. It will include prohibitions on contacting or even coming near his past victims. It may include additional restrictions on contact with his victim types, like children, or frequenting locations where his victim types are present, like playgrounds. These conditions not only prevent access to potential victims, they also provide strong incentives to the offender to implement relapse prevention techniques that he has learned by avoiding those situations that have been conducive to his offending in the past. He may also be subject to urine analysis to check for prohibited substances, like alcohol or drugs that may be associated with his reoffending, and to electronic monitoring and random home visits. Random polygraph exams are also given to deter and detect any violations of these conditions.

Treatment Required

The offender must also participate in treatment provided by approved therapists. This treatment, often provided in group settings, emphasizes cognitive restructuring,[55] which changes how the offender thinks about his offending, and relapse prevention,[56] which helps him identify and avoid recurring sexual fantasies or high-risk situations. The offender may pay for some or all of his treatment.

Surveillance and Compliance

The team meets regularly to ensure that the offender is following his plan and to determine whether the offender poses any threat to public safety. Specialized surveillance officers help to ensure compliance by monitoring the offender through intensive fieldwork. This may include searching the cars and homes of offenders and monitoring their daily routine. If the offender violates the conditions of his parole or probation, the team can impose a range of sanctions. These may include increased restrictions on his daily routine, more intensive surveillance or more frequent polygraphs, home visits, or urine analysis. He may be required to attend more treatment sessions, or even to live in a halfway house, or if necessary, to return to jail or prison on revocation of probation or parole.

---

[55] See chapter 3 for a discussion of cognitive restructuring.
[56] See chapter 3 for a discussion of relapse prevention.

These graded sanctions allow the team to increase control over the offender if appropriate in light of new information it learns about his behavior in the community.[57] Conversely, the team can also loosen the intensity of control it exercises over him if his behavior indicates less risk; thus, the community containment approach provides powerful incentives for sex offenders not to reoffend.

Interagency Communication

The team also keeps the court updated on the offender's compliance or noncompliance. This not only keeps the judge informed, it also impresses on the offender that he may be swiftly returned to jail or prison if he does not comply with the conditions of his plan. The public, too, may have more confidence in this strategy because of the judge's ongoing involvement in community containment.

Caseloads

Needless to say, this approach can be successful only if the team has a limited number of offenders to supervise, because it requires intensive and effective monitoring of sex offenders.

Effectiveness

The research to date suggests that community containment is effective in reducing sexual victimization. Among offenders, including sex offenders, released through the community corrections system (probation and parole) who did reoffend, as measured by a new criminal charge, those not subject to postrelease supervision tended to reoffend more quickly than those subject to community supervision.[58] Of course, more research is needed to determine specifically whether the community containment approach is effective in reducing sexual recidivism. So far, it shows great promise.

Lifetime Probation

Arizona law authorizes offenders to be placed on probation for life.[59] Creative prosecutors in Maricopa County, which includes Phoenix, Scottsdale, and Tempe, have used this law to create a special lifetime probation program for sex offenders.

---

[57] English, *supra* note 1.
[58] Suzanne Gonzalez Woodburn & Kim English, *Community Corrections in Colorado: A Report of Findings,* (2002), *available at* http://dcj.state.co.us/ors/pdf/docs/2002COMCOREPORT.pdf (last visited Feb. 12, 2004).
[59] Ariz. Rev. Stat. §13-604.01 (2003).

Preliminary Evaluations

In selected cases, prosecutors and defense counsel agree to have the defendant evaluated to determine whether he is an appropriate candidate for probation and, if he is, to determine appropriate probation conditions. If this evaluation indicates that probation is a suitable disposition, prosecutors allow the sex offender to plead guilty, and they agree not to seek his incarceration. In exchange, these offenders agree to be subject to lifetime probation for their crime.

Team Management

This program uses an approach very similar to the community containment program in Colorado. Teams consisting of probation officers, treatment providers, and polygraph examiners develop a full understanding of each sex offender's criminal and sexual history and develop a probation plan designed to prevent reoffending. These plans may include no contact or limited contact with children, periodic polygraph testing and urine analysis, and other limitations, such as no access to computers and a waiver of confidentiality. In addition, each probationer must participate in treatment, including an intensive 35-hour class on human sexuality and sexual deviancy. Less intensive treatment will continue thereafter; it may be terminated if a periodic assessment so indicates. Polygraph tests typically are given every 6 months. Surveillance officers make unannounced visits to their homes, workplace, and family to ensure offender compliance. The team meets frequently to discuss and evaluate their cases. Quarterly reports are provided to an advisory committee.

Prosecutors, judges, law enforcement personnel, and victim advocates informally participate in the system and are often invited to specialized training sessions. As a result, these players understand how the system works and are more likely to trust it and rely on it.

The Numbers

As a result of this plea agreement, Arizona prosecutors can effectively engage in intensive risk management supervision of sex offenders who are not at high risk of committing another sex crime and are living in the community. The relevant offender population includes 200 adult offenders, as well as adolescent offenders as young as 14 who are sentenced to adult probation for their sex offenses.[60]

---

[60] CENTER FOR SEX OFFENDER MANAGEMENT, CASE STUDIES ON THE CENTER FOR SEX OFFENDER MANAGEMENT'S NATIONAL RESOURCE SITES, (2d ed., rev. 2001), *available at* http://www.csom.org/pubs/casestudies2.pdf (last visited Feb. 12, 2004).

The probation department has 23 specialized probation officers who supervise an average of 52 offenders. It also has 19 surveillance officers who each keep track of about 63 offenders. In addition, the office has an intensive probation unit, which supervises about 200 sex offenders. Each officer has a caseload of no more than 25. Most probationers begin in intensive probation and, if successful after several years in that program, move into maintenance-level probation.

The Results

Maricopa County has analyzed 2,344 offenders supervised by these units from May 1993 through August 2000. It found that about 40% of them had been returned to court for a probation violation at least once. Of these nearly 1,000 offenders, more than 30% had not complied with treatment; 30% had used alcohol or drugs; and approximately 27% had had unauthorized contact with children. A total of 350 offenders from this group were sent to prison, whereas approximately 330 were placed in intensive parole. More important, just under 7% (160 offenders) had committed new crimes, and only 42 of them were sex crimes, including 17 cases of indecent exposure, 3 cases of viewing child pornography, and 22 various contact crimes. Many of the contact crimes had occurred after family or friends had allowed offenders access to children.

On balance, it appears that the Maricopa County lifetime probation program has been successful in allowing sex offenders to live in the community, while protecting the community from sexual reoffending. This risk management approach also seems to be cost-effective. The costs of monitoring a sex offender in this program are reportedly about $1,400 a year, compared with a cost of $16,000 to keep a sex offender in prison and about $100,000 to keep an SVP in an institution.

Lifetime Parole

Arizona had also passed a law that allowed judges to include lifetime parole as part of the sentence they could impose on offenders who committed serious crimes against children.[61] However, the Arizona Supreme Court struck down the law, holding that it violated Arizona's constitutional provisions on separation of powers. The court concluded that the law improperly gave judges the power to grant parole. In the court's view, only the legislature can set the length of criminal sentences and only the executive branch can

---

[61] ARIZ. REV. STAT. §13-914 (2004). *See also* Arizona Judicial Department, Overview and Summary of Community Punishment Program, 1996.

grant parole.[62] The court suggested that this defect in the law might be correctable but that, as written, the Arizona statute authorizing lifetime parole violated the state constitution.

Although the Arizona law violated the state constitution because of how the law was written, this does not mean that similar laws could not be enacted by other states. In some cases, lifetime parole will be essential to protect the community against sex offenders released from the prison system. States should seriously consider this strategy.

Sex Offender Reentry Courts

Professor Bruce J. Winick and I have proposed the creation of *sex offender reentry courts* that would be based on the concept of therapeutic jurisprudence and the community containment approach to risk management.[63] A primary goal of our correctional process should be the successful reentry into the community of an offender as a law-abiding member.[64] Reentry courts, which were first proposed by the director of the National Institute of Justice, Jeremy Travis,[65] facilitate that goal. They contemplate reentry as a process that begins with sentencing and continues until the offender is safely reintegrated into the community.[66]

Reentry court is one kind of "problem-solving court," a system that can deal with various offender populations, including drug offenders, mentally ill offenders, and domestic violence abusers,[67] as well as sex offenders. In all of these courts, the judge plays a central role in a collaborative, interdisciplinary approach to community protection and offender rehabilitation.[68]

Therapeutic Jurisprudence

Therapeutic jurisprudence is an interdisciplinary approach to law. It believes legal principles, procedures, and roles can have positive or negative psychological impact on people involved in the legal system.[69] Legal systems

---

[62] *See* State v. Wagstaff, 794 P.2d 118 (Ariz. 1990); *see also* State v. Byrd, 793 P.2d 1093 (Ariz. 1990); *and* Ariz. Const. art. III.

[63] La Fond & Winick, *supra* note 5.

[64] Jeremy Travis, *But They All Come Back: Rethinking Prisoner Reentry*, Sentencing & Corrections: Issues for the 21st Century (May 2000) *available at* http://www.ncjrs.org/pdffiles1/nij/181413.pdf (last visited Feb. 12, 2004).

[65] *Id.*

[66] T. Saunders, *Staying Home: Effective Reintegration Strategies for Parolees*, 41 The Judges' J. 34 (2002); Joan Petersilia, *When Prisoners Return to the Community: Political, Economic, and Social Consequences*, Sentencing & Corrections: Issues for the 21st Century (Nov. 2000) *available at* http://www.ncjrs.org/pdffiles1/nij/184253.pdf (last visited Feb. 12, 2004).

[67] Bruce J. Winick, *Therapeutic Jurisprudence and Problem Solving Courts*, 30 Fordham Urban L. J. 1055 (2003).

[68] *Id.*

[69] *See generally*, David B. Wexler, Therapeutic Jurisprudence (1990); David B. Wexler & Bruce J. Winick, Essays in Therapeutic Jurisprudence (1991).

should use sound social science research to maximize positive psychological effects while minimizing negative effects. Therapeutic jurisprudence also urges social scientists to study legal systems in order to measure these effects, wherever possible.

Community Containment

As we saw earlier in this chapter, community containment uses an interdisciplinary team to prepare a strict plan for each sex offender released into the community. The plan denies him access to victims and to opportunities for offending. Parole officers closely monitor his behavior in the community, and trained polygraph examiners periodically question the offender to ensure that he has rigorously complied with his release plan. Failure by the offender to do so can lead to serious consequences, including more restrictive conditions on his movements and even reincarceration.

The Role of the Judge

The judge plays a key role in a sex offender reentry court. He or she is intimately involved in the interdisciplinary team that establishes the risk management plan and is a key person in adjusting it in light of ongoing risk assessments. He or she also plays a pivotal role in motivating the offender, shaping his successful performance by praise and other positive reinforcement and, if necessary, punishing the offender if he fails to adhere to his risk management plan. Anecdotal evidence and preliminary research indicate that there is a "kind of magic in the judicial robe; that the judge's direct participation and interaction with the offender makes an important difference in offender compliance and rehabilitation."[70]

A primary role for the judge is to enter into a behavioral contract with the offender.[71] This contract sets forth specific intermediate and long-term goals for the offender. It provides agreed upon rewards for his successful performance of goals, such as participating effectively in treatment, not using alcohol or drugs, and avoiding situations that could lead to his sexual reoffending. It also stipulates agreed upon penalties if he should fail to keep the contract, such as not being able to leave his home for a specified period or, in serious cases of breach, return to prison. A behavioral contract harnesses human psychology to spur the offender to comply with its terms and to attain the goals it sets out. These principles include goal setting effect, intrinsic motivation, and the psychological value of choice.[72]

---

[70] La Fond & Winick, *supra* note 5.
[71] Travis, *supra* note 64.
[72] La Fond & Winick, *supra* note 5; *see also* Bruce J. Winick, *Harnessing the Power of the Bet: Wagering With the Government for Social and Individual Change,* 45 U. OF MIAMI L. REV. 737 (1991) (describing behavioral contracting or contingency management, analyzing the psychological principles that underlie it, and illustrating its application to achieve individual and social goals).

Sex Offender Court in Action

Sex offenders must agree to participate in sex offender courts. If they do not, offenders will be processed through the ordinary criminal process.

Pleading and Acceptance of Responsibility. Sex offender courts create a process for eventually returning the offender to the community. The process begins at the beginning, with the defendant's plea. Offenders in this court must accept full responsibility for their actions by fully acknowledging in a colloquy with the judge all the crimes they committed. Many sex offenders deny, minimize, or rationalize their criminal behavior, thereby perpetuating psychological attitudes that enable sex offending. *Nolo contendere* pleas, in which a defendant does not acknowledge his crime but does not contest the charges, and *Alford* pleas, in which the defendant maintains his innocence but admits that the prosecutor could prove its case, further allow the offender to downplay his own culpability. For this reason, such pleas are not accepted in sex offender courts. Insisting that the defendant plead guilty to the charged sex crimes begins to break down an offender's defense mechanisms and forces him to confront and acknowledge what he did.[73]

Presentencing Treatment. Sex offenders who have pled guilty may decide to enter treatment *before* they are sentenced. A judge can consider presentencing factors, such as treatment, when setting a sentence.[74] This option can provide a potent incentive for offenders to start the process of change as soon as possible. If a thorough risk assessment indicates a very low risk of recidivism, perhaps in cases involving first-time nonviolent offenders, diversion to a community treatment program,[75] together with an aggressive risk management plan based on community containment principles, may be in order.

Sentencing and Reentry. For offenders who will be sentenced to jail or prison, the judge can discuss reentry with the offender. He or she can motivate the offender to accept treatment if available in the prison system, noting that this factor may be important in determining whether the offender should be paroled to the community or serve his full prison sentence. If authorized, the judge can sentence the offender to a term in prison to be followed by a period of community release subject to the court's supervision.[76] In short, sentencing provides a unique opportunity for the judge and the

---

[73] Jeffrey A. Klotz et al., *Cognitive Restructuring Through Law: A Therapeutic Jurisprudence Approach to Sex Offenders in the Plea Process*, 15 U. PUGET SOUND L. REV. 579 (1992).

[74] Bruce J. Winick, *Redefining the Role of the Criminal Defense Lawyer at Plea Bargaining and Sentencing: A Therapeutic Jurisprudence/Preventive Law Model.* 5 PSYCHOL. PUB. POL'Y & L. 1034 (1999).

[75] *See, e.g.,* WASH. REV. CODE §9.94A.670 (2004) (authorizing a special sex offender sentencing alternative allowing community treatment rather than incarceration).

[76] Travis, *supra* note 64.

offender together to develop a plan for his reentry into society as a law-abiding citizen.[77]

Community Release. If possible, the judge would retain wide sentencing discretion for offenders in this court and could allow early release into the community if a risk assessment were to indicate a reduced risk of reoffending, subject to aggressive monitoring and an appropriate risk management plan. A prisoner might first leave the prison for part of the day, subject to continuous observation by a parole officer. If successful, he might then be assigned to a halfway house, subject to strict rules about when he may leave and where he may go. Again, if the prisoner convincingly demonstrates by his daily behavior that his risk has diminished, he might then be allowed to live at home, perhaps subject to electronic monitoring or surveillance by GPS.[78] Ongoing risk assessments, using the polygraph and other information measures, perhaps including urinalysis for drug and alcohol use, would be conducted, and the conditions of release would be adjusted in light of those assessments. The judge could impose punishment for any failure to comply with the conditions of release; in cases of serious breach, he or she could return him to prison.

Support Network. The judge could involve other stakeholders in the sentencing process. He or she could ask the offender's family, friends, and others to help the offender successfully and safely reintegrate into the community on release and help develop a reentry plan for the offender, including specifying what roles they would play in the plan. Victims or victim advocates could participate in formulating the reentry plan and in monitoring to ensure compliance, as is done in New Haven, Connecticut.[79]

Advantages

Sex offender reentry courts could prove invaluable both to community protection and to sex offender control and treatment. Even though sex offenders are being sentenced to longer prison terms and serving a greater percentage of these sentences, most sex offenders will return to the community. When they do, some of them will still be at risk of sexually reoffending, but for the most part, we simply cannot identify which individuals will

---

[77] La Fond & Winick, *supra* note 5.

[78] *See supra* notes 34–39 and accompanying text.

[79] Connecticut has created a Sex Offender Intensive Supervision Unit, which was established cooperatively by the Connecticut Office of Adult Probation and the Center for the Treatment of Problem Sexual Behavior, a nonprofit community-based treatment program. The New Haven Approach uses a team, consisting of probation officers, treatment providers, and victim advocates, to monitor high-risk sex offenders in the community and to ensure community safety. For more information, *see* http://www.theconnectioninc.org/safet.htm and http://www.csom.org/pubs/ct.html (last visited Feb. 14, 2004).

reoffend if left unsupervised. Consequently, a "best practice" would be to subject many sex offenders to aggressive risk management in the community, while providing ongoing opportunities for change and the reduction of individual risk.

Sex offender reentry courts allow the criminal justice system to affect sex offenders' attitudes early on, creating incentives for offenders to understand the significance of the harm they have caused and to undertake the arduous process of change. These courts will combine an aggressive risk management system based on the community containment approach with powerful strategies for behavioral change. Thus, incentives and opportunities for treatment will be counterbalanced by ongoing monitoring and risk assessment. Offenders will have to prove over time, by sustained effort, that they have earned the opportunity to transition through a graduated series of release placements. No one believes these courts will not make mistakes or that some released sex offenders will not commit more sex crimes. But at least this model provides a strong component of community protection together with positive and negative reinforcements for sex offenders.

Restorative Justice

An innovative program based on restorative justice is currently being tried in Arizona as an alternative to prison for sex offenders who have committed nonpenetration sex crimes. *Restorative justice* is a response to criminal behavior that seeks to restore the losses suffered by crime victims and to facilitate peace and tranquility among victims, offenders, and communities.[80] Its basic principles include healing those who have been injured and allowing those who have been harmed by the crime, including the community, the opportunity to participate fully in the response. Through this process, the community tries to build and maintain a just peace.[81]

Some scholars believe that offenders who are treated do better than nontreated offenders and that the treatment provided in an outpatient setting is more effective than treatment provided in prisons.[82] Examples of outpatient treatment programs include victim–offender reconciliation or mediation, community conferencing, victim–offender panels, victim assistance, and community crime prevention.[83] Proponents of restorative justice

---

[80] Kevin I. Minor & J.T. Morrison, A *Theoretical Study and Critique of Restorative Justice*, in RESTORATIVE JUSTICE: INTERNATIONAL PERSPECTIVES 117 (Burt Galaway & Joe Hudson eds., 1996).
[81] Restorative Justice Online, Principles of Restorative Justice, *available at* http://www.restorativejustice.org/rj3/Introduction-Definition/Tutorial/Principles_of_Restorative_Justice.htm (last visited Feb. 12, 2004).
[82] Mary P. Koss et al., *Restorative Justice for Sexual Violence: Repairing Victims, Building Community, and Holding Offenders Accountable*, in 989 SEXUALLY COERCIVE BEHAVIOR: UNDERSTANDING AND MANAGEMENT 386 (Robert A. Prentky et al., eds., 2003).
[83] Restorative Justice Online, *supra* note 81.

argue that these programs have advantages over the traditional criminal justice system because they recognize that offenders harm victims, communities, and even themselves. These programs also measure success differently; they measure how much harm has been repaired or prevented as opposed to how much punishment has been inflicted. Most important, these programs recognize the importance of community involvement and initiative in responding to and reducing crime, rather than leaving the problem of crime to the government alone.[84]

Pima County, Arizona, has a program based on restorative justice for sexual offenders, called *RESTORE* (Responsibility and Equity for Sexual Transgressions Offering a Restorative Experience). It is a community conferencing program that brings together victims, offenders, and their supporters for a face-to-face meeting under the guidance of a facilitator. Everyone is encouraged to discuss the effects of the crime on each of them and to make a plan to repair the damage done and to minimize the likelihood of further harm.[85]

In the RESTORE program, the victim must elect to participate in the program or it will not be offered to the offender.[86] Offenders usually agree to participate in the RESTORE program because they will not be incarcerated or have criminal records if they successfully complete the program. Nor will they have to register as sex offenders unless they commit another sex crime.[87] The offender must pay a fee to participate and, more important, he must acknowledge that the sexual act occurred.[88]

In the preparatory stage, a case manager meets with the victim to decide which reparations are appropriate. The victim can chose from a list of options, including compensation for lost time from work and for any medical and counseling expenses. The victim can also ask the offender to sign a "stay-away" agreement, perform community service, or issue a formal apology.[89] All redress plans require the offender to be evaluated by a state licensed sexual offender treatment provider and to participate in treatment.[90]

The conference is then held in a secure location, and all participants are required to sign a confidentiality agreement.[91] The conference begins with the offender telling what he did to the victim. Then, the victim describes how his actions harmed her or him. The redress plan is then discussed and signed by both the victim and the offender.[92]

---

[84] *Id.*
[85] Koss et al., *supra* note 82, at 388.
[86] *Id.* at 389.
[87] *Id.* at 389–90.
[88] *Id.* at 390.
[89] *Id.*
[90] Koss et al., *supra* note 82, at 390.
[91] *Id.*
[92] *Id.* at 391.

After the conference, a case manager is assigned to each offender and is responsible for supervising each of them for 12 months following the conference.[93] Offenders who complete their program appear personally before the board for closure and reintegration into the community. The victim and his or her community are also welcome to attend.[94]

Although not a typical risk management approach that emphasizes aggressive control of the offender in the community, RESTORE creates powerful incentives for sex offenders to make amends to the person they hurt and to the community and to participate in treatment. Failure to complete the program can lead to criminal prosecution and conviction, with all of their damaging consequences. This alternative seems particularly useful for first-time offenders who have committed minor sex offenses. Of course, further research will be necessary to determine whether the program reduces sexual recidivism.

CONCLUSION

Society cannot—and should not—keep massive numbers of sex offenders locked up forever. It is cruel, expensive, and unnecessary. Most sex offenders will return to the community, and most of them will pose little risk of committing another sex crime. However, some will continue to pose a significant risk of reoffending. Strategies have been developed that combine ongoing risk assessment with aggressive community surveillance and treatment and show great promise of reducing sexual recidivism. These strategies are both tough and smart. We should use them when appropriate to significantly reduce the risk of sexual violence, thereby protecting our loved ones.

---

[93] Id.
[94] Id. at 392.

8

RECOMMENDATIONS

The public's fury over violent sex crimes, especially those committed against vulnerable children by convicted sex offenders, is understandable. Many of these cases were given extensive media coverage, expanding the intensity and breadth of community outrage. It was no surprise that the public insisted that their elected representatives take action to make sure that crimes like these would never be committed again. Legislators and other policymakers passed new laws designed to protect the community against sexual violence, often targeting convicted sex offenders. Sexual predator laws, registration and community notification laws, and castration laws in particular were aimed at preventing convicted sex offenders from committing more sex crimes.

The context for this cycle of law reform certainly made the task of lawmakers very difficult. Horrible and high-profile sex crimes committed by convicted sex offenders against young children captured the public's attention and spawned firestorms for law reform that swept the nation. Americans wanted quick, sure-fire solutions to very complex public policy issues. Public anger was not conducive to thoughtful deliberation on how best to improve community protection against sexual violence, and in truth, what we knew about sex offending was incomplete. Too often, agitation for law reform and the process of law reform assumed that these unusual cases were typical cases. As a result, law reform often was crafted to promise that the worst case would never happen again.

With the passage of time, we have had an opportunity to see how many of these laws work in the real world, and we have also learned much more about sex offenders and the crimes they commit. Now is a good time to look back and see whether these laws have performed as promised or whether a rebalancing of crime control measures is in order.

Some of the newly crafted strategies adopted since 1990 to protect the community against sexual offending show great promise and, on the basis of preliminary research, have contributed significantly to a reduction in sexual violence. Unfortunately, too many of them simply ignore what we now know about sex offenders, their victims, and their patterns of offending. As a result, some of these newly minted public safety measures overtarget by a wide margin. Many are too expensive or ineffective. Some laws may actually make future victims worse off than if lawmakers had done nothing. It is time to put aside our understandable fear of sex offenders and consider more carefully what we now know about them and their victims. Only then can we craft cost-effective legal strategies that really can prevent sexual violence.

In this concluding chapter, I candidly review the most important legal strategies enacted in the past decade to see whether they have stood the test of time and experience. When appropriate, I recommend what society should do—and what it should not do—to protect our loved ones from sexual violence.

GETTING THE FACTS STRAIGHT

Sound legal policies that will protect the community against dangerous sex offenders must rest on facts, not fiction. What are those facts?

Most Sex Offenders Are Not Dangerous

Many of these new laws assume that all sex offenders are especially dangerous and more likely than other criminals to commit more crimes. Contrary to this current mythology, most sex offenders are *less likely* to commit new crimes than many other types of offenders. As we saw in chapter 2, criminals who commit assault, burglary, and kidnapping are much more likely to commit another crime.

However, it is also true that research probably *underreports* sexual recidivism significantly. By how much, researchers do not know. It is also true that some sex offenders are more likely to commit another *sex crime* than some other crime, when compared with nonsex offenders. In short, sex offenders are less "dangerous" than many other violent criminals, but they are more "sexually dangerous" than all other offenders.

Greater Harm to Victims May Justify Special Laws for Sex Crimes

The claim that sex crimes are more damaging to their victims than other crimes may justify strategies that are specific to sex offenders. Sex crimes can be very damaging to their victims, especially to children. Sex crimes against children can wreak havoc with their emotional and sexual development. Sexual assaults can inflict serious physical harm on victims and damage their sense of security. They also violate individuals' right to choose with whom they will share sexual intimacy.

On balance, special laws for sex offenders cannot be justified empirically by the claim that sex offenders as a group are more likely to commit another crime than other offenders. However, they may be justified if society believes that preventing *sex* crimes (as opposed to other crimes) is worth the enactment of crime-specific laws and the special allocation of resources they require. Society has seemingly concluded that the damage to victims caused by sex crimes is of a special magnitude, requiring special crime control efforts. This value judgment is certainly reasonable. Having said that, many of these recently enacted laws should be dramatically reformed in light of what we now know.

All Offenders Are Not Equally Dangerous

Because many of the recent initiatives designed to prevent sexual violence assume that *all* sex offenders are dangerous, they have treated all sex offenders alike. These crime control measures should not include all sex offenders. Instead, they should concentrate on that small number of sex offenders who really do pose a significant risk of committing more sex crimes. Experts have made significant progress in identifying a group of convicted sex offenders, who—as a group—have a much greater statistical probability of sexual reoffending when compared with the vast majority of convicted sex offenders.

As I pointed out in chapter 2, by examining large numbers of serious repeat sex offenders, researchers have been able to identify common characteristics shared by this group. These characteristics can be used to develop actuarial instruments that have significant predictive power in identifying a group of sex offenders who are at high risk of committing more sex crimes. These instruments can and should be used to identify those convicted sex offenders who ought to be subjected to aggressive measures to protect the community. Because we can now identify the most dangerous sex offenders accurately and at a reasonable cost, applying expansive and costly control measures to all sex offenders is a waste of time and effort. Legal strategies to safeguard the community should focus primarily on dangerous sex offenders.

Most Sex Crimes Are Committed by Offenders Who Know Their Victims

Research clearly establishes that perpetrators who have a relationship with their victims commit most sex crimes. Far too many sex crimes are committed within the family by other family members or by offenders who know their victims. Too often, this repetitive violation of trust occurs over a long period, subjecting victims not only to continual sexual abuse and emotional damage, but also to the psychological destruction of never-ending fear. This experience can be devastating, especially for young children.

Yet some of these new laws cannot be used against offenders who commit sex crimes against family members or friends. And those laws that can be used against these offenders, such as registration and notification laws, may discourage the reporting and successful prosecution of sex crimes committed within the family.

Public safety measures must take into account the real possibility that victims will not report family sex crimes or assist in their prosecution if their father, stepfather, or other close family member will be sent to prison or committed indefinitely as a sexual predator. But a fine line must be drawn between measures that discourage detection, investigation, and prosecution of sex crimes committed by familiars and those that appropriately target those sex offenders who commit most sex crimes. Excluding these dangerous perpetrators from public safety measures may send them the wrong message about the wrongfulness of their conduct and their personal responsibility. It may also magnify the harm suffered by their victims. So far, public policy debates about this balance have been based primarily on intuitive judgments. Much more research is needed to provide sound knowledge to inform these debates and to shape legal strategies. The goal should be to decrease the number of sex crimes committed within the family and by offenders who know their victims.

Strangers Do Not Commit Most Sex Crimes

Recently enacted laws may misdirect community vigilance. Sexual predator laws apply exclusively to offenders who commit sex crimes against strangers or against victims with whom they have established a relationship in order to gain access and opportunity for committing sex crimes. Community notification laws, which inform the public that sex offenders reside nearby, reinforce the popular fear that sex crimes are committed by strangers rather than people they know. These laws may encourage parents to protect their children from the "dangerous stranger" rather than recognize that their children are much more likely to be sexually victimized by a family member or friend. This emphasis is misplaced.

Additional resources should be spent on public education, alerting parents to the more significant risk to their children posed by family and friends and to help children understand what is inappropriate touching by anyone. Prompt intervention is essential when sex crimes are committed within the family. This is especially important if we want to help children who have been sexually victimized to recover and to avoid doing to others what was done to them.

We Do Not Know What Causes Sex Offending

Unfortunately, we still do not have sound research to explain fully and with complete accuracy the etiology of sex offending. In all probability, there are multiple causes that will require multiple solutions.

We do know that many sex offenders report that they were sexually abused as children. Yet most children who were sexually abused do not become sex offenders. Because there appears to be a significant correlation between early sexual abuse and subsequent sexual abusing, we need to spend more resources identifying child sexual abuse and intervening with abusers and treating their victims. Often, this means that whole families must receive appropriate intervention. It seems very likely that these preventive efforts will be successful in stopping much present sexual abuse and in preventing future sexual abuse.[1] Certainly, this area should receive much more attention from policymakers, mental health providers, public safety and social service agencies, and researchers.

Treatment May Reduce Sexual Reoffending

Policymakers, experts, mental health professionals, and virtually everyone involved in the criminal justice system during the 1970s and 1980s had reached the seemingly indisputable conclusion that sex offenders were not sick and that treatment for sex offenders was not effective in reducing sexual recidivism. Indeed, these fundamental conclusions led to repeal or disuse of virtually every sexual psychopath commitment law in the United States. The new wisdom that emerged in the 1980s firmly taught that sex offenders are responsible moral agents who should be punished for their behavior. Treatment, or at least an opportunity to change their attitudes and behavior,

---

[1] William D. Pithers & Alison Gray, *The Other Half of the Story: Children With Sexual Behavior Problems*, 4 PSYCHOL. PUB. POL'Y & L. 200 (1998).

was offered in some states to sex offenders who wanted it while they served their time in prison.

Nonetheless, during the 1990s, some mental health professionals argued that they could provide new treatment for these offenders that would significantly reduce, though not completely eliminate, sexual recidivism. These new claims of expertise were made even though researchers had not yet determined what causes sex offenders to commit sex crimes. Mental health professionals sincerely believed that new approaches, especially cognitive–behavioral and relapse prevention strategies,[2] were effective in reducing sexual recidivism. These approaches, borrowed from treatment strategies developed for alcoholics, relied heavily on cognitive restructuring, relapse prevention, and correcting deviant sexual interests.

As discussed in chapter 3, researchers have not yet found conclusive evidence establishing clearly that treatment professionals can change sex offenders' attitudes, interests, and behavior to reduce sexual recidivism. Nonetheless, there is some basis for optimism that sex offenders who want to change can be provided with strategies that can enable them to avoid committing another sex crime.[3] More research on sex offender treatment methods and treatment efficacy is sorely needed. In the meantime, it is shortsighted not to continue efforts to develop new treatment strategies and to provide treatment to sex offenders as quickly as possible after they have been identified. Delaying treatment can have a serious negative impact on an offender's attitudes toward his offending. It allows him to deny to himself that he did anything seriously wrong or that he was responsible for what happened. Delay lets these distortions harden, making it more difficult to change them later on.

Of course, treatment efficacy must be rigorously evaluated, and it should take into account whether patients had volunteered for treatment or were coerced into it by laws like sexually violent predator (SVP) statutes. Internationally known experts in this field have started a collaborative effort to determine whether treatment for sex offenders reduces sex reoffending.[4] These efforts and similar efforts must receive significant financial support. It is an investment that has enormous potential to reduce sexual violence and victimization.

One aspect of these efforts is worth mentioning. Some of the researchers currently engaged in evaluating whether treatment for sex offenders reduces subsequent sex offending are also premier designers and providers of the

---

[2] See chapter 3.
[3] See R. Karl Hanson et al., *First Report of the Collaborative Outcome Data on the Effectiveness of Psychological Treatment of Sex Offenders*, 14 Sexual Abuse: A. J. of Res. and Treatment 169 (2002), discussed in chapter 3.
[4] *Id.*

treatment programs that are being evaluated. Policy-makers would have more confidence in this research if investigators evaluating treatment efficacy did not have any stake in the programs being evaluated.

WHAT SOCIETY SHOULD DO

Preventive Programs

Too much money and energy are spent on preventing sexual violence *after* it has occurred. Society should get smart and try harder to *prevent* it. Although this book has not extensively analyzed preventive strategies, some are obvious and deserve more funding.

Treat Children Who Have Sexually Inappropriate Behaviors

Most children who were sexually victimized do not become sex offenders. However, a disproportionate number of them do, and there is a significant correlation between sexual victimization and becoming a sexual victimizer.[5] These children are not responsible for their victimization, and society should do whatever it can to ensure that they do not themselves become sex offenders. More resources should be spent treating children with sexually inappropriate behavior and their families. This preventive strategy should prevent many sex crimes. It is also less costly than confining large numbers of adult sex offenders in prison or in secure mental health facilities.[6]

Education Programs

We should continue to educate children and parents about inappropriate sexual behavior.[7] These programs should not only consider a risk posed by strangers but also stress the more likely risk posed by people whom children know. Today too much emphasis is placed on "stranger danger."

The Criminal Justice System

The criminal justice system can do the job of protecting the community against dangerous sex offenders. It can, and should, punish sex offenders for

---

[5] *See* chapter 1.
[6] Pithers & Gray, *supra* note 1.
[7] Many local police departments conduct safety programs at schools, day care centers, community centers, and other places or provide videos to organizations wishing to provide such training. Additionally, there are numerous "stranger danger" Web sites, some of which stress that nonstrangers can be dangerous as well. *See, e.g.,* http://www.mcgruff.org/mcgruff/mcgruff/?pg=13364-14072 (last visited Feb. 12, 2004).

the sex crimes they commit, thereby reaffirming individual responsibility for the choice the offender made. The system can also incapacitate dangerous offenders for as long as necessary.

However, it is in need of fundamental reform. Simply put, too many sex offenders who are *not* dangerous are being confined longer than necessary to prevent them from committing another sex crime. Conversely, too many sex offenders who *are* dangerous are being released back into the community without adequate supervision. The balance between confinement and control in the community must be recalibrated.

In addition, the system must develop the necessary flexibility to match the appropriate response to the risk posed by each offender. Increased expertise in risk assessment should allow the system to use more aggressive control measures for those offenders who are most likely to commit another sex crime, and conversely, less control for those offenders who are not dangerous. We will now consider specific ways to accomplish these goals.

Correct Sentencing Flaws

There is no doubt that many states, like Washington, Minnesota, and Wisconsin, had set sentences for serious sex crimes far too low when they initially enacted determinate sentencing schemes. All states should review their sentences for sex crimes, including provisions for repeat sex offenders and for sex crimes against children, to make sure they are proportionate to the harm done and the dangerousness of the offender. If criminal sentences for sex crimes are set appropriately, there should be no need to resort to the subterfuge of "civil commitment" to confine dangerous sex offenders.

SVP laws victimize victims a second time by sending the false message that the offender was "sick" and therefore not really responsible for what he did. It also sends the wrong message to the offender, discouraging him from taking responsibility for his crimes and engaging in treatment while in prison.[8] The criminal justice system is fully capable of exercising aggressive control over sex offenders released from prison for as long as necessary.[9] Some changes must be made in the criminal justice system, however.

"Three-Strike" Laws

Many states have three-strike laws that impose mandatory minimum sentences, including in some cases a life sentence, for repeat serious offenders. This approach is also used to sentence sex offenders. However, these laws often tend to be overly harsh in proportion to the crimes committed and

---

[8] Bruce J. Winick, *Sex Offender Law in the 1990s: A Therapeutic Jurisprudence Analysis,* 4 PSYCHOL. PUB. POL'Y & L. 505 (1998).
[9] *See* chapter 7.

do not individualize justice in any meaningful sense. More important, they do not use reliable methods for making risk assessments and identifying the most dangerous sex offenders. Too often, prosecutors misuse these laws to induce plea bargains to other charges that avoid the statutorily prescribed sentence. On balance, they are mechanical and inflexible, and result in needless overkill.

Reform the Sentencing Process

A better approach is to use criminal sentencing to fashion a punishment that fits both the crime and the criminal. The length of the sentence can, and should, be based on the severity of the crime committed and the harm done to the victim. A repeat offender should be punished more severely than a first-time offender. Sex offenders who commit more sex crimes should be sentenced to extended prison terms. By deliberately choosing to harm another victim, they have earned enhanced punishment to pay them back for the terrible wrongs they have committed. They have also manifested their increased dangerousness and the need for extended incapacitation. The guiding principle should be the more crimes committed, the longer the sentence. A firm but proportional scheme of escalating punishments should be established for repeat sex offenders.

Incapacitate Dangerous Sex Offenders

Chapter 2 demonstrated that the best predictors of sexual recidivism are fixed, historical facts, such as the age of the offender's initial sex crime, the number of sex crimes committed, the gender of the victim, and other similar information. All of these data are available for use at sentencing in the criminal justice system. If society truly wants to protect itself against high-risk sex offenders—and it should—judges should sentence these repeat violent sex offenders to long prison terms. In unusual cases, the criminal sentence can be set beyond the normal sentence, provided the prosecutor can prove that the offender is dangerous and very likely to commit another sex crime if not in restraint.

Washington State has adopted a new sentencing scheme that shows promise in keeping dangerous sex offenders in prison. If an offender is convicted of a serious sex crime, the judge can find that he or she is a "sexually violent predator" and then sentence the offender to the maximum term provided by law and also to a minimum sentence. The offender *must* serve that minimum sentence. When the mandatory minimum sentence is about to expire, the Indeterminate Sentence Review Board, which is very similar to a parole board in other states, reviews the individual's record and determines whether he can be released under supervision or whether he must serve *another* mandatory minimum term. This process continues until the offender has been released under supervision or has served the statutory maximum sentence.

Give Indeterminate Sentences to Extremely Dangerous Sex Offenders

In the most dangerous cases, involving criminals who have a well-established history of repeated violent sex crimes, an indeterminate sentence is appropriate. The very same evidence that is currently used to establish dangerousness in a commitment hearing for a sexual predator is available to prove the same element in a criminal sentencing hearing. In such cases, the individual will not be released back into the community until there is evidence that he is not dangerous. Canada uses this approach, albeit sparingly, and it seems to work well.

A parole board could determine when to release an offender who has satisfactorily completed treatment. Most offenders would then be paroled to intensive community supervision. Offenders who had no interest in reforming themselves would simply remain in prison. Because the political pressure to use this option would be powerful, effective safeguards would be needed to insulate a prosecutor's charging decision under this law. One approach would be to legislate that these cases may be filed only if actuarial instruments indicated a very high risk that the individual would commit another sex crime.

Provide Prison Treatment

Treatment for all sex offenders who want it should be made available in the prison system. This strategy would have the advantage of providing appropriate treatment for offenders as soon as the need for it became obvious. Some evidence suggests that patients who choose treatment are more likely to benefit from it than those who have it imposed on them.[10] Unlike under SVP laws, therapy would not be deferred for many years, which allows sex offenders to deny or rationalize what they did. Consequently, it should be more effective in changing offenders' attitudes and behavior.[11]

Some states that have enacted SVP laws are spending an extraordinary amount of money on a small number of sex offenders. As noted in chapter 5, these costs average about $100,000 per patient per year; in some cases it is even more. And no one knows how expensive these laws ultimately will be. This money would be better spent on providing treatment for many more sex offenders in prison who want to change their attitudes and behavior. Treatment in prison is more likely to be effective than it is under SVP laws.[12]

---

[10] Winick, *supra* note 8.
[11] Robert M. Wettstein, *A Psychiatric Perspective on Washington's Sexually Violent Predator Law*, 15 U. Puget Sound L. Rev. 597 (1992).
[12] *Id.*

Postrelease Supervision

The criminal justice system has proven capability to ensure aggressive control over sex offenders after they are released from prison. Long-term parole (and even lifetime parole in exceptional cases) should be a standard component of a criminal sentence for a dangerous sex offender. This permits the use of strategies like community containment to closely monitor the behavior of these offenders while they live in the community. It also permits the reincarceration of sex offenders who engage in behaviors that are precursors to sexual offending, thus permitting effective preventive steps to be taken.

The criminal justice system can be used to confine and to monitor after their release many more sex offenders than sexual predator laws could ever hope to reach. Unlike registration and warnings, which are really symbolic (and probably futile) gestures, intensive supervision requires the police and other public safety personnel to take "hands on" responsibility for keeping an eye on high-risk sex offenders living in the community. Of course, effective crime prevention is not cost free. Parole officers will have to be trained in sex offender risk management, and their caseloads must be low because their supervision is so intensive.

Community Containment

Several states use multidisciplinary teams, including police and parole officers, mental health professionals, and lie detector specialists, to control and monitor released sex offenders who live in the community. These approaches appear to be effective in preventing new sex crimes.[13] They are also much less costly than civil commitment.

Aggressive surveillance of dangerous sex offenders in the community should be at the forefront of our public safety agenda. This strategy allows individual offenders who have served their prison term to live in the community, subject to supervision as intensive as their risk of reoffending requires. It also provides them with incentives to reintegrate into our society. At the same time, it assures both past and potential future victims that society is taking effective measures to safeguard them.

Community containment also allows the use of a risk management approach to the danger posed by sex offenders. State officials can adjust, more or less intensively, their control over sex offenders living in the community, depending on the offender's behavior and consideration of continually updated information about him. Officials are not relegated to

---

[13] Kim English et al., *Managing Adult Sex Offenders in the Community—A Containment Approach*, National Institute of Justice Research in Brief, Jan. 1997, *available at* http://www.ncjrs.org/pdffiles/sexoff.pdf (last visited Feb. 11, 2004).

making a one-time prediction about future dangerousness and choosing a single course of action from the extremes, such as turning the offender loose, perhaps with an ineffective public warning, or confining him in a secure prison-like hospital indefinitely. Money now spent on warehousing several thousand men (and a handful of women and juveniles) under SVP laws would be better spent controlling a much larger number of dangerous sex offenders while they lived in the community.

Community containment is cost-effective. In 1997, it cost $9.16 per day to provide intensive supervision for adult sex offenders in Colorado. This cost for juvenile sex offenders was $18.11; juveniles cost more because more treatment and programs were provided. Lie detector tests can be administered for under $300. Intensive monitoring of an offender's every movement by global positioning satellite can be provided for about $10 a day.[14] Community containment will cost more than registration and notification laws, but it should be much more effective in preventing sexual violence. It will certainly cost much less than incarceration in prison and commitment to a secure mental health facility.

Special Sex Offender Courts

During the past decade or so, creative problem-solving courts have been established throughout the United States to deal with diverse populations of offenders like drug addicts, people with mental illness, and domestic abusers. These courts are based both on risk management and therapeutic jurisprudence[15] approaches to offenders. It is time to establish sex offender courts, which will try many sex offense cases.[16]

Risk management allows judges to closely monitor offender behavior in the community and to adjust the degree of control the judge exercises over the offender on the basis of ongoing information provided to the court. If new information indicates increased risk of reoffending, the judge can impose more restraint on the offender. In serious cases, the offender may be returned to custody. Because it allows decision makers to make ongoing

---

[14] *See* chapter 7.

[15] Therapeutic jurisprudence postulates that the legal system, including its rules and procedures and how legal participants perform their roles, can have a positive or negative psychological impact on individuals who come into contact with it. Therapeutic jurisprudence recommends that legal systems take social science research into account in improving the legal system. It also believes that researchers should study how the law operates to determine its impact on the psychological well-being of individuals involved in that system. *See generally,* DAVID B. WEXLER, THERAPEUTIC JURISPRUDENCE (1990), *and* DAVID B. WEXLER & BRUCE J. WINICK, ESSAYS IN THERAPEUTIC JURISPRUDENCE (1991).

[16] John Q. La Fond & Bruce J. Winick, *Sex Offender Reentry Courts: A Cost Effective Proposal for Managing Sex Offender Risk in the Community,* 989 ANNALS N.Y. ACAD. SCI. 300 (2003); John Q. La Fond & Bruce J. Winick, *Sex Offender Reentry Courts: A Proposal for Managing the Risk of Returning Sex Offenders to the Community,* 34 SETON HALL L. REV. 1173 (2004).

risk assessments in light of current information, and to adjust control over the offender in light of those assessments, risk management is superior to the prediction model of social control, which requires judges to make a one-time decision about the future based only on the offender's past behavior.

These courts would also use *therapeutic jurisprudence*, which builds on well-known research about human psychology. Sex offender courts can create incentives for offenders to change their attitudes and behavior in order to earn more freedom in the community and their eventual release from state control. Offenders who participate in community treatment, avoid risky situations, and develop strong support systems should need less monitoring. Offenders who drop out of treatment, go near places or people they should avoid, possess inappropriate erotic material in their homes, or engage in other behavior indicating increased risk of reoffending can be subjected to much more aggressive control. If necessary, they can be returned to jail or prison.

EVALUATING LAW REFORM

Understandably, horrendous sex crimes, especially those against children, provoke rage, an instinctive urge for revenge, and unconditional demands that such crimes will never be committed again. Unfortunately, we cannot make the world perfectly safe. We can, however, exercise wise judgment in creating new strategies to prevent sexual violence and improve community safety. Most important, we must build those strategies on a sound empirical foundation, not on the latest tragic sex crime showcased by the media. Enacting new laws like registration and notification laws, SVP laws, and chemical castration laws may satisfy our psychological need to "do something." Unfortunately, they will not make our world appreciably safer. They may even make it more dangerous.

Enough time has passed since the enactment of many new laws designed to protect the community against dangerous sex offenders. It is time to use what we know to fashion cost-effective strategies to protect future victims against sexual violence.

TABLE OF AUTHORITIES

AUTHOR INDEX

Williams, L. M., 65n27
Wilson, J. A., 112n156, 113n162
Wilson, J. Q., 161n151
Winick, B. J., 62n13, 82n100, 110n143,
    n150, 111n153, 112n154,
    122n212, 123, 155n129,
    163n161, 202n5, 203n5, 205n15,
    213n32, 219n54, 224, 225n70,
    n72, 226n74, 227n77, 238n8,
    240n10, 242n15, n16
Winslade, W., 71n59, 169n11, n12,
    170n16, 171–172, 175n48, n51,
    n56, 177n61

Wong, C. M., 168n6
Wood, R. M., 67n39, 70n52, n54, n56
Woodburn, S. G., 221n58

Yap, F., 147n82, n85, n87

Zevitz, R. G., 90n24, 105n116, 109n142,
    110n146, n147, 114n173,
    115n174, 118n189, n196

SUBJECT INDEX

253

ABOUT THE AUTHOR

John Q. La Fond, JD, holds the Edward A. Smith/Missouri Chair in Law, the Constitution, and Society at the University of Missouri—Kansas City School of Law. A graduate of Yale College and Yale Law School, he is an internationally recognized scholar in mental health law, criminal law and procedure, and constitutional law. He has written extensively on involuntary hospitalization of people with mental illness, the criminal responsibility of offenders with mental illness, substantive criminal law, U.S. mental health law and policy, sex offender law and public policy, and therapeutic jurisprudence. La Fond is coauthor of *Back to the Asylum: The Future of Mental Health Law and Policy in the United States* and *Criminal Law: Examples and Explanations*, and coeditor of *Protecting Society From Sexually Dangerous Offenders: Law, Justice, and Therapy* (American Psychological Association, 2003). La Fond has served as a consultant to several major studies funded by the National Institute of Mental Health, including an investigation of the effect of expanding the statutory criteria for civil commitment, how to assess outcomes in the public welfare domain for people with serious mental disorders, and the impact of mental-health-related advance directives. He was coeditor of "Sex Offenders: Scientific, Legal, and Policy Perspectives," published in the journal *Psychology, Public Policy, and Law* and is co-initiator of a proposal to establish sex offender reentry courts. La Fond has convened and served as coeditor of a national symposium, "On Preventing Intimate Violence: Have Law and Public Policy Failed?" He has also written and argued briefs challenging the constitutionality of Washington State's groundbreaking law on committing sexual predators. La Fond previously practiced law with Debevoise and Plimpton in New York City and served in the U.S. Army.